ACT® Mastery
Reading

Student Workbook

4th Edition

MasteryPrep

Inquiries concerning this publication should be mailed to:

MasteryPrep
7117 Florida Blvd.
Baton Rouge, LA 70806

MasteryPrep is a trade name and/or trademark of Ring Publications LLC.

10 9 8 7 6 5 4 3 2 1

ISBN-13: 978-1-948846-06-6

Table of Contents

Get ready to master the ACT° test!

You are about to take part in the most effective and broadly used ACT prep program in the nation! With ACT Mastery, you will learn the most frequently tested content on the ACT test and develop the skills and strategies necessary to achieve the score you desire.

With practice in all four subjects, you will be fully prepared.

The ACT Mastery Reading workbook is just one part of a larger program that includes four core subject books, each in line with a subtest found on the ACT: English, math, reading, and science. Each book works to build your mastery of the content most frequently tested on the ACT by providing thorough subject reviews and hundreds of ACT practice questions. By completing this book, you will be prepared for the reading subtest; the rest of the program will prepare you for the English, math, and science subtests.

Test prep is a team effort.

Although you may be tempted to jump ahead, this workbook should be used in conjunction with your teacher's instructions and is not intended for self-guided practice. Each lesson is designed so that the majority of the direction and some of the content is delivered by an instructor either verbally or visually by way of slide presentations. Working ahead will limit your understanding of the ACT content and may actually lead to confusion. Follow your teacher's instructions during the lesson and only work on practice as directed. This will maximize your understanding of the material and, ultimately, your score.

The score you want is within your reach!

The ACT test is a rigorous, challenging marathon of an exam. It can be intimidating. Of the more than two million students who take the test each year, many feel that it is uncoachable—that whatever score they earn on the test is the best they can do. The ACT Mastery program has proven this assumption to be *completely false.* Students dedicated to the program routinely see substantial improvement on their test scores. It will take hard work and determination, but with the content and strategies available to you, anything is possible.

You *can* master the ACT test.

The keys to success with ACT preparation are content, practice, and strategy. As your teacher leads you through the lessons, focus on the content. Take notes on all of the definitions and rules, ask questions to clarify any points of confusion, and participate in all of the activities.

Once you begin to master the content, practice the problems in your workbook. Give your best effort on every question no matter how hard or easy it may seem. Complete any homework your teacher assigns and make sure you ask questions if you do not fully understand a concept.

Finally, as you develop content mastery and practice the ACT questions, work on building your test-day strategy. Look for trends in the questions and answer choices, determine your strongest and weakest areas, and decide how you will pace yourself on the day of the test.

Good luck!

Locate Part 1

CAPTION:

1.1 Entrance Ticket

Read the passage and answer the questions.

Science, to the ordinary reader of newspapers, is represented by a varying selection of sensational triumphs, such as wireless telegraphy and airplanes, radioactivity and the mar-
5 vels of modern alchemy. It is not of this aspect of science that I wish to speak. Science, in this aspect, consists of detached, up-to-date fragments, interesting only until they are replaced by something newer and more up-to-date, dis-
10 playing nothing of the systems of patiently constructed knowledge out of which, almost as a casual incident, have come the practically useful results that interest the man in the street. The increased command over the forces of nature,
15 which is derived from science, is undoubtedly an amply sufficient reason for encouraging scientific research, but this reason has been so often urged and is so easily appreciated that other reasons, to my mind quite as important,
20 are apt to be overlooked. It is with these other reasons, especially with the intrinsic value of a scientific habit of mind in forming our outlook on the world, that I shall be concerned in what follows.

25 The instance of wireless telegraphy will serve to illustrate the difference between the two points of view. Almost all the serious intellectual labor required for the possibility of this invention is due to three men—Faraday, Maxwell, and
30 Hertz. In alternating layers of experiment and theory, these three men built up the modern theory of electromagnetism and demonstrated the identity of light with electromagnetic waves. The system that they discovered is one of pro-
35 found intellectual interest, bringing together and unifying an endless variety of apparently detached phenomena and displaying a cumulative mental power that cannot but afford delight to every generous spirit. The mechanical details
40 that remained to be adjusted in order to utilize their discoveries for a practical system of telegraphy demanded, no doubt, very considerable ingenuity but had not that broad sweep and that universality that could give them intrinsic inter-
45 est as an object of disinterested contemplation.

From the point of view of training the mind, of giving that well-informed, impersonal outlook which constitutes culture in the good sense of this much-misused word, it seems to be gener-
50 ally held indisputable that a literary education is superior to one based on science.

Entrance Ticket   Learning Targets   How to Skim   How to Scan   ACT Practice   Sum It Up

1.1 Entrance Ticket

1. According to the narrator, an ordinary reader of newspapers considers that science is represented by:
   A. a gradually increasing understanding of the world around us.
   B. a varying selection of sensational triumphs.
   C. a mad scientist in a lab coat.
   D. a sophisticated system of carefully assembled knowledge.

2. The author indicates that it is a generally held belief that compared to an education based on science, a literary education is:
   F. superior.
   G. inferior.
   H. elaborate.
   J. under-appreciated.

3. In paragraph 1, (lines 1–24), the author cites all of the following as examples of sensational scientific triumphs EXCEPT:
   A. airplanes.
   B. wireless telegraphy.
   C. radioactivity.
   D. electromagnetic theories.

Entrance Ticket   Learning Targets   How to Skim   How to Scan   ACT Practice   Sum It Up

1.2 Learning Targets

1. Skim passages effectively

2. Scan passages effectively

3. Locate basic facts and simple details in reading passages

Self-Assessment

Circle the number that corresponds to your confidence level in your knowledge of this subject before beginning the lesson. A score of 1 means you are completely lost, and a score of 4 means you have mastered the skills. After you finish the lesson, return to the bottom of this page and circle your new confidence level to show your improvement.

Before Lesson

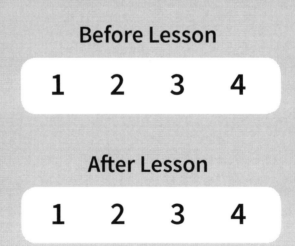

1   2   3   4

After Lesson

1   2   3   4

1.3.1 How to Skim

Follow your teacher's instruction to fill in the blanks.

1. _____ everything as _____ as possible.

2. If you are confused by a word or sentence, _____ _____.

3. _____ or _____ the unique element in each _____.

4. Get _____ and get _____. Read the whole _____ in _____ minutes.

5. If you are running behind, just read the first and last _____ of _____ _____.

1.3.1 How to Skim

Luther Burbank lived in California, where this renowned wizard of plant life continually played tricks on Mother Nature. He transformed her vegetables into different shapes, making them no longer recognizable in their original forms. Like fairies in Irish mythology, Burbank stole away the plant babies, but instead of leaving sickly elves in their places, he brought into the world healthy offspring that grew into full maturity and developed superior traits to those they supplanted. Burbank transformed the ugly, thorny, insipid cactus of the western desert into a smooth, succulent beauty that is now known as the "desert rose." Burbank's acclaim as a creator of new plants is worldwide.

Burbank essentially combined two plant species to create superior *hybrids*. He was meticulous in his selection, choosing only superior plant species to mate. Though he occasionally mated plants of the same species, he preferred to combine those of different species. Burbank's hypothesis was that neither plant in its current environment would thrive to its full potential.

From the early days of his career, Burbank had been fascinated with the potato. In fact it was his hybrid potato, the "Burbank potato," that first brought the plant wizard into worldwide prominence. Introduced into Ireland, it promised to be the agricultural salvation of the country where the potato was a diet staple. The Burbank potato is the hardiest of all varieties and is well-suited for colder climates.

Apart from the potato that bears his name, Burbank produced many other hybrids. Burbank's greenhouses were home to a wide array of cross-produced potatoes that are truly remarkable in shape, size, and color. One of Burbank's most vibrant creations is a potato that, far from its humble beginnings, is magenta in color and reveals concentric geometric figures when cut. Some have even noted the artistic aspect of the vegetable, which when cut often reveals likenesses of human and animal faces. Burbank's experiments were not for the purpose of novelty, however. His primary objective was to cultivate richer, superior vegetables for the food supply. Burbank's famed "pomato" is the product of such determination.

In his first attempt to cross-breed the potato and the tomato, Burbank began by grafting a potato vine with a large tomato plant. This yielded what he called "aerial potatoes" of very peculiar, twisted shapes. Then reversing this operation he grafted a tomato plant with the aerial potatoes to yield a strange-looking potato with marked tomato characteristics. He was encouraged by this start.

After further experimentation, Burbank succeeded in producing what some consider the most unique fruit in the world: the pomato. The fruit first emerges as a tiny green ball on top of the potato. As the growing season progresses, the ball gradually enlarges and finally develops into a fruit which is the size and shape of an ordinary tomato. Its flesh is white and contains only a few tiny, white seeds. Its flavor is exceedingly unique, a perceived combination of various fruit flavors, though difficult to fully define. Like the tomato, the pomato can be eaten raw or cooked. It is said to be especially well-suited for preservation, or canning. The production of the pomato is one of the crowning triumphs of California's plant wizard, likely the most novel of the hybrids Burbank has produced.

By Burbank's example, agriculturists, botanists, and horticulturists have continued

Entrance Ticket   Learning Targets   How to Skim   How to Scan   ACT Practice   Sum It Up

1.3.1 How to Skim

to experiment with the role that humans play in nature. By revealing the numerous possibilities created by plant manipulation, Burbank's
80 work led to the passing of the Plant Patent Act in 1930, which made it possible to patent new varieties of plants. As a *modern magician* of his time, Burbank planted the seed of possibility within the plant world.

1.3.1 How to Skim

This page is intentionally left blank.

Lesson 1 – Locate Part 1

1.3.1 How to Skim

Pepin had two sons, Charles and Carloman. After their father's death, they ruled together, but a few years later, Carloman died and Charles became sole king.

5　Charles was the most famous king of the Franks. He did so many great and wonderful things that he was called Charlemagne, which means Charles the Great.

Charlemagne was a great soldier. For 10 thirty years he waged war against the Saxons. Finally Charlemagne conquered the Saxons, and their great chief, Wittekind, submitted to him. The Saxons were a people of Germany who lived near the land of the Franks. They spoke 15 the same language and were of the same race as the Franks, but they had not been civilized by contact with the Romans.

They were still pagans, just as the Franks had been before a previous king, Clovis, 20 became a Christian. As part of pagan ritual, the Saxons offered human sacrifices.

After Charlemagne conquered the Saxons, he made their lands part of his kingdom. A great number of them, including Wittekind, were bap-25 tized as Christians, and soon they had churches and schools in many parts of their country.

Another of Charlemagne's wars was against the Lombards. Pepin, Charlemagne's father, had defeated the Lombards and had 30 given part of their country to the pope. The Lombard king then invaded the pope's lands and threatened Rome itself, so the pope asked Charlemagne for help.

Charlemagne quickly marched across the 35 Alps and attacked the Lombards. He drove them out of the pope's lands and took possession of their country.

After Charlemagne's victory over the Lombards, he waged war in Spain in 778. A large 40 portion of Spain was then held by the Moorish Saracens, but a Mohammedan leader from Damascus was invading, and the Moors invited Charlemagne to help them. He therefore led an army across the Pyrenees. Leading an army 45 across the Pyrenees Mountains, Charlemagne successfully defeated the enemy, restoring the land to his Moorish allies. Then he began the journey home.

Charlemagne's returning army was di-50 vided into two parts. The main body was led by Charlemagne himself, and the rear guard was commanded by a famous warrior named Roland. While marching through the narrow Roncevaux Pass in the Pyrenees, Roland's divi-55 sion was attacked by a tribe called the Basques, who lived on the mountain slopes of the neighboring region.

High cliffs walled in the pass on both sides. From the tops of these cliffs the Basques hurled 60 rocks and trunks of trees down upon the Franks and crushed many of them to death. The wild mountaineers also descended into the pass and attacked the Franks with weapons. Roland fought bravely; nevertheless, he was overpow-65 ered, and he and all his men were killed.

Roland had a friend and companion named Oliver, who was as brave as Roland. Many stories and songs tell of their wonderful adventures and deeds in war.

1.3.1 How to Skim

70   The work of Charlemagne in Spain was quickly undone. Abd-er-Rahman, the leader of the Mohammedans, who had come from Damascus, soon conquered almost all the territory south of the Pyrenees.

1.3.1 How to Skim

- [ ] king
- [ ] princess
- [ ] Jewish
- [ ] Charlemagne
- [ ] war
- [ ] church
- [ ] Romans
- [ ] Spain
- [ ] Germany
- [ ] France
- [ ] bravery
- [ ] guillotine

This page is intentionally left blank.

1.3.1 How to Skim

In appearance, the gods were supposed to resemble mortals, whom, however, they far surpassed in beauty, grandeur, and strength; they were also more commanding in stature, height being considered by the Greeks an attribute of beauty in man or woman. They resembled human beings in their feelings and habits, intermarrying and having children, requiring daily nourishment to recruit their strength, and refreshing sleep to restore their energies. Their blood, a bright ethereal fluid called *ichor*, never engendered disease, and, when shed, had the power of producing new life.

The Greeks believed that the mental qualifications of their gods were of a much higher order than those of men, but nevertheless, as we shall see, they were not considered to be exempt from human passions, and we frequently behold them actuated by revenge, deceit, and jealousy. They, however, always punish the evildoer and visit with dire calamities any impious mortal who dares to neglect their worship or despise their rites. We often hear of them visiting mankind and partaking of their hospitality, and not infrequently both gods and goddesses become attached to mortals, with whom they unite themselves, the offspring of these unions being called heroes or demi-gods, who were usually renowned for their great strength and courage. But although there were so many points of resemblance between gods and men, there remained the one great characteristic distinction, which was that the gods enjoyed immortality. Still, they were not invulnerable, and we often hear of them being wounded and suffering in consequence such exquisite torture that they have earnestly prayed to be deprived of their privilege of immortality.

The gods knew no limitation of time or space, being able to transport themselves to incredible distances with the speed of thought. They possessed the power of rendering themselves invisible at will and could assume the forms of men or animals as it suited their convenience. They could also transform human beings into trees, stones, animals, etc., either as a punishment for their misdeeds, or as a means of protecting the individual, thus transformed, from impending danger.

Their robes were like those worn by mortals but were perfect in form and much finer in texture. Their weapons also resembled those used by mankind; we hear of spears, shields, helmets, bows and arrows, etc. being employed by the gods. Each deity possessed a beautiful chariot, which, drawn by horses or other animals of celestial breed, conveyed them rapidly over land and sea according to their pleasure.

Most of these divinities lived on the summit of Mount Olympus, each possessing his or her individual habitation and all meeting together on festive occasions in the council-chamber of the gods, where their banquets were enlivened by the sweet strains of Apollo's lyre, whilst the beautiful voices of the Muses poured forth their rich melodies to his harmonious accompaniment.

Magnificent temples were erected to their honor, where they were worshiped with the greatest solemnity; rich gifts were presented to them, and animals, and indeed sometimes

1.3.1 How to Skim

human beings, were sacrificed on their altars.

    The most important of these divinities may have been something more than the mere cre-
75 ations of an active and poet imagination. They were possibly human beings who had so distinguished themselves in life by their preeminence over their fellow mortals that, after death, they were deified by the people among whom they
80 lived and the poets touched with their magic wand the details of lives, which, in more prosaic times, would simply have been recorded as illustrious.

1.3.1 How to Skim

Question: _____

_____

Answer: _____

_____

Question: _____

_____

Answer: _____

_____

Question: _____

_____

Answer: _____

_____

Reading Tip

Skimming: Skim the passage quickly before answering the questions. Underline key words or jot short notes about each paragraph. Knowing the general topic of each paragraph will help you scan and locate details more quickly when it comes time to answer the questions.

Entrance Ticket　　Learning Targets　　How to Skim　　How to Scan　　ACT Practice　　Sum It Up

1.3.2 How to Scan

Follow your teacher's instruction to fill in the blanks.

1. Find the _____ in the _____.

2. Start _____ that topic by _____.

3. _____ your finger along with the _____.

4. _____ for anything that _____ the topic.

5. Read _____ _____ around that _____ to understand the _____.

1.3.2 How to Scan

Passage 1

Term 1: _____

Term 2: _____

Term 3: _____

Passage 2

Term 1: _____

Term 2: _____

Term 3: _____

Passage 3

Term 1: _____

Term 2: _____

Term 3: _____

Reading Tip

Scanning: Questions that require you to find details include words such as *indicate*, *state*, *refer*, *present*, *establish*, *claim*, *mention*, *describe*, *illustrate*, *identify*, *demonstrate*, and *inform*. When you see these words, you know to go back and scan the passage for the detail asked about in the question.

This page is intentionally left blank.

Lesson 1 – Locate Part 1

1.4.1 Set One

Passage II

SOCIAL SCIENCE: This passage is adapted from *Jewelry* by H. Clifford Smith (©1908 by Methuen & Co.). A brooch is a piece of jewelry attached to clothing at or near the neck.

The brooch, an ornament of very considerable importance, can be traced back to the earliest civilization and is a valuable criterion in questions of ethnic movements. The story, however, of the growth of each of
5 the different classes into which primitive brooches may be divided, the periods at which these ornaments made their appearance, and the deductions of ethnographical interest that may be drawn therefrom, must of necessity lie outside the scope of the present work.

10 All brooches originated from the simple pin, which itself was probably derived from a thorn. At an early period this pin, after having been passed through the garment, was for greater security bent up, and its point caught behind the head. Later, in order that the point might be held more
15 securely in the catch, the pin was given a complete turn, which produced the spring, as seen in the common form of our modern safety pin. Thus constructed, the brooch, though in one piece, may be said to consist of four parts: the acus or pin; the spring or hinge; the catch or locking
20 apparatus, which forms the sheath of the pin; and the bow or back—the framework uniting the spring with the catch.

From this primitive safety pin, which is the foundation form of all brooches with a catch, developed the numerous varieties and patterns of the brooch or fibula
25 of succeeding ages. Amongst these is the Roman fibula, which instead of being made of one piece of metal, is of two pieces—the bow and the acus. This pin works on a hinge. From the brooch hinged in this manner originated the Roman provincial fibula of the T-shaped type common
30 in early France and Britain, and later, the cruciform brooch of Anglo-Saxon times. The brooch with a hinge was exclusively used until the 19th century revival of the safety pin, which amazed people as though it were an entirely new invention.

35 In addition to the above brooches or fibula—all developments of the safety-pin type—there are three other large groups of brooches: the circular disc type; the penannular or Celtic brooch; and the ring brooch. The first of these—the type generally worn at the present
40 day—may be described as a flat disc fitted with a hinged pin. In cemeteries belonging to the Early Iron Age in Southern Europe, circular plates have been found fitted with a pin. These plates appear to have been developed by the conversion of a primitive disc of spiral concentric
45 wire into a circular plate. From the brooch of this type sprang the circular brooches of the Roman period—often made of iron or bronze inlaid with enamel, glass, coral, or

bone—as well as the splendid circular brooches of Anglo-Saxon times and all other disc-shaped brooches. In all
50 early periods and even in Roman times, the bow or safety-pin type of brooch was more common than the disc and also more practical, as it offered room for the gathered folds of the garment. In modern times, the disc-shaped brooch fitted with a hinge or sometimes with a spring pin
55 has been principally used.

The two remaining groups of brooches, the Celtic brooch and the ring brooch, are both developments of the simple pin in combination with a ring—in the former case, penannular, and in the latter, annular. The Celtic brooch,
60 with penannular, or open-circled, ring and long pin, is apparently the result of fitting a pin to a prehistoric form of fastening for the dress—a penannular ring terminating with knobs, known as a mammillary fibula. The ring brooch, with complete ring and pin of the same length as
65 the diameter of the ring, which was popular in medieval times, is the outcome of fitting a complete ring of wire to a pin to prevent the head of the pin from slipping through the material. Over time the ring became the more important member. It is improbable that the Celtic brooch
70 originated in the same way, from the union of a long pin with a small ring. Nor is it likely that these two forms of brooches were evolved, the one out of the other, by the shortening or lengthening of the pins. As a matter of fact, the two appear to have arisen independently side by side.

1. According to the passage, a brooch worn by a person in early France would be most accurately described as:

   A. oblong.
   B. penannular.
   C. T-shaped.
   D. cruciform.

2. Based on the passage, the original safety-pin brooch design was made up of all of the following pieces EXCEPT:

   F. the acus.
   G. the spring.
   H. the bow.
   J. the disc.

3 ▬▬▬▬▬▬▬▬▬▬▬▬▬▬▬▬▬▬▬▬▬ **3**

3. The passage states that the attitude toward the safety-pin brooch in the 19th century was one of:

   A. misplaced amazement.
   B. indifference.
   C. curiosity.
   D. unrealistic jealousy.

4. The first three paragraphs (lines 1-34) establish all of the following about brooches EXCEPT that:

   F. they have an extensive and important history.
   G. the first brooch most likely originated from a thorn.
   H. the ring brooch preceded the Roman brooch.
   J. the spring is produced by a turn in the pin.

5. The passage states that all of the following are materials inlaid to decorate brooches during the Roman era EXCEPT:

   A. bone.
   B. glass.
   C. bronze.
   D. enamel.

END OF SET ONE
STOP! DO NOT GO ON TO THE NEXT PAGE
UNTIL TOLD TO DO SO.

Entrance Ticket   Learning Targets   How to Skim   How to Scan   ACT Practice   Sum It Up

1.4.2 Set Two

Passage II

SOCIAL SCIENCE: This passage is adapted from *The Lobster Fishery of Maine* by John N. Cobb (© 1899 by the United States Fish Commission).

Ever since the early Puritan settlers first learned from the Native Americans how to utilize the lobster, it has been one of the most prized articles of food in the New England states. The early town records of Massachusetts contain
5 frequent references to this valuable crustacean, and efforts were made at an early date to conserve the supply.

At first, as most settlers lived on or near the coast, each family could easily secure its own supply, but as the settlements gradually extended farther inland, this
10 became inconvenient, and it soon became customary for certain persons living on the coast to attend to supplying the wants of the inland settlers, and thus the American commercial fishery was established.

The coast of Maine is very favorably situated for
15 this fishery. In its eastern and middle sections the shore is bold and rocky, and it is cut up by large, deep inlets and coves that are studded with numerous islands large and small. Groups of islands are also numerous farther offshore, like the Fox and Matinicus islands and the Deer
20 and Mount Desert islands. Large and small freshwater rivers are numerous, and the granite bottoms of these channels and inlets form admirable breeding grounds. In the western end the shores are not so rocky, being broken frequently with sandy reaches, while the rivers are small
25 and comparatively shallow. West of Casco Bay the islands are infrequent. As a result of this conformation of coast, the best fishing grounds in Maine are between Cape Elizabeth and Quoddy Head.

As early as 1830, smacks—small boats that
30 transported live lobster—from Boston and Connecticut visited Harpswell, Maine, for fresh prizes, and it is very probable that even before this time they had visited the points farther west in the state. The history of the fishery, so far as known, shows that it gradually worked eastward.
35 This was doubtless owing to the fact that the trend of settlement in the early part of the century was in that direction. It is also probable that, for some time before the people along the coast took up the fishery, the smackmen themselves did their own fishing. This is easily believed
40 when the great abundance is considered. It is known for certainty that this was done in Massachusetts.

During summer the lobsters were common close to the shore and could easily be gaffed by boys at low water; but this could hardly be called a regular fishery.

45 The regular fishery began with the use of hoop-net pots, which were traps of generally very crude construction, and the facility with which the lobsters escaped from them led to their disuse soon after the lath pots began to be introduced. The lath pots were essentially
50 the same in construction as those now used on the coast of Maine, and each pair of fishermen then handled between 25 and 50.

Up until about 1865 it was the custom to set the traps singly, and two smackmen were usually employed
55 in the fishery, one to haul up, empty the pot, rebait it, and drop it overboard, while the other handled the boat. In the latter years it was discovered that by setting the pots on trawls, more pots could be set and only one man would be required to work them. This invention, which was claimed
60 by several different persons, proved quite successful for a while. After a time, when the supply of lobsters began to drop off, better results were secured by scattering the pots over a greater area and shifting their position each time they were fished, which was very easily done. As a result
65 of this, the use of trawls decreased very rapidly.

6. According to the passage, a lath is a type of:

F. lobster trap that replaced hoop-net pots.
G. fishing boat that transports live lobsters.
H. net used to trawl in rivers and lakes.
J. rocky mouth of a coastal inlet.

7. According to the passage, until 1865 it was customary in the fishery to set traps:

A. close enough to shore to be reached without boats.
B. individually with two-person boat crews.
C. on trawls that could be hauled in quickly by one man.
D. by scattering pots in different locations.

8. Based on the passage, smacks first visited Harpswell in:

F. 1825.
G. 1830.
H. 1850.
J. 1865.

3 ▬▬▬▬▬▬▬▬▬▬▬▬▬▬▬▬▬▬▬▬▬▬▬▬▬ **3**

9. According to the passage, the best fishing grounds in Maine are located:

    A. near Fox Island.
    B. between Deer and Mount Desert Islands.
    C. between Cape Elizabeth and Quoddy Head.
    D. west of Casco Bay.

10. According to the passage, Maine's fishery can trace its history:

    F. from the west of the state and toward the shore.
    G. from the shore and into the east of the state.
    H. around the shore of the state only.
    J. around the rivers in the west of the state.

END OF SET TWO
STOP! DO NOT GO ON TO THE NEXT PAGE
UNTIL TOLD TO DO SO.

Entrance Ticket   Learning Targets   How to Skim   How to Scan   ACT Practice   Sum It Up

1.4.3 Set Three

Passage I

PROSE FICTION: This passage is adapted from the short story "The Song of My Grandmother" by Sam Windbourne (©2015 by MasteryPrep).

Ada Summers had never been a great singer, but what she lacked in raw talent she made up for in heart and dedication. She liked to tell her granddaughter that singing was about lifting her own spirits, never about pleasing a
5 crowd. She began singing while working on her family farm, and she kept right on singing through a string of factory jobs and housework. After church one summer a man had approached her to say that she could make some money singing her gospel music, but nothing ever came
10 of it. However, Ada was content to sing as she swept or cooked, dreaming of far off lands that she'd never see on her pension.

When she was a young girl just off her father's farm, Ada worked for a garment factory that made a variety of
15 uniforms for blue-collar workers. She would carefully stitch the seams, humming all the while, and her quality of work was quickly identified as beyond compare. After a year she was promoted to fixing other seamstresses' mistakes; to Ada, however, it never felt like a promotion,
20 since it was especially tedious. Still, she did not mind the work because, as she never hesitated to point out, it sure beat walking up and down the rows of sugar cane in the blazing sun.

When World War II came, the factory where
25 Ada worked was converted from producing outfits for machinists to producing uniforms for soldiers. Ada often thought about the young men across the world fighting and dying in the clothing that she made, and she would lead the other seamstresses in patriotic songs. She liked
30 to think that their cheerful singing helped to embed a bit of hope into the garments and that maybe those soldiers could sense the care that went into each stitch.

By the end of the war, Ada had married her own soldier, Donald, and the pair moved to St. Louis. They
35 lived in an apartment—so small it could hardly be called such—above a little automobile shop where Donald worked as a mechanic. They'd stash their money in a shoe box under the bed, saving up for the day when they could own their own shop and home. After a little under a year
40 living in the small apartment, Donald and Ada added a bassinet to the corner and welcomed their only daughter, Emily, to the world. With her sweet curls and tinkling laugh, Emily was the light of her parents' life. Ada would rock Emily, swaddled in her hand-sewn blankets, and sing
45 lullabies as she drifted to sleep.

Cradling Emily, Ada would remember the winter day she first met Donald, a dashing aircraft mechanic dressed in one of the olive uniforms that she'd sewn herself. After spending the day working a long shift, she went to the
50 market to buy groceries for her mother. When she reached for a bag of rice, she nearly knocked over the entire stack; thankfully, the young soldier was there to keep the pile from tumbling down, and the two shared a small laugh. Ada was struck by the man's wide smile and gave him
55 one to match. After a few moments that felt like hours, he offered to walk her home.

On the way Ada told him about her seamstress job and how she and the other girls would sing as they sewed. The young soldier seemed touched by the gesture and told
60 her of his time overseas and how thankful he was now to be stationed stateside. Donald asked her if she would sing one of her songs. Blushing, Ada sang him *America the Beautiful*, and when she looked over she saw him wipe a tear from his eye. She looked up and finally felt
65 confirmation that her work in the factory had made an impact. She also felt that she had met someone whom she very much wanted to know better, so she invited him for dinner. Mama always had extra biscuits, and Ada doubted she would mind a visit from a soldier just back from the
70 front.

---

11. Which of the following is NOT mentioned as a place where Ada liked to sing?

   A. On her family's farm
   B. In the market
   C. In her apartment in St. Louis
   D. At the garment factory

12. According to the passage, Ada began working at the garment factory:

   F. after World War II ended.
   G. during World War II.
   H. before World War II began.
   J. just as World War II was coming to a close.

Entrance Ticket · Learning Targets · How to Skim · How to Scan · ACT Practice · Sum It Up

3 ▓▓▓▓▓▓▓▓▓▓▓▓▓▓▓▓▓▓▓▓▓▓▓▓▓▓▓▓▓▓▓▓ **3**

13. The passage mentions which of the following positive effects of singing?

   A. It provides an outlet for stress.
   B. It is a good way to become famous.
   C. It is a good way to pass the time.
   D. It helps to lift the singer's spirits.

14. According to the passage, all of the following were aspects of Ada's work at the garment factory EXCEPT:

   F. she was promoted based on the quality of her work.
   G. the factory began making uniforms for soldiers when World War II began.
   H. she led the other seamstresses in patriotic songs.
   J. the demand for garments slowed at the end of World War II.

15. According to the passage, when did Ada move to St. Louis?

   A. After marrying Donald
   B. Before World War II began
   C. After her father sold the family farm
   D. When the garment factory shut down

END OF SET THREE
STOP! DO NOT GO ON TO THE NEXT PAGE
UNTIL TOLD TO DO SO.

Entrance Ticket   Learning Targets   How to Skim   How to Scan   ACT Practice   Sum It Up

Sum It Up

Skimming

1. Read the passage as fast as possible before looking at the questions.
2. If you are confused by a word or sentence, just keep moving.
3. Find the unique element in each paragraph.
4. Get in and get out! Read the whole passage in three minutes or less.
5. If you are running behind, just read the first and last sentences of each paragraph.

Scanning

1. Find the topic in the question.
2. Start searching for that topic by paragraph.
3. Move your finger along with the text.
4. Look for anything that matches the topic.
5. When you find the topic, read five lines above and below to understand the context.

Locate Part 2

CAPTION:

2.1 Entrance Ticket

Read the passage and answer the questions.

By "Cheat the Prophet," the author refers to the phenomenon where people attentively listen to wise predictions about the future and "then go out and do something else."

In the beginning of the 20th century, the game of Cheat the Prophet was made far more difficult than it had ever been before. There were so many prophets and so many prophecies
5 that it was difficult to elude all their ingenuities. When a man did something free and frantic and entirely his own, a horrible thought struck him afterward; it might have been predicted. Whenever a duke climbed a lamppost, when a dean
10 acted recklessly, he could not be really happy: he could not be certain that he was not fulfilling some prophecy.

In the beginning of the 20th century, you could not see the ground for clever men. They
15 were so common that a stupid man was quite exceptional, and when they found him, they followed him in crowds down the street and treasured him up and gave him some high post in the state. And all these clever men were at work
20 giving accounts of what would happen in the next age, all quite clear, all quite keen-sighted and ruthless, and all quite different. And it seemed that the good old game of hoodwinking your ancestors could not really be managed
25 this time, because the ancestors neglected meat and sleep and practical politics, so that they might meditate day and night on what their descendants would be likely to do.

But the way the prophets of the 20th cen-
30 tury went to work was this: they took something or other that was certainly going on in their time and then said that it would go on more and more until something extraordinary happened. And, very often, they added that in some odd
35 place that extraordinary thing had indeed happened and that it showed the signs of the times.

For instance, there were Mr. H. G. Wells and others who thought that science would take charge of the future; just as the motorcar was
40 quicker than the coach, so some lovely thing would be quicker than the motorcar, and so on forever. And there arose from their ashes Dr. Quilp, who said that a man could be sent on his machine so fast around the world that he could
45 keep up a long, chatty conversation in some old-world village by saying a word of a sentence each time he came 'round. And it was said that the experiment had been tried on an apoplectic old major who was sent around the world so
50 fast that there seemed to be (to the inhabitants of some other star) a continuous band 'round the earth of white whiskers, a reddish complexion and tweeds—a thing like the ring of Saturn.

2.1 Entrance Ticket

1. In the fourth paragraph (lines 37–53), the predictions of H. G. Wells and Dr. Quilp could best be characterized as anticipating that:

    A. scientific advances would dramatically improve transportation.
    B. man would return to a more natural state.
    C. the motorcar would be replaced by the carriage.
    D. Earth would eventually become a planet more like Saturn.

2. The narrator claims that in the 20th century, it was difficult to play "Cheat the Prophet" because:

    F. people were becoming far too cynical to believe in prophecies.
    G. people were becoming more merciful, which meant they would do what the prophet said.
    H. people were making so many predictions that it was inevitable some would come true.
    J. so many people were making accurate predictions.

3. The first three paragraphs (lines 1–36) of the passage establish all of the following EXCEPT that:

    A. the passage is discussing the beginning of the 20th century.
    B. various people were engaged in hoodwinking their ancestors.
    C. some of the predictions made in the 1900s were based on occurrences that were already taking place.
    D. many people who thought themselves clever were predicting the future.

Entrance Ticket · Learning Targets · Decoding the Language of Detail Questions · Justifying Support · ACT Practice · Sum It Up

35

2.2 Learning Targets

1. Master skimming and scanning passages effectively

2. Locate and interpret minor or subtly stated details in passages

Self-Assessment

Circle the number that corresponds to your confidence level in your knowledge of this subject before beginning the lesson. A score of 1 means you are completely lost, and a score of 4 means you have mastered the skills. After you finish the lesson, return to the bottom of this page and circle your new confidence level to show your improvement.

Before Lesson

1   2   3   4

After Lesson

1   2   3   4

Entrance Ticket | Learning Targets | Decoding the Language of Detail Questions | Finding Supporting Details | ACT Practice | Sum It Up

2.3.1 Decoding the Language of Detail Questions

1. Throughout the passage, the phrase *burning bridges* is mentioned primarily to:

   ☐ word-for-word   **or**   ☐ interpretation   **Keyword:** _____

2. According to the narrator, which of the following best describes Bixby's experience at the veterinarian's office?

   ☐ word-for-word   **or**   ☐ interpretation   **Keyword:** _____

3. The author calls the tendency to omit specific plants a result of:

   ☐ word-for-word   **or**   ☐ interpretation   **Keyword:** _____

4. Which of the following statements about technological advances is best supported by the passage?

   ☐ word-for-word   **or**   ☐ interpretation   **Keyword:** _____

5. The author indicates that one flaw in traditional dieting is:

   ☐ word-for-word   **or**   ☐ interpretation   **Keyword:** _____

6. The passage notes that George Park's occupation was:

   ☐ word-for-word   **or**   ☐ interpretation   **Keyword:** _____

Entrance Ticket   Learning Targets   Decoding the Language of Detail Questions   Finding Supporting Details   ACT Practice   Sum It Up

37

2.3.1 Decoding the Language of Detail Questions

When it came my turn to speak—realizing that the average man is profoundly ignorant of the history of the women's movement because the press has never adequately nor truthfully

5 chronicled the movement—I told the jury, as briefly as I could, the story of the forty years' peaceful agitation before my daughters and I resolved that we would give our lives to the work of getting the vote for women and that we

10 should use whatever means necessary to accomplish this goal.

"We founded the Women's Social and Political Union in 1903," I said. "Our first intention was to try and influence the particular political

15 party that was then coming into power, to make this issue of the enfranchisement of women their own and to advance it. It took some little time to convince us—and I need not weary you with the history of all that has happened—but

20 it took some time to convince us that it was no use; that we could not secure things in that way. Then in 1905, we faced the hard facts. We realized that there was a press boycott against women's suffrage. Our speeches at public meetings

25 were not reported, and our letters to the editors were not published even when we implored the editors; even the things relating to women's suffrage in Parliament were not recorded. They said the subject was not of sufficient public in-

30 terest to be reported in the press, and they were not prepared to report it. Then, with regard to the men politicians in 1905, we realized how shadowy were the fine phrases about democracy and human equality used by the gentlemen

35 who were then coming into power. They meant to ignore the women—there was no doubt whatsoever about that. For in the official documents coming from the Liberal Party on the eve of the 1905 election, there were sentences like this:

40 'What the country wants is a simple measure of Manhood Suffrage.' There was no room for the inclusion of women. We knew perfectly well that if there was to be franchise reform at all, the Liberal Party, which was then coming into

45 power, did not intend upon instituting votes for women in spite of all the pledges of its members. In spite of the fact that a majority of the House of Commons, especially on the Liberal side, were pledged to it—it did not mean that

50 they were going to put it into practice. And so we found some way of forcing their attention to this question.

"Now I come to the facts with regard to militancy. We realized that the plans we had in our

55 minds would involve great sacrifice on our part, that it might cost us all we had. We were at that time a small organization, composed mainly of working women and the wives and daughters of working men. And my daughters and I took a

60 leading part, naturally, because we thought the thing out, and, to a certain extent, because we were of better social position than most of our members, and we felt a sense of responsibility."

I went over the whole matter of our peaceful

65 committees and of the violence with which they were invariably met; of our arrests and the farcical police court trials, where the mere evidence of policemen's unsupported statements sent us to prison for long terms; of the falsehoods told

70 of us in the House of Commons by responsible members of the government—tales of women scratching and biting policemen and using hatpins. I accused the government of making these attacks against women who were powerless

75 to defend themselves because they feared the women and desired to crush the agitation represented by our organization.

Entrance Ticket · Learning Targets · Decoding the Language of Detail Questions · Finding Supporting Details · ACT Practice · Sum It Up

38

2.3.1 Decoding the Language of Detail Questions

1. Which of the following best describes the role of the author and her daughters in the women's suffrage movement in Great Britain?

_____

_____

_____

2. Which statement most nearly describes the police response to the author and her organization's protests?

_____

_____

_____

3. The author repeatedly mentions the peaceful nature of her work primarily to:

_____

_____

_____

Entrance Ticket   Learning Targets   Decoding the Language of Detail Questions   Finding Supporting Details   ACT Practice   Sum It Up

39

2.3.2 Finding Supporting Details

Physics, being one of the inductive sciences, received little attention until modern times. True, the Greeks were familiar with some fundamental facts of solid and fluid mechanics, and they had some notions about various physical forces, but their knowledge of what is now known as natural philosophy was extremely limited. Aristotle, Pythagoras, and Archimedes were among the most successful investigators of their time regarding the laws and properties of matter. They contributed materially to the advancement of knowledge regarding the phenomena of the material universe, but the sum total of their data, what we now would call physics, could be told in a few pages.

In light of these facts, we should not expect to find women engaged in the study—much less in the teaching—of physical science during ancient times. And yet if we are to credit Boccaccio, who bases his statements on those of early Greek writers, there was at least one woman who earned distinction by her knowledge of natural philosophy as early as the days of Socrates. In his work, *De Laudibus Mulierum*, the genial Boccaccio gives special praise to Arete of Cyrene for the breadth and variety of her attainments. She was the daughter of Aristippus, the founder of the Cyrenaic school of philosophy, and she is represented as being a veritable prodigy of learning. Among her many claims to distinction, she is said to have publicly taught natural and moral philosophy in the schools and academies of Attica for thirty-five years, to have written forty books, and to have counted 110 philosophers among her pupils. She was so highly esteemed by her countrymen that they inscribed on her tomb an epitaph declaring that she was the splendor of Greece and possessed the beauty of Helen, the virtue of Thirma, the pen of Aristippus, the soul of Socrates, and the tongue of Homer.

This is high praise, but when we remember that Arete lived during the golden age of Greek learning and culture, she had exceptional opportunities of acquiring knowledge in every field; when we recall the large number of women who, in their time, distinguished themselves by their learning and accomplishment and reflect on the advantages they enjoyed as pupils of the ablest teachers of the Lyceum, the Portico, and the Academy; when we remember further that they lived in an atmosphere of intelligence that has since been unknown; when we call to mind the success that rewarded the pursuit of knowledge by the scores of women mentioned by Athenæus and other Greek writers and the eminence that they attained in science, philosophy, and literature, we can realize that the character and amount of Arete's work as an author and as a teacher must have been excelling, indeed, to receive such recognition eighteen centuries later.

In an age of vast mental activity, when both women and men were overcome by an abiding love of knowledge for its own sake, there is nothing surprising in finding a learned and eloquent woman like Arete commanding the admiration of her countrymen. Was not the learned and eloquent Aspasia her contemporary? And did not Theano, the wife of Pythagoras, take charge of her husband's school after his death? And does not history credit Theano with being not only a successful teacher of philosophy but also a writer of books of recognized value? Such being the case, what is incredible in the statements made by ancient writers regarding the literary activity of Arete and her eminence as a teacher of science and philosophy? She was but one of many of the Greek women of her age who won acclaim for her gifts of intellect and for her contributions to the educational work of her time and country.

Entrance Ticket   Learning Targets   Decoding the Language of Detail Questions   Finding Supporting Details   ACT Practice   Sum It Up

40

2.3.2 Finding Supporting Details

Better known than Arete, but probably not superior to her as a teacher or writer, was the illustrious Hypatia of Alexandria. She, like her distinguished predecessor in Athens, was an instructor of natural philosophy as well as other branches of science. We know more of her than we do of the daughter of Aristippus, but even our knowledge of the acquisitions and achievements of Hypatia is, unfortunately, meager. However, we do know from the historian Socrates and from Synesius, bishop of Ptolemais—who was her pupil—that Hypatia was a very wealthy woman. "Her knowledge," writes Socrates, "was so great that she far surpassed all the philosophers of her time. And succeeding Plotinus in the Platonic school which he had founded in the city of Alexandria, she taught all the branches of philosophy with such great success that students flocked to her in crowds from all parts." Her home, as well as her lecture room, was the resort of the most noted scholars of the day and was, with the exception of the library and the museum, the most frequented intellectual center in the great city of learning and culture. It is a small wonder, then, that her contemporaries lauded her as an oracle and as the most brilliant luminary in Alexandria's splendid galaxy of thinkers and scholars—*sapientis artis sidus integerrimum.*

1. Some women were known to take over philosophy schools following the death of their husbands.

_____

_____

_____

2. Learning for its own sake was greatly valued in the Golden Age of Greece.

_____

_____

_____

3. Physics was not well understood during the time of Aristotle and Pythagoras.

_____

_____

_____

4. Arete of Cyrene authored many books.

_____

_____

_____

Entrance Ticket   Learning Targets   Decoding the Language of Detail Questions   Finding Supporting Details   ACT Practice   Sum It Up

41

2.3.2 Finding Supporting Details

5. Many women during the Golden Age of Greece were known for their intellect and educational contributions.

_____

_____

_____

6. Hypatia of Alexandria was very well regarded by Socrates.

_____

_____

_____

7. Arete of Cyrene was said to have the soul of Socrates.

_____

_____

_____

8. Plotinus founded his school in Alexandria.

_____

_____

_____

9. Arete and Hypatia were likely equals in terms of skill in writing and teaching.

_____

_____

_____

10. Boccaccio wrote about Arete's many achievements in his book _De Laudibus Mulierum._

_____

_____

_____

Entrance Ticket   Learning Targets   Decoding the Language of Detail Questions   Finding Supporting Details   ACT Practice   Sum It Up

42

This page is intentionally left blank.

2.4.1 Set One

Passage I

LITERARY NARRATIVE: This passage is adapted from the epic *The Odyssey* by Homer. The passage begins with a narrator following Odysseus on his final journey back to his home after a long absence.

The waves pause enough to allow Odysseus glimpses of land, visual reminiscences of a life that has been long on hold. Odysseus regularly sees creeping danger hidden in the sea or the shoreline ahead of his boat. As
5 he nears the port in his home country of Ithaca, he tries to recall his old subjects, to remember their faces or habits. The names slowly come back ... *Eurycleia ... Eurymachus ... Penelope.*

Alone on his couch Odysseus begins to fall asleep,
10 too many memories coming to his mind. Like a clairvoyant he dreams of his reunion with his wife and son. He believes these dreams amount to something—some greater significance or warning about all the struggles it took to return home—and his sleeping mind tries to voice these
15 beliefs, but it is unable to. He eventually gives up, sighs, leaves his dreams, and sleeps more deeply.

Yet now Odysseus is awake, presiding over Greece's craggy shores once more. Athens—even Sparta—seems not so far away. Remarkably soon, in the early morning
20 hours, his ship arrives at the port, Ithaca, the land he once ruled as king.

Unexpectedly, upon setting foot on the island, Odysseus is reminded of his threatening dreams. The goddess Athena appears to Odysseus, warning him: "Your earliest
25 care must be to rid your house of the suitors who seek to marry Penelope, your wife of old. Can you sweep this stain from your home?"

* * *

Odysseus prepares diligently for battle in the coming days. Nightly he sits in Eumaeus's cottage discussing the
30 enemy and tactics, learning of all that has changed since his departure from Ithaca twenty years before. In his own time Odysseus daydreams about his home as it was back then. He remembers the joy he and Penelope shared and the youthful exploits of his boy Telemachus. In his dream
35 world, he rebuilds the glory of his father Laertes's house to what it had been before he left Ithaca; he removes the vile suitors from his home; he undoes the changes time has brought upon the land itself. He restores the vibrancy of youth to his old dog, and Eumaeus reminds him of the
40 hope the people used to have. But soon his daydreams are sidetracked and ideas are left half-remembered as he

struggles to recall the names of his people: old-what's-his-name, the butcher; Eurycleia, the old servant; and Telemachus, his son.

45 Late at night, as Odysseus attempts to sleep in Eumaeus's hut, he listens with rage to the sounds of his country at night and falls asleep counting all that has changed: the suitors invading his home, the distrust held amongst neighbors, the craftsmen that have sprung up in the town.
50 The people of Odysseus's youth are gone. It seems that trust and friendship have left Ithaca. These changes can be seen in none so strongly as their king. Absent now of kindness, optimism, and joy, Odysseus wants only revenge.

* * *

Odysseus decides to pose as a beggar and arrive
55 home in disguise, hoping to trick the suitors into underestimating him. It works for a while. Several hours pass, but then the men who stole his home turn their contempt toward Odysseus. He tries to remain calm, but the men are persistent. Ithaca is a place where his father and his fa-
60 ther's father ruled before him, and he is still remembered. Odysseus knows he is home, and he wants it back.

Withstanding their insults, Odysseus finally sees his opportunity to strike when Penelope—believing her husband to be dead—announces a competition to win her
65 hand in marriage. The first man to bend Odysseus's prized bow and shoot a target would be declared the winner and the new king of Ithaca. Despite the fervent protestations of the suitors, Odysseus takes his turn and accomplishes the feat with ease. He then begins his rampage with the
70 bronze-tipped arrows, killing Eurymachus and the other suitors who would usurp his kingdom. After twenty long years, Odysseus finally reclaims his home and kingdom.

In the aftermath of his victory, Odysseus reflects on all that has changed in his absence and considers how he
75 has returned, after all, to his rightful place in the world. He exhibits great joy—he smiles in the company of his dear wife and son. He seems to have returned in full. One has to wonder if he has truly returned as the Odysseus of old or if he sailed along shores where time advanced
80 without him.

(Entrance Ticket) (Learning Targets) (Decoding the Language of Detail Questions) (Finding Supporting Details) (ACT Practice) (Sum It Up)

44

3 ⬛ 3

1. The passage contains repeated allusions to all of the following EXCEPT:

   A. sailing.
   B. suitors.
   C. hunting.
   D. dreams.

2. According to the passage, Odysseus is related to the individuals listed in lines 7–8 in what way?

   F. All of the individuals traveled extensively.
   G. They all are family members of Odysseus.
   H. All of the individuals sail regularly to Athens.
   J. They all resided in Odysseus's kingdom.

3. The passage supports the idea that by the time Odysseus returns to Ithaca, he has been deprived of all of the following emotions EXCEPT:

   A. kindness.
   B. joy.
   C. optimism.
   D. rage.

4. Which of the following does the passage suggest was true about Ithaca before Odysseus left twenty years earlier?

   F. Telemachus taught Odysseus how to string a bow.
   G. Laertes's home was filled with glory.
   H. Suitors competed for Penelope's hand.
   J. Many of the townspeople were fine artisans.

5. According to the passage, Odysseus's move to eliminate the suitors from his home was a result of:

   A. Athena's warning upon his return to Ithaca.
   B. Penelope's plea sent out to neighboring kingdoms.
   C. Telemachus finding Odysseus and begging for his help.
   D. Odysseus's own desire to attain power in Ithaca.

END OF SET ONE
STOP! DO NOT GO ON TO THE NEXT PAGE
UNTIL TOLD TO DO SO.

Entrance Ticket   Learning Targets   Decoding the Language of Detail Questions   Finding Supporting Details   ACT Practice   Sum It Up

2.4.2 Set Two

Passage I

PROSE FICTION: This passage is adapted from *Peter and Wendy* by James M. Barrie (©1911 by Charles Scribner's Sons). The narrator is a young girl named Wendy, who is in the fantasy world of Neverland.

As the day began to fade, I was still "mother" to the Lost Boys. They sat in the home under the ground, the children squabbling as only children can. I tried to focus on mending patches in a few boys' shirts. A few
5   hours later, I watched my children playing, joy on their faces, laughter on their lips, and their limbs dancing in the firelight. I remembered my earlier irritation, but their joy was so easy it seemed natural. *How charming!* I thought. I remained in my chair with all thoughts of sewing quick-
10 ly falling away. Finally I heard a step nearing the door. Rising from my seat I gathered the children and sent them to the door to greet their "father." In my mind I still heard their joyous laughter.

Peter Pan strolled through the door and brought
15 me back to reality. While the children mobbed Peter, I vaguely remembered a life gone by. It was a life that I had lived—and not so long ago. Lives are often measured in years alive from birth to death. I had never considered another way to measure them. Greeting my "husband" at
20 the door, my mind focused again on my children's joy.

The fire cast a warm glow throughout our cozy home as the children sat eating the nuts Peter brought home for them. The treats would surely spoil the children, but I hardly noticed. I felt as though I was hypnotized. Return-
25 ing to the fire, I thought again of Mr. and Mrs. Darling— parents of a life gone by, nearly forgotten. Comfortable in my chair, I let my mind remember my parents ... *remember I am a parent* ... as if losing my mind. Returning to the moment my past slipped away. I tried to focus on
30 the mayhem around me and remembered how *my* children and husband needed me. Relaxing again in front of the fire, I closed my eyes, feeling content but remembering the love of my parents.

Several minutes later the children began to ask Peter
35 and me to dance. We initially protested, encouraging them to dance among themselves. Their requests became insistent, as Peter truly is the best dancer among them.

We discarded our excuses of old bones and too many children and relented to the children's pleas. Michael, the
40 baby of our group, broke us down with a reminder that it was a Saturday night. We had long ago lost track of the days—any special request came on a Saturday night. The children changed into their pajamas, their half of the bargain, and we began to dance.

45 Peter and I danced and danced as the children tired among us. The children began to settle down near the fire, and we began to talk—first of our contentment, but not for long. We noted Peter's nose on our son Curly and Michael's resemblance to me. The children snacked on mammee
50 apples and tappa rolls, and they sloshed and gulped calabashes of poe-poe. Peter asked if the Lost Boys being "our children" was only make-believe. I assured him that they weren't "truly ours, but all the same they *are* ours." Peter insisted he felt like a devoted son to me, and his questions
55 reminded me of my earlier thoughts. Mr. and Mrs. Darling back in England returned a plain and normal childhood to my mind. That life was less exciting, of course, but it was becoming increasingly beautiful.

Peter talked and talked as I realigned my thoughts,
60 made a decision, and summoned my children to bed. I began to tell the children my story. With great care I weaved the picture and brought to life once again my *real* mother and father. Very slowly, Mr. and Mrs. Darling appeared in the minds of my children. I was back in my old
65 life, further connecting the Darlings to my life in Neverland, carefully reminding John and Michael that they once knew them as parents as well. With thoughtless enthusiasm, I strengthened the connection. This was the most dangerous time for me—making my old life feel real—
70 because of the difficulty I'd imagined came with trying to return to a life I thought was lost. Peter's ire enhanced the danger, but to fight the memory was unthinkable. I focused on my parents and on our dog Nana, who was the most diligent nursemaid who ever lived. As I neared
75 the end of my memory, I encouraged the Lost Boys to remember the love of the parents they once knew. Carefully I tried to draw each of my "sons" into their comforting memories, but they were only able to picture the Darlings. I recognized Peter's anger, greater than ever before. My
80 nerves were undeniable, and I felt a bit ashamed. Yet the love from my old life filled my soul, and it was impossible to will away.

Entrance Ticket   Learning Targets   Decoding the Language of Detail Questions   Finding Supporting Details   ACT Practice   Sum It Up

46

3 ▨▨▨▨▨▨▨▨▨▨▨▨▨▨▨▨▨▨▨▨▨▨▨▨▨▨▨▨▨▨ **3**

6. The author lists details about all of the following traits of her "family" EXCEPT:

   F. the number of boys Wendy cares for.
   G. that Peter acts as the father.
   H. that Wendy sews the boys' clothes.
   J. that the children are happy and energetic.

7. According to the passage, which of the following must the boys do before Wendy and Peter dance?

   A. They must listen to Wendy's story.
   B. They must put on their pajamas.
   C. They must finish their snacks.
   D. They must state the day of the week.

8. Regarding the evening described in the passage, the author does NOT make clear:

   F. whether Peter enjoyed reminiscing about the past.
   G. what foods the Lost Boys snacked on near the fire.
   H. what role Peter plays in the make-believe family.
   J. why the Lost Boys are unable to remember their families.

9. According to the passage, calabashes served as which of the following for the children?

   A. The name of the dance Peter and Wendy perform
   B. A vessel through which they use to drink poe-poe
   C. The type of nut Peter brought them
   D. The instruments they play while Peter and Wendy dance

10. In the passage, the narrator suggests that all of the following were memories from Wendy's former life EXCEPT:

    F. the Darlings.
    G. her husband Peter.
    H. John and Michael.
    J. the dog Nana.

END OF SET TWO
STOP! DO NOT GO ON TO THE NEXT PAGE
UNTIL TOLD TO DO SO.

Entrance Ticket   Learning Targets   Decoding the Language of Detail Questions   Finding Supporting Details   ACT Practice   Sum It Up

2.4.3 Set Three

Passage II

SOCIAL SCIENCE: This passage is adapted from *Lives of our Forefathers* by Nancy McNeese (©2015 by MasteryPrep).

George Washington was born on February 22, 1732. He was born in a farmhouse situated on Bridges Creek Plantation near the Potomac River. The son of a wealthy planter and landowner, Washington was schooled by the
5 sexton of the local church in three subjects: basic reading, basic writing, and ciphering. This simplistic education did little to limit Washington's endeavors in his later life, although he always struggled with spelling.

Washington's youth was marked by tragedy. The
10 death of his father when he was only eleven was the most notable sorrow, which sparked several key developments: one of his brothers left home to operate the Mount Vernon plantation, and Washington became the head of a plantation on the Rappahannock River. He remained under the
15 tutelage of his mother; fortunately, she was kind, firm, and practical. The two shared a deep bond marked by great care and even greater respect. Washington's character also benefitted from the presence of his brothers: Lawrence, who taught him how to be a cultured gentleman, and Au-
20 gustine, who helped provide a more traditional education.

Washington was a spirited youth who was enraptured by military campaigns. While he was in school, he heard many stories about wars, particularly those between the English or French and the Native Americans. His in-
25 terest was only heightened by Lawrence, who had been a soldier in a war between England and Spain. After hearing these stories the young Washington organized his childhood friends into military companies that he led in drills, parades, and sham schoolyard battles. Washington quickly
30 bored of the quiet Virginia setting, and Lawrence's stories inspired aspirations of becoming a sailor. He had all but boarded the ship as a fourteen-year-old when his mother talked him out of it. Even without going to sea, Washington's youth was still replete with outdoor activities.

35 By the time he was sixteen, Washington's love for the outdoors and his methodical studying (his motto was,"Whatever is worth doing is worth doing well.") lent him a natural capacity for surveying. Surveying, the practice of establishing relationships between different land-
40 marks, often for mapmaking purposes, became the prime area of study in which he excelled. Thus, Washington's diligent application of his skills commanded the confidence of others in his ability as a trustworthy surveyor. Eventually he left Rappahannock and moved to the plan-
45 tation at Mount Vernon, which his brother Lawrence was still operating. It was there that Washington met the extremely influential Lord Fairfax.

Although Lord Fairfax was thirty-nine years older than George Washington, the two quickly struck a close
50 friendship that greatly aided the youth's development. The two enjoyed a variety of activities together: surveying, fox hunting, horse riding, discussing English life, and reading literature. Lord Fairfax also introduced Washington to his cousin, George William Fairfax, and assigned
55 the two a monumental task. It was estimated that Lord Fairfax owned land that equated to nearly one-fifth of present-day Virginia. He asked his cousin and Washington to explore a swath of uncharted land beyond the Blue Ridge Mountains that was part of his estate. The young
60 men faced many difficulties in their journey: they traveled alone on horseback, hunted for their primary food supply, had only the stars for a roof, and gathered all their water from streams.

Washington so impressed Lord Fairfax with his
65 work during the campaign that he then found the young man work as a public surveyor. For three years Washington spent much of his time at Lord Fairfax's wilderness home, helping him take care of his land. This work allowed Washington to develop an intimate knowledge
70 of both the woods and outdoor life, as well as develop fearlessness, patience, self-reliance, and leadership skills. However, the most significant outcome of his time as a public surveyor was that the governor of Virginia appointing Washington as a major in the state militia.

75 Washington went on to serve with distinction in the French and Indian War: he traveled 1,000 miles in winter, forded an icy Allegheny River, built Fort Necessity to secure a key location, and served on British General Edward Braddock's staff. General Braddock ultimately
80 died in combat, ignoring Washington's wisdom regarding woodland warfare. With Braddock's death, Washington was placed in charge of all the Virginian troops. When Washington and his troops assailed Fort Duquesne—the fort General Braddock died attacking—the French fled in
85 terror upon hearing of his approach.

Entrance Ticket   Learning Targets   Decoding the Language of Detail Questions   Finding Supporting Details   ACT Practice   Sum It Up

3 **3**

11. The author provides all of the following details about George Washington's youth EXCEPT:

   A. what his mother nicknamed him.
   B. the occupation of his father.
   C. what day he was born.
   D. the location of his birth.

12. According to the passage, for which purpose was Washington employed in the field of surveying?

   F. To measure land for mapping
   G. To plan battle strategies
   H. To dispute lands held by the French
   J. To trace rivers to their source

13. According to the passage, George Washington gained command of all Virginian troops when:

   A. General Edward Braddock died in combat.
   B. Washington built Fort Necessity.
   C. the governor first gave him an officer position.
   D. he successfully captured Fort Duquesne.

14. Regarding Washington's friendship with Lord Fairfax, the author does NOT make clear:

   F. how much older Lord Fairfax was than George Washington.
   G. how much land it is estimated that Lord Fairfax owned.
   H. what geographical feature Washington and George William Fairfax were asked to explore.
   J. why Lord Fairfax introduced his cousin to George Washington.

15. According to the passage, Washington's brothers influenced him by:

   A. encouraging him to join the military.
   B. serving as his teachers after his father's death.
   C. organizing him and his friends into mock military companies.
   D. applauding his enthusiasm for outdoor activities.

END OF SET THREE
STOP! DO NOT GO ON TO THE NEXT PAGE
UNTIL TOLD TO DO SO.

Entrance Ticket   Learning Targets   Decoding the Language of Detail Questions   Finding Supporting Details   ACT Practice   Sum It Up

49

Sum It Up

Locate Part 2

Scanning
The process of looking back to find a specific fact or detail in the passage

---

Skimming
The process of reading through a passage quickly, only determining the most important details rather than reading carefully

Entrance Ticket   Learning Targets   Decoding the Language of Detail Questions   Finding Supporting Details   ACT Practice   Sum It Up

50

Locate Part 3

CAPTION:

3.1 Entrance Ticket

What is wrong with the picture below? Why do many people miss it at first glance?

3.2 Learning Targets

1. Quickly identify where to locate details in a passage

2. Practice and master skimming and scanning passages for details

Self-Assessment

Circle the number that corresponds to your confidence level in your knowledge of this subject before beginning the lesson. A score of 1 means you are completely lost, and a score of 4 means you have mastered the skills. After you finish the lesson, return to the bottom of this page and circle your new confidence level to show your improvement.

Before Lesson

1   2   3   4

After Lesson

1   2   3   4

3.3.1 Building a Passage Map

The stocky, short-legged appearance of penguins has endeared them to people world-wide. On average they are approximately four-teen inches in height and two pounds in weight.
5 Most are black on their backs and white on their stomachs, often with black lines across their upper breasts or white spots on their heads. Color is rare and is limited to red or yellow irises of the eyes in some species, red beaks or feet in
10 a few species, yellow brow tufts in the three spe-cies of *Eudyptes*, and orange and yellow areas on the heads, necks, and breasts in the emperor king (*A. patagonica*) penguins.

Many features of the penguin life cycle
15 vary with body size and geographic distribution; the chronology of breeding may also vary within a species in relation to latitude. The majority of species breed only once per year. Certain spe-cies, such as African penguins, breed twice per
20 year. King penguins only breed twice every three years. The emperor and king penguins only lay one egg at a time; all others lay two or occa-sionally three eggs at a time. Most penguins begin breeding in the spring or summer. King
25 penguins are on a fourteen- to eighteen-month cycle, and the timing of an individual pair de-pends on the success or failure of the previous breeding attempt. Some populations of gentoo penguins breed in winter. The breeding of em-
30 peror penguins begins in autumn and yields a long developmental period that produces young in midsummer, when their chances for survival are greatest.

The total populations of some species,
35 such as the emperor penguin, are estimated in the hundreds of thousands, but most species of smaller penguins have populations in the mil-lions. Immense island breeding colonies—some teeming with hundreds of thousands of nesting
40 pairs—represent a large potential food resource, but the economic importance of penguins is neg-ligible. Whalers and seal hunters in the 19th cen-tury visited some penguin colonies for meat and eggs, and a penguin oil industry once took large
45 numbers of the birds. By the early 20th century, however, this exploitation was no longer profit-able, and most colonies were either left alone or actively protected. Some species are now increasing in numbers, apparently as a result
50 of the mid-20th century's decimation of the Ant-arctic whale population, which competed with penguins for crustacean food sources. Penguin populations, however, remain highly vulnerable to changes in climate and ocean temperature.
55 Penguins also are very vulnerable to the deple-tion of local fish populations by humans.

3.3.1 Building a Passage Map

Main idea of passage: _____

Main idea of first paragraph: _____

Main idea of second paragraph: _____

Main idea of third paragraph: _____

appearance _____   breed _____

numbers _____   weight _____

color _____   egg _____

height _____   populations _____

millions _____

3.3.1 Building a Passage Map

It was beautiful spring weather, but neither the sled dogs nor the humans were aware of it. Each day the sun rose earlier and set later. It was dawn by three in the morning, and twilight
5 lingered until nine at night. The whole long day was a blaze of sunshine. The ghostly winter silence had given way to the great spring murmur of awakening life. This murmur arose from all the land, fraught with the joy of living. It came from
10 the things that lived and moved again—things that had not moved during the long months of frost. The sap was rising in the pines. The willows and aspens were bursting out in young buds. Shrubs and vines were putting on fresh garbs
15 of green. Crickets sang in the nights, and in the days all manner of creeping, crawling things rustled forth into the sun. Squirrels were chattering, birds were singing, and overhead honked the wild geese flying up from the South in wedges
20 that split the air.

From every hill slope came the trickle of running water, the music of unseen fountains. All things were thawing, bending, and snapping. The Yukon was straining to break loose the ice
25 that bound it down. It ate away from beneath; the sun ate from above. Air holes formed and fissures sprang and spread apart, while thin sections of ice fell through into the river. Amid all this bursting, rending, throbbing of awakening life,
30 under the blazing sun and through the soft-sighing breezes, like wayfarers to death staggered the two men, the woman, and the huskies.

With the dogs exhausted, Mercedes weeping and riding, Hal swearing innocuously, and
35 Charles's eyes wistfully watering, they staggered into John Thornton's camp at the mouth of White River. When they halted, the dogs dropped down as though they had all been struck dead. Mercedes dried her eyes and looked at John Thorn-
40 ton. Charles sat down on a log to rest. He sat down very slowly and painstakingly due to his great stiffness. Hal did the talking. John Thornton was whittling the last touches on an axe handle he had made from a stick of birch. He whittled
45 and listened, gave monosyllabic replies, and— when it was asked for—terse advice. He knew this type of people, and he gave his advice in the certainty that it would not be followed.

3.3.1 Building a Passage Map

Main idea of passage: _____

Main idea of first paragraph: _____

Main idea of second paragraph: _____

Main idea of third paragraph: _____

key word: _____   paragraph: _____

key word: _____   paragraph: _____

key word: _____   paragraph: _____

key word: _____   paragraph: _____

key word: _____   paragraph: _____

3.3.1 Building a Passage Map

Cesar Chavez was one of America's fiercest fighters for civil rights, even if he didn't necessarily appear ferocious. The grandson of humble Mexican immigrants, Chavez stood just five
5 feet, six inches tall, with deep brown eyes and a quiet, unassuming demeanor. But his small stature belied a mountain of strength, evidenced in his quest to win rights for migrant farm workers in California. His major accomplishment was to
10 establish the first successful labor union of such workers who, prior to that time, had had virtually no protection under American law. With this accomplishment Chavez brought a degree of stability and economic security to their lives for the
15 first time. His work also inspired dozens of key activists and leaders in subsequent movements for social justice, including immigrant rights, feminism, and environmental protection. In fact there is hardly a progressive movement in Amer-
20 ica today uninfluenced by Chavez's legacy.

For Latinos especially Chavez was a hero. The civil rights movement of the 1960s is today remembered largely for its advances on behalf of African-Americans, but all non-whites had been
25 subject to segregation in the era of Jim Crow. Chavez and his family grew up being harassed by the police, being denied service in restaurants, and being made to sit in the "colored" sections at movie theaters. Martin Luther King Jr.
30 and Malcolm X have achieved mythical status in American history—and deservedly so for the incredible progress they helped bring about— but Chavez's gains were just as vital to millions of disenfranchised Latino people, who made up
35 the majority of America's migrant workers. He rallied them with a simple Spanish phrase: "Si, se puede," meaning "Yes, we can."

However, it wasn't just Latinos who lined up behind Chavez. His struggle was for work-
40 ers' rights, no matter what race or ethnicity the workers happened to be. Throughout the 1960s and 1970s, his United Farm Workers union won concessions from the conservative, behemoth U.S. agribusiness industry, and this drastically
45 improved the lives of Chinese, Japanese, Filipino, African-American and white laborers, as well as Latinos.

Reading Tip

Keep Your Pencil Moving: If you find yourself struggling to concentrate while reading a passage, try to make a brief passage map as you read. If you train yourself to do this well, you can create the map just by underlining the author's main points as you read them.

3.3.1 Building a Passage Map

Main idea of passage: _____

Main idea of first paragraph: _____

Main idea of second paragraph: _____

Main idea of third paragraph: _____

key word: _____   paragraph: _____

key word: _____   paragraph: _____

key word: _____   paragraph: _____

key word: _____   paragraph: _____

key word: _____   paragraph: _____

3.3.2 Skimming and Scanning

We first witness theater when we are very young, as audience members watching the dramas and comedies of our own families. As toddlers we pay close attention as the acts unfold. Before we are old enough to play central roles ourselves, we watch others. Some stories play out in mere minutes; others stretch over the course of days, weeks, or years. Parents fight and make up. Older siblings experience emotions and confusions that we dimly understand are previews of our own. Neighbors and relatives make entrances and exits, bringing news of the world outside. We take all this in from our positions in the gallery, leaning forward to get a better view, trying to understand the significance of a look, a smile, a slouch. We learn to heed the details and to make connections between moments. And then, suddenly, it is our turn to take the stage.

As young children we gradually become aware of ourselves as actors. For the first time we influence the action taking place. We learn what effects our own glances, words, and touches have on others. Crucially we also learn to distinguish true from false and sincere from disingenuous. Some of us try our hands at pretending. We imagine ourselves in situations different from our own and try to feel what it would really be like to be somewhere else in another time as another person.

Two aspects of performance influence our early appreciation of acting, as well as the expectations we bring to it later. The first is reality or believability. Do we believe in the truth of what we see, hear, and feel? Does it pass our inner test for authenticity? Do we trust it? The second is empathy. Does this matter to me? Can I see myself in this person? Does it reveal something to me about myself? I believe it is at the intersection of these two constructs that great acting is realized.

Let's face it: if it seems fake, we're not interested. However, just because it seems real, doesn't mean we're necessarily interested in it. A man straightening his tie while waiting for a bus is perfectly real—and perfectly forgettable. But a man straightening his tie while waiting to receive news about his sick mother is something else entirely because we automatically put ourselves in his position—that is, if we buy into his reality. A performance has to be both authentic and relatable for us to invest our interests.

What if *we're* the ones performing on stage? How do we place ourselves into an alternate reality? What's more, how do we do it on cue? Ah, this is trickier, to say the least, but it asks for the same two ingredients, believability and empathy.

First we must accept our given circumstances. If I am playing Hamlet, I must accept that I live in Denmark, that I am a prince, that my father was murdered, and that I have reason to believe my uncle did it. That's all fine. It is given to me by the play, and I must accept it as fact. I may later come to actually believe it, but for the moment, let me just accept it as the set of "rules" by which I must play.

Now comes the challenging part. How can I empathize with this character? I'm not a prince, but I can remember what it feels like to have expectations placed on me at a young age, and I can remember feeling the pressure of living up to them. I can remember what it feels like to represent my family in the eyes of others. Thankfully, my own father wasn't murdered, but I can recall the ache I once felt at seeing him in pain and the shock of imagining him being gone. I have these

3.3.2 Skimming and Scanning

experiences on which to draw, but they are ap-
proximations. I still haven't connected the facts
80 of the play to the facts of my own life. I have both
reality and empathy but not at the same time.

Bridging this gap takes practice. It takes
memory, both of words and feelings. It takes
learning lines so thoroughly that they lose their
85 meaning, giving one the chance to discover
them anew. This is the process of rehearsal,

where the real work of acting happens. It takes
humility, in a way, to believe that circumstances could be different and yet just as true as our
90 actual experiences. It calls one's attention to the
commonalities and differences between people
and the mysteries of each. Above all, though, it
takes faith. It takes faith to believe that what we
are doing and the story we are telling will cap-
95 ture our audience and transport it somewhere
else—different yet familiar.

Main idea of passage: _____

Main idea of first paragraph: _____

Main idea of second paragraph: _____

Main idea of third paragraph: _____

Main idea of fourth paragraph: _____

Main idea of fifth paragraph: _____

Main idea of sixth paragraph: _____

Main idea of seventh paragraph: _____

Main idea of eighth paragraph: _____

3.3.2 Skimming and Scanning

Einstein's theory of general relativity holds that massive objects in space cause a distortion in the continuum of space-time, which is felt as gravity. If we think of space-time as the surface of a trampoline and imagine placing a 500-pound medicine ball at its center, we have a reasonable approximation of this phenomenon. The fabric of the trampoline would stretch and bend around the ball, causing the once-flat surface to dimple. A marble then rolled around the trampoline's outside edge would gradually spiral toward the center, pulled inward by the gradually increasing curvature of the surface.

In the case of Earth and all the planets in our solar system—not to mention the sun—the warping of space-time manifests as a gravitational field that pulls objects in as they enter its orbit. However, if the central object is much more massive and dense than a planet or a star, its gravitational pull becomes so strong that not even light can escape it. The result is a black hole, observable only by the extreme warp it causes in space-time since it obviously does not emit any light.

Supermassive black holes—with masses ranging from hundreds of thousands to billions of times the mass of our sun—actually reside at the center of every galaxy, including our own Milky Way. How they form in the first place is still a matter of debate, but astrophysicists agree that they grow over time, mostly by pulling interstellar gas into themselves. These episodes of rapid gas accretion are observable as quasars—very remote objects nonetheless distinguished by their extreme luminosity (the effect of so much energy spinning toward the black holes at their centers).

Because black holes warp the fabric of space-time so drastically, the light around them is observed as if through a highly distorted lens, which magnifies more distant objects so they appear more clearly. A prime example of so-called "gravitational lensing" occurs in a quasar known as Einstein's Cross. It is roughly 8 billion light-years from Earth and sits directly behind a galaxy 400 million light-years away. If not for gravitational lensing, the quasar would be obscured by the galaxy in front of it. Instead, the galaxy's gravity bends the light from the more distant quasar around it, resulting in four separate images of the quasar around the galaxy. Each appears as a distinct object, but the "four quasars" are actually all the same quasar refracted differently through the lens of space-time.

Most supermassive black holes are distant enough from each other that their respective fields of gravity exert little effect on one another. However, in a distant galaxy known as PG 1302-102, two supermassive black holes appear to be heading for a cosmic collision of a mind-boggling scale. The impact, projected to take place in as little as 100,000 years, could release as much energy as a combined 100 million of the violent supernova explosions in which stars end their lives. This would effectively obliterate the galaxy that surrounds it.

Flanked by a pair of smaller galaxies, PG 1302-102 lies about 3.5 billion light-years from Earth in the constellation Virgo, and it has a quasar at its center. Astrophysicists first detected evidence of the impending black hole collision in a rhythmic flickering of the quasar's light. They found it wavered by about 14 percent every 1,884 days, or roughly five years, and they deduced that the only thing that could so signifi-

Entrance Ticket · Learning Targets · Building a Passage Map · Skimming and Scanning · ACT Practice · Sum It Up

3.3.2 Skimming and Scanning

cantly affect the energy pull of a giant black hole would be another giant black hole.

In the event of such a collision, most of the resulting energy would be released as gravita- 80 tional waves, the violent ripples of space-time that are predicted but not yet directly detected by Einstein's theory. Theoretically, the twisting merger of the black holes would fling nearby stars away, like shingles flying off a roof in a tor- 85 nado. Of course no one knows what will actually happen until they are able to observe the effects. Whether or not humans are around to witness the event, though, it should provide a preview of what will happen in a few billion years when our 90 own Milky Way galaxy collides with the neighboring Andromeda galaxy, merging the black holes at the heart of each.

Main idea of passage: _____

Main idea of first paragraph: _____

Main idea of second paragraph: _____

Main idea of third paragraph: _____

Main idea of fourth paragraph: _____

Main idea of fifth paragraph: _____

Main idea of sixth paragraph: _____

Main idea of seventh paragraph: _____

Reading Tip

Finding details questions are the easiest questions on the ACT if they are approached in the correct way. You can recognize these questions because they usually ask about the *who*, *what*, *where*, *when*, *why*, and *how* of a passage. If you see this type of question, you should scan the passage and select the answer that best matches the information in the passage.

Entrance Ticket   Learning Targets   Building a Passage Map   Skimming and Scanning   ACT Practice   Sum It Up

3.4.1 Set One

Passage II

SOCIAL SCIENCE: This passage is adapted from *My Grandmother's Egypt* by Miriam Zarzour (©2015 by MasteryPrep).

I can remember where I was when I first learned about Egypt. I was very young—four or five years old—and I was staying with my grandmother for the summer. I still cannot believe this was my first time learning of my

5 family's homeland. My parents had neglected to teach me about the place that bore us and the amazing people who formed the roots of our family tree. My grandmother was happy to enlighten me, and I was a willing pupil.

"We Egyptians are a race different from both

10 the dark-skinned people of Africa and from the paler Europeans. We have olive skin, very dark almond-shaped eyes, and dark, straight hair. Most of the men shave their heads and wear a tarboosh as a covering. Both the men and the women wear several loose garments, which cover

15 the whole body from the neck to the feet. Traditional women fasten a veil below their eyes, which falls over the lower part of their face. It is as though this veil hides many secrets, but the truth is in their eyes.

"In the place where I grew up, there were a great

20 many people—some very rich and others very poor. The city appeared very beautiful because the houses were built of white or light-colored stone or brick. But they were close together, and the streets were very narrow and dirty. The houses were built in stories—one room on top of

25 another—with steps leading to the upper rooms. Often there was a courtyard in the middle of the house so that all the rooms had windows and light. Remember this was before every household could afford electric lighting!

"Until just before I was born, in the early 1920s,

30 all Egyptians who had enough money had slaves do their work. These slaves could be bought or sold, or married or given away, as if they were things instead of people. Often slaves were content if they had good employers, but it is unfair to take away a person's freedom and treat him

35 as if he has no soul. Can you imagine a life in which you are treated as a possession? Simply being content is not happiness.

"My father used to tell me of the time he looked into the eyes of a boy his age who was enslaved. My father

40 was kicking a ball in the street as the boy passed him in a wagon. My father said he would still see the boy's face in his dreams. He could still feel the pain in the other boy's eyes, and it would shake him from his sleep. The boy's truth was in his eyes.

45 "By the time I was born, Egyptians had done away with slavery. Instead of slaves people had servants who received fair wages for their work. These people were free to leave their employers if they did not treat them well. Although slavery had died out in Egypt, there were

50 still other parts of North Africa where the old customs persisted. But people are happiest in countries where there are no slaves and everyone is free to do the work that makes them most happy.

"Most Egyptian men had multiple wives; together,

55 they lived in one harem, a section of the house that was devoted to them. Each of the wives—in order to secure her position—was expected to bear her husband a son. Surely this led to tension, resentment, and even quarrelling among the women and confusion among the children.

60 My own mother, who grew up in such a household, often warned me of the difficulties of an unhappy marriage.

"You must know, though, my child, that this could not be more untrue of my marriage to your grandfather. Knowing the ways of our ancestors and how the seeds

65 of unhappiness could be sown, we have chosen our own path, adhering to many of the old customs but remaining separate from others. In this home we have built together—just the two of us—there is respect, there is support, and above all, there is love. It is these Egyptian roots from

70 which you are born."

I looked at my grandmother. She was appreciative of her Egyptian ancestry and brutally honest about all aspects of the culture that reared her. She loved Egypt. She was proud of Egyptians—herself included. This truth

75 was in her eyes.

Entrance Ticket   Learning Targets   Building a Passage Map   Skimming and Scanning   ACT Practice   Sum It Up

3   **3**

1. In the passage, the narrator's grandmother states that the city she grew up in appeared beautiful because:

   A. each building had its own courtyard.
   B. the people themselves were gorgeous.
   C. its citizens were very wealthy.
   D. the houses were built with white or light stone and brick.

2. According to the passage, the narrator's grandmother describes most traditional Egyptian households in her town in each of the following ways EXCEPT that they:

   F. contained a separate area for the women of the house.
   G. were situated on narrow, dirty streets.
   H. were equipped with electric lighting.
   J. were built one room on top of another.

3. According to the passage, which of the following traditions does the narrator's grandmother say she and her husband deviate from most?

   A. Taking pride in Egyptian culture
   B. Settling down in a big city
   C. Living with multiple wives
   D. Paying servants to work for them

4. According to the passage, who did the narrator's great grandfather often see in his dreams as described in lines 38–44?

   F. A woman in a veil
   G. Himself kicking a ball
   H. His wives
   J. A slave his own age

5. According to the passage, one's experiences can be boiled down to a singular truth that is visible in which part of them?

   A. Hands
   B. Eyes
   C. Temperament
   D. Shoulders

END OF SET ONE
STOP! DO NOT GO ON TO THE NEXT PAGE
UNTIL TOLD TO DO SO.

Entrance Ticket   Learning Targets   Building a Passage Map   Skimming and Scanning   ACT Practice   Sum It Up

3.4.2 Set Two

Passage I

PROSE FICTION: This passage is adapted from the short story "The Price of Nostalgia" by Charles Frank (©2015 by MasteryPrep).

It's a slow day at the shop. Just as I'm about to call it a day, a smartly dressed elderly man walks in. This strikes me as odd because the types I usually get in the shop don't even own a tie.

5 "What's the price of that set of '57 Cadillac hubcaps?" he asks, gesturing to a set of gorgeous chrome caps with that iconic Caddy emblem in red at the center.

"Oh, I'm not selling those," I say. "Actually, all the old hubcaps behind the desk here are just for show." It's
10 not that I'm emotionally attached to them. I just like the look of old chrome hubcaps from before the 1980s, and they make cool decorations for the shop.

He looks a little upset and then counters, "What about four hundred dollars? Are they for sale now?"

15 My interest is certainly piqued, but then I remember that the clasps on the back that attach them to the wheels are bent, and, in some cases, broken off. I could probably fix them for him, but I do like having them in the shop. "Those really aren't in great condition. You wouldn't even
20 be able to use them as real wheel covers," I say.

"That's alright. Would you take six hundred dollars? I just like them, that's all."

Now, it's possible that I just don't know my hubcaps and wheel covers like a real expert should. But I get the
25 funny feeling that he's not an expert either; he's just a guy who sees something he wants. He doesn't have the usual vibe of a collector. I can sniff out collectors from a mile away by how coolly and calmly they bid on items in the shop or in the scrapyard. They act like it's no big
30 deal and always keep an upper hand in the negotiations. At this point, the old man is almost begging just to be able to buy them.

"Alright, fine," I finally say, breaking open a big smile. "I'm telling you, though, they're not usable.
35 They're just for show. You've been warned."

"So you must collect old hubcaps?" I ask after helping the man to his pickup truck with his haul. I'm thinking he's about to tell me that I could have gotten away with asking for ten times what he paid for them.

40 "Nope. I had an uncle with a '57 Cadillac Coupe Deville. I have a picture of him leaning on that car in my den. And I thought it'd be neat to hang these babies up next to the picture."

Hearing this I'm suddenly happy I sold them to him.
45 I've been in his shoes before. I know what it's like to want something for no other reason than that it brings up good memories. It's an odd thing, really. When we have something as kids, the monetary value of it never even occurs to us. And then, as adults, nostalgia multiplies its
50 value by a hundred.

A friend of mine has turned her scrapyard into a museum of sorts. It isn't advertised as that, but people treat it as such. My friend has curated her collection of odd auto parts to tell a story of not only the history of
55 automobiles but also how they fit into our lives. Walking through, you may see only the driver's side door of a '63 Ford Falcon Futura, simply because that's the only part she has. Next to it she's placed a drive-in speaker pole and a poster of Alfred Hitchcock's "The Birds," and
60 in a second, you're a kid again, sitting in the backseat, terrified, and hiding under a blanket.

I know that cars aren't central to everyone's experience growing up and that not every scrap or piece jogs a memory. But just to see the back seat of your
65 mom's Honda that you saw every day from age zero to six, to see the seatbelt of your grandpa's Lincoln—"The Commander"—where you rode up front for the first time, to see the back fender of your dad's Dodge that he was driving when he scraped the side of the house backing
70 out—believe me—it would take you back to those moments. And for maybe just a second, you'd feel the same warmth, the same pride, the same shock of those moments in a way that you'd forgotten.

There's a quote that always makes me feel like my
75 scrapyard is more than what meets the eye. The great writer Florence King once said, "True nostalgia is an ephemeral composition of disjointed memories." Well, there's nothing more disjointed than the parts in my yard. You might call the parts in my care "auto ephemera."
80 Although it might take a little digging, when you find the right part, it'll drive you somewhere special.

⬭ Entrance Ticket ⬭   ⬭ Learning Targets ⬭   ⬭ Building a Passage Map ⬭   ⬭ Skimming and Scanning ⬭   ⬛ ACT Practice ⬛   ⬭ Sum It Up ⬭

3   **3**

6. The narrator indicated that he collects hubcaps from before the 1980s because they:

    F. remind him of a simpler time.
    G. help him remember his uncle's cars.
    H. make good decorations for his shop.
    J. keep going up in value.

7. The author states that he knows the man who walks into his shop is not a collector because he:

    A. does not know how much the hubcaps are truly worth.
    B. maintains a cool distance from the transaction.
    C. keeps the upper hand during negotiations.
    D. practically begs to purchase the hubcaps.

8. In response to the buyer bidding six hundred dollars for the hubcaps, the narrator:

    F. tells the man they are not for sale.
    G. accepts his bid and helps the man carry them to his truck.
    H. explains the importance of nostalgia to the man and tells him about his friend's museum.
    J. tries to sell him the rear fender of an old Dodge instead.

9. According to the passage, who or what is "The Commander"?

    A. The narrator
    B. The narrator's grandfather
    C. The nickname of a Lincoln
    D. One of the narrator's first automobile purchases

10. According to the passage, who likes to refer to old car parts as *auto ephemera*?

    F. The buyer
    G. The narrator
    H. Florence King
    J. The friend who owns the museum

END OF SET TWO
STOP! DO NOT GO ON TO THE NEXT PAGE
UNTIL TOLD TO DO SO.

Entrance Ticket   Learning Targets   Building a Passage Map   Skimming and Scanning   ACT Practice   Sum It Up

3.4.3 Set Three

Passage I

LITERARY NARRATIVE: This passage is adapted from *The Luck of Barry Lyndon* by William Makepeace Thackeray, which first appeared serially in *Fraser's Magazine for Town and Country* (©1844 by George William Nickisson).

I presume that there is no gentleman in Europe who has not heard of the house of Barry of Barryogue in the kingdom of Ireland. As a man of the world, I have learned to despise the claims of my countrymen who boast that
5 they are descendants from kings of Ireland when their genealogy indicates nothing of the kind. And truth compels me to assert that my family, the Barry family, was the noblest of the island and, perhaps, of the world. This was true in land holdings, livestock, precious jewels,
10 servants and wait staff, arms, trophies of sport, and—if I may be so bold—in wit, beauty, and temperament. The land at Barryogue was legendary for its lush pastures, its interconnected lakes and rivers, and its rolling hills, which are said to have given birth to the red Irish temper itself.

15 Our land used to stretch vastly outward and embrace many counties at a time when Ireland was more prosperous than it is now. Today Barrys' possessions are now insignificant, having been torn from us by war, treachery, ancestral extravagance, and the passage of
20 time. We are princes of the land no longer. I know the origin of our fate to be fact, for my mother has often told it to me, and she had worked it in a stitched tapestry,which hung up in the yellow parlor at Barryville where we lived.

Rory Barry of Barryogue owned the estate during
25 Elizabeth I's reign and was the Barry at the time. As history tells it, the Barrys were always in feud with the O'Mahonys during those decades. It is said that the latter's men were forever envious of the fairness of the women at Barryogue, who were known as the loveliest
30 in all of Ireland. The sparring between the two clans was continuous, one passionately determined to usurp the other's possessions.

As it happened, a certain young English colonel, Roger Lyndon, happened to pass through the Barry's
35 country with a band of soldiers just as the O'Mahonys had snuck upon our territories and carried off a frightful plunder of our flocks and herds. This young English colonel, Roger Lyndon, having been most hospitably received by the Barrys, learned that they were just at
40 the point of carrying out their own mission into the O'Mahonys' land—a craggy, fallow, rocky wasteland compared to the Barryogue—and offered the aid of himself and his men. Lyndon succeeded, as it appeared that the O'Mahonys were entirely overcome, all the
45 Barrys' property was restored, and twice as much of the O'Mahonys' goods and cattle were added to it.

As it was winter, the Barry pressed the young English Lyndon and his men to remain at his house of Barryogue. They remained there for several months and
50 were housed with the mercenary warriors hired by the Barrys. But Lyndon and his men conducted themselves with the most intolerable insolence toward the Irish—so much so that fights and murders continually ensued, and the Irish then vowed to defeat Lyndon and the English
55 altogether.

The Barry's son, Phaudrig Barry, from whom I descend, was as hostile to the English as any other man on his domain and was determined to destroy these people, each and every one of them. But the Irish had made the
60 mistake of letting another into their plot, and this was the Barry's daughter. She was in love with the English Lyndon and broke the whole secret to him. As a result, the dastardly English prevented the rightful massacre of themselves by attacking the Irish and destroying
65 Phaudrig Barry and many hundreds of his men. The cross at Barrycross near Carrignadihioul is the spot where the battle took place.

Who knows, if not for the fault of one deceitful woman, I might be wearing the Irish crown now? Had
70 there been a gallant chief to lead my countrymen, instead of disloyal knaves who bowed to King Richard II, my countrymen might be free, and we could have shaken off the English forever.

That very estate which the Lyndons now possess in
75 Ireland was once the property of my family. It pains me to think of the untold riches and acreage that would be under my realm were it not for one treasonous affront. Instead I find myself here at Kill   arney, deposed from the land that is rightly my family's, no crown on my head, and no
80 coat of arms. The modest earnings of a machinist are the jewels in my vault, but I say, again, my genealogies to the highest thrones of Ireland are true. And I take it as a personal indignity that any commoner should dispute it, or worse—make claims that he himself is more worthy of
85 the throne than I.

Entrance Ticket   Learning Targets   Building a Passage Map   Skimming and Scanning   ACT Practice   Sum It Up

3 **3**

---

11. Which of the following events does the narrator NOT cite as a contributing factor to his family's fall from nobility?

    A. The O'Mahonys' capture of the Barry's land
    B. The arrival of Roger Lyndon
    C. Rory Barry's daughter divulging the secret of the plan to the English
    D. Englishmen preventing their own massacre

12. According to the passage, all of the following were formerly holdings of the Barry family EXCEPT:

    F. land where the Irish temper is said to have originated.
    G. elaborate jewels that few in the land had seen.
    H. wealth accumulated from an ancestor's modest machinist wages.
    J. large holdings of flocks and herds.

13. The passage does NOT identify which of the following as a feature of the Barryogue?

    A. Craggy, fallow, rocky terrain
    B. Lush pastures
    C. Interconnected waterways
    D. Hills where the Irish temper came from

14. According to the passage, the woman whom the author blames for the downfall of his family was in love with:

    F. a member of the rival O'Mahony family.
    G. Phaudrig Barry, the ancestor of the narrator.
    H. King Richard II.
    J. an Englishman named Roger Lyndon.

15. The author states that the O'Mahonys were jealous of the Barrys because of their:

    A. trophies of sport.
    B. fair women.
    C. landholdings and livestock.
    D. coat of arms.

END OF SET THREE
STOP! DO NOT GO ON TO THE NEXT PAGE
UNTIL TOLD TO DO SO.

Entrance Ticket   Learning Targets   Building a Passage Map   Skimming and Scanning   ACT Practice   Sum It Up

Sum It Up

Locate Part 3

Detail
A particular fact or piece of information

Main Idea
The most important or central thought of a paragraph or larger section of text that tells the reader what the text is about

Tips and Techniques

Keep Your Pencil Moving: If you find yourself struggling to concentrate when you read a passage, try to create a brief passage map while you read. If you train yourself to do this well, you can create the map just by underlining the author's main points as you read them.

Finding details questions are the easiest questions on the ACT if they are approached in the correct way. You can recognize these questions because they usually ask about the *who*, *what*, *where*, *when*, *why*, and *how* of a passage. If you see this type of question, you should scan the passage and select the answer that best matches the information in the passage.

Drawing Conclusions Part 1

CAPTION:

4.1 Entrance Ticket

Read the passage and answer the following questions.

Tamara turned the wheel clumsily. The man in the passenger seat eyed her, pursed his lips, and made several marks on his clipboard. She had hoped to carefully inch out of her parking spot, but when her foot slipped and fell hard on the gas pedal, the car lurched back and bumped straight into a pole in the parking lot. The man grimaced and quietly marked another check on his clipboard. "Turn left," he said gruffly as beads of sweat began to drip down Tamara's brow. She timidly exited the parking lot and pulled out onto a busy boulevard, traveling almost twenty miles per hour below the speed limit. The man glanced in the mirror disapprovingly as traffic accumulated behind them. He scribbled a few more things on his clipboard and muttered, "Turn right at this stoplight." Tamara swung the car right, but she did not stop first at the light. Several cars honked and slammed on their brakes behind her. She hit a curb and bumped into a railing trying to swerve out of their way. The man hastily made several more marks and scribbles. "That is sufficient," he said. "Please pull over. I will drive us back to the facility."

1. What is Tamara doing? How do you know?

_____

_____

2. Who is the man with Tamara? How do you know?

_____

_____

3. What information is the man writing on his clipboard? How do you know?

_____

_____

4. What do you expect will be the results of Tamara's actions? Why?

_____

_____

Entrance Ticket   Learning Target   Understanding Inferences   Inferences vs. Assumptions   ACT Practice   Sum It Up

4.2 Learning Target

1. Recognize good and bad inferences from written passages

Self-Assessment

Circle the number that corresponds to your confidence level in your knowledge of this subject before beginning the lesson. A score of 1 means you are completely lost, and a score of 4 means you have mastered the skills. After you finish the lesson, return to the bottom of this page and circle your new confidence level to show your improvement.

Before Lesson

1   2   3   4

After Lesson

1   2   3   4

Entrance Ticket   Learning Target   Understanding Inferences   Inferences vs. Assumptions   ACT Practice   Sum It Up

73

4.3.1 Understanding Inferences

1. Martin stepped out of his house, squinting as he looked at the sky.

    What can you infer? _____

    What is the conclusion? _____

    What is the evidence? _____

    Martin slept late: _____

    _____

    Martin has spent the day inside: _____

    _____

    It is morning: _____

    _____

    It is very hot outside: _____

    _____

Reading Tip

Sounds Right: If you notice that a choice sounds strange or out of place, it is most likely an incorrect answer. If that is the case, eliminate it.

Entrance Ticket   Learning Target   Understanding Inferences   Inferences vs. Assumptions   ACT Practice   Sum It Up

74

4.3.2 Inferences vs. Assumptions

1. LaShawn's pet goldfish died last week after three years of life.

   LaShawn's goldfish died of old age. Assumption   Inference

   LaShawn was extremely upset. Assumption   Inference

   LaShawn no longer has any goldfish. Assumption   Inference

   LaShawn has had to grieve the death of a pet. Assumption   Inference

2. Jared danced the night away at the dance party.

   Jared did not have school the next day. Assumption   Inference

   Jared was a great dancer. Assumption   Inference

   Jared was dancing with other people. Assumption   Inference

   Jared danced late at night. Assumption   Inference

   Jared danced with his date. Assumption   Inference

3. Garrett cut his finger chopping onions.

   Garrett was preparing food. Assumption   Inference

   Garrett is a very inexperienced chef. Assumption   Inference

   Garrett's finger was bleeding. Assumption   Inference

   Garrett needed stitches. Assumption   Inference

Reading Tip

Scanning: Since drawing a conclusion is always based on the evidence in the passage, you should always scan through the passage to find the evidence. It may feel like it is taking a long time, but it will help you answer questions more quickly and accurately.

Entrance Ticket   Learning Target   Understanding Inferences   Inferences vs. Assumptions   ACT Practice   Sum It Up

75

3   3

4.4.1 Set One

Passage I

PROSE FICTION: This passage is adapted from the short story "Candid Lemonade" by Phoebe Gellrich (©2015 by MasteryPrep).

I think about how Uncle Ralph's neighbors all remember the same things a little differently. Mama says that all memories are just versions of the truth and that sometimes they're more important than what actually
5 happened. If Uncle Ralph and his neighbors remember things differently, then there's probably a little bit of truth in everyone's version. It must be that when folks reminisce about old times, they're softly reshaping each other's memories.

10 Uncle Ralph sands a chair leg on the steps while Mama waters plants in the garden. I look across the street and see Louise Erstad sitting on her porch. She smiles at me and holds up her glass of lemonade in greeting. I go across the street to show her my camera.

15 Louise Erstad's face is wrinkled and tanned, and she has the same dark brown eyes as Uncle Ralph. She always wears a dress—I've never seen her in anything else. Mama sometimes wears jeans or khaki pants, but on Louise I think that would look strange.

20 She's definitely one of the quickest people I know, both in the way she moves and talks. She has a way of listening to you and then saying something that lets you know she understands exactly what you mean.

She's sitting in a rocking chair on her porch, saying,
25 "I saved my pennies for a camera just like that! Sometimes I felt bad because my daddy needed money, but I never gave it to him. I remember I was so excited when I got it, I took it to bed with me for a week. I put it under my pillow and laid my head on the mattress!"

30 "I still forget to change the f-stop on mine," I say. "Sometimes I'll take a picture and it'll come out so light I can barely tell what it is. And other times I can't get it focused in time to take the picture I want."

Louise flicks her hand. "Just keep taking lots of pic-
35 tures. Don't worry whether they're good or bad. After a while you'll get the kinks worked out, and it'll be like second nature to you."

I aim the camera at a squirrel on the oak tree in Louise's yard and peer through the viewfinder. It's out of
40 focus. I twist the ring, but the image only gets blurrier. I quickly twist it back the other direction, but by the time I've got it sharp, the squirrel has scrambled back up into the branches. I drop my shoulders and let out a frustrated groan.

45 When I turn around, Louise is watching me. "May I hold it for a minute?" She takes the camera and looks through the viewfinder, then clicks the f-stop a few times and adjusts the focus. Before I know it, she snaps a picture of me.

50 "It's best to do it quickly before the person knows you're taking it," she laughs. "Now you take one of me." I carefully accept the camera from her and hold it up to my eye. Louise gazes out across the yard. I press the button, and the shutter claps.

55 Louise smiles. "Photograph folks when they're not paying attention. You'll get more honest pictures that way."

Across the street, Mama looks up, sees us together, and cocks her head. Louise grins and waves.

60 "I remember when your mama and your Uncle Ralph first moved into that house. It was in 1954, right after the accident that took your grandparents. For a long time, they would just come and go and never speak to anybody. We all knew the story and felt horrible. For a
65 little girl to lose her parents so young, and for your uncle to lose his brother and sister-in-law—it was too awful."

Mama strolls across the street and up the steps to Louise's front porch. She stands there for a moment, eyeing Louise's lemonade. I quickly raise the camera and
70 tap the shutter release button.

Mama's short and slim, with gray eyes that hold a quiet intensity. She's had to do a lot of things for herself that most people never do. She picks up the glass of lemonade from the table next to Louise and takes a swig.

75 I start to take another picture, but I'm worried Mama will get mad. Instead I ask, "How did you two first meet?" Maybe if they get to talking, they won't mind me taking pictures.

Mama shrugs. "I think you brought something over
80 to our house, like a casserole or something. So that was when we met, I guess, but we didn't get to really know each other until that summer after Uncle Ralph and I moved in."

Louise's eyes sparkle. "I heard about you from
85 people at church. They told me about the tragedy and how Ralph had taken responsibility for your upbringing. They said, 'The girl's name is Marigold.' I had never heard that name before, and I thought it sounded pretty nice."

Mama drains the lemonade and says, "You had me
90 over here to weed your backyard. I was grateful 'cause I needed the money. I didn't want to ask Uncle Ralph for

Entrance Ticket   Learning Target   Understanding Inferences   Inferences vs. Assumptions   ACT Practice   Sum It Up

76

3

money 'cause his carpentry wasn't bringing in much back then." She pauses. "It wasn't an easy time."

"And that's when you became friends?"

95 "Mm-hmm. She had a lot of weeds back there, and it took me a few days. Every day when I was done, she would invite me up to the house and give me lemonade." A smile flashes across her face. "With mint! Louise was the first person I knew who put mint in her lemonade."

100 Louise grins as I snap another picture. "It's the best way to drink it."

Mama goes inside to Louise's kitchen and retrieves the pitcher of lemonade from the fridge. Louise doesn't ask what she's doing or even turn around. She just looks
105 across at Uncle Ralph, still sanding away.

I want to make a whole album of pictures on my own. I know that someday I'll want to remember these times when Mama and I visit Uncle Ralph and Louise and everybody else in Lexington. I'd like to have some pic-
110 tures to go with the memories if I can. They're evidence of moments that really happened, but they'll also remind me of what the people were like, what they sounded like, how they moved. I was going to give Mama a birdfeeder for her birthday, but maybe I'll make her a photo album
115 instead. I'll give her some new memories.

1. It can most reasonably be inferred that Marigold is the name of:

   A. the narrator.
   B. the narrator's mother.
   C. one of Uncle Ralph's neighbors.
   D. one of Louise's children.

2. It is reasonable to infer that, when she first received the camera, the narrator:

   F. used it constantly and became well-versed in its components.
   G. did not use it much because she found it difficult to understand.
   H. shared it with her mother, who had an interest in photography.
   J. immediately had the idea to make a photo album.

3. It is most reasonable to infer from the passage that the narrator's plan to make a photo album is primarily the result of:

   A. her desire to document the present moment.
   B. her wish to learn how to use the camera.
   C. encouragement from her mother.
   D. her conversation with her uncle.

4. It can reasonably be inferred from the passage that the "quiet intensity" (line 72) in Mama's eyes is the result of:

   F. an interest in gardening.
   G. growing up in the company of her uncle.
   H. having to make her way in life without her parents.
   J. taking care of her daughter.

5. It can reasonably be inferred from the passage that Mama's act of drinking from Louise's glass:

   A. is offensive to Louise.
   B. is a compulsive habit of Mama's.
   C. is a ritual the two of them have.
   D. is something Louise doesn't mind at all.

END OF SET ONE
STOP! DO NOT GO ON TO THE NEXT PAGE
UNTIL TOLD TO DO SO.

Entrance Ticket   Learning Target   Understanding Inferences   Inferences vs. Assumptions   ACT Practice   Sum It Up

4.4.2 Set Two

Passage II

SOCIAL SCIENCE: This passage is adapted from the article "Grassroots Forest Conservation in Mexico" by Hector R. Cadenas (©2015 by MasteryPrep).

In the southern tail of Mexico, bordered by the Gulf of Mexico and the Pacific Ocean, a small mountain community is making a global impact. Ixtlán de Juarez, Oaxaca, has received a "gold star" from the United
5 Nations as a leader in environmental conservation and natural resource management. All of its commercial timber is certified by the Forest Stewardship Council, an international body that guarantees the wood is harvested legally and in an environmentally conscious method.

10 "This forest belongs to the Zapotec people," says Piedro de Val, a member of the indigenous community in Ixtlán. "This land has been ours for nearly 600 years, and we intend that our children's grandchildren also enjoy our inheritance and cultivate it."

15 The forest enterprise in Ixtlán is distinct in that it is operated entirely by the local community. No aspect of the enterprise—administration, financial planning and profit distribution, marketing, oversight—are contracted out to private companies.

20 However, this was not always the case. Half a century ago, the Mexican government prioritized industrialization for its rural states. In Ixtlán, this translated into 25-year contracts in which the government "rented" its forests to a national newspaper manufacturing plant. Promises
25 that industrialization would bring much-needed upgrades instead resulted in paved roads that only led to the logging camp, a rapidly "balding" mountainside, few jobs, and a crumbling infrastructure.

When the contract expired in the early 1980s and
30 the government made to renew at another astounding long term, the people of Ixtlán revolted. Worker strikes, logging road blockades, protests throughout the state of Oaxaca, and political pressure on the national government resulted in a victory for the local people. They now legally own the
35 pine-oak forest.

At the time, they had very little else: inadequate training and no experience managing forests, operating a large-scale business, or sourcing and storing funds for future growth. In order to survive, Ixtlán joined nine other
40 communities in Oaxaca in the same situation. Together, they sought international help and learned how to operate an environmentally conscious, successful forest enterprise.

"I can't believe I'm able to return home," testified
45 Alejandro Garcia Corral. Corral, like many residents of Oaxaca, had left to find work in the United States. With the improved economy, the wave of migration is changing course back to Oaxaca.

"If you look at the global scale, what these people
50 have accomplished is remarkable," said Helen Mauer, spokesperson for the Forest Stewardship Council. "In the face of rampant deforestation, there's Ixtlán de Jaurez. This community has bridged the capitalist motive with the benefits only a joint community can provide. It's why
55 we chose to recognize them specifically."

This "joint community" is a traditional practice as ancient as the Zapotec people. According to custom, no property is owned and therefore cannot be purchased or sold. People live in communes, or *ejidos*, and share
60 all things in common. Some community members raise cattle, others grow crops, and now, more are able to participate in the forest management enterprise. All business decisions are decided by assembly vote.

"Assemblies are notorious for taking several hours,"
65 chuckles Guillermo León, a community member. "But it is the safest way. The last time we ceded the right to decide what was best for our community, we nearly lost everything." It also creates an incentive to preserve Ixtlán's business model: any member who helps illegal
70 logging, a multi-million dollar industry ravenous for such prized resources, faces strict discipline from the *ejido*. "He loses all rights to the community profits," explains León. "Anyone who would take from his brothers to give to a private company does not deserve the privilege of
75 participating in the *ejido*."

In contrast, there is much incentive to remain with the *ejido* and its somewhat laborious assembly rule. Jobs with decent wages abound. The profit from the forest enterprise returns to Ixtlán in the form of new schools,
80 paved roads, electricity, and clean drinking water. There is the opportunity to learn business management, financial accounting, and, of course, the highly valued skill of producing handmade furniture.

Thanks to the endorsement from the Forest
85 Stewardship Council, all furniture produced by Ixtlán is labeled as "certified wood," meaning it was harvested ecologically, without illegal interferences. This stamp makes the furniture highly valued by national and international consumers, including the Oaxacan state
90 government, either seeking to avoid international sanctions for illegal trading or to support a more environmentally conscious enterprise.

Of course, not every endangered locale can copy Ixtlán's model. "If your natural resource is, say diamonds
95 or coal, you may not have the same means or organizational protection on your side," admits Howard McAlister, chair of the U.N. committee that awarded the forest enterprise a gold star. "But it's a start. If we can execute protections for a major natural resource such as lumber, we can then set our
100 sights on the smaller and more vulnerable resources."

Entrance Ticket   Learning Target   Understanding Inferences   Inferences vs. Assumptions   ACT Practice   Sum It Up

78

6. It can be most reasonably inferred from the passage that regarding Ixtlán, the author feels:

   F. skeptical of the enterprise's aims.
   G. disheartened by the enterprise's partial reliance on government aid.
   H. supportive of the enterprise's goals.
   J. confident that the enterprise could be replicated in other areas.

7. It can reasonably be inferred from the last paragraph that the author believes Ixtlán represents:

   A. a positive change in protecting endangered natural resources.
   B. the best-case version of a fundamentally unsustainable situation.
   C. simply the latest in a series of flawed attempts to protect vulnerable locations.
   D. an indication that Mexico is on the cutting edge of tropical forest conservation.

8. It can most reasonably be inferred from the passage that the system of community governance in the *ejido*:

   F. isn't worth the time it takes to get everyone to agree.
   G. was a radical idea when it was first implemented.
   H. has been updated and reshaped as the enterprise's production has increased.
   J. has benefits that outweigh its disadvantages.

9. It can reasonably be inferred from the third paragraph (lines 15–19) that the author thinks that, in the future, governments aiming to conserve tropical forests should:

   A. designate them as protected areas.
   B. establish contracts with successful private companies.
   C. allow local communities to have a central role in their management wherever possible.
   D. have harsher punishments for people who destroy them.

10. It can most reasonably be inferred from the passage that which of the following is a direct expression of the Ixtlán community's long-term commitment to its forestry businesses?

   F. The investment of profits in future generations of foresters and managers
   G. The sale of its furniture to the Oaxacan government
   H. The revocation of property rights for community members who assist illegal loggers
   J. The community's public recognition by international forestry experts

END OF SET TWO
STOP! DO NOT GO ON TO THE NEXT PAGE
UNTIL TOLD TO DO SO.

Entrance Ticket   Learning Target   Understanding Inferences   Inferences vs. Assumptions   ACT Practice   Sum It Up

3

3

4.4.3 Set Three

Passage IV

NATURAL SCIENCE: This passage is adapted from the article "Elephant Dung and Ivory: How One May Save the Other" by Herbert Finster (©2015 by MasteryPrep).

The director of the University of Washington's Center for Conservation Biology is leading the latest effort to crack down on Africa's elephant poaching epidemic. Dr. Samuel Wasser's innovative approach is effective, if
5 unglamorous: he and his assistants spend much of their time analyzing elephant dung.

African elephant populations have been in steady decline for the past several years as international market demands for their ivory have made a lucrative business
10 for poachers. In 2013, an estimated 50,000 elephants were killed for their ivory tusks. Two years prior, the number was 40,000. Less than 450,000 African elephants currently remain in the wild.

International sales of ivory were banned in 1989
15 by the Convention of International Trade in Endangered Species (CITES), a decision that was backed by the United Nations. However, in countries where wildlife management authorities are chronically under-funded, poaching is still a persistent, significant problem.
20 International demand from Southeast Asia has also driven up the costs of illegal trade and allowed corruption to seep into the local enforcement agencies. For many consumers, especially in China and the Philippines, carved ivory pieces are a symbol of wealth, carrying a sense of prestige.
25 Although ad campaigns have specifically targeted such consumers to educate them on the reality of where their extravagant art comes from, the market dynamic of "less supply, higher demand" is hard to overcome. The end result of such a situation is the extinction of all African
30 elephants.

"It's an epidemic," explains Camellia Rosenberg, a senior analyst in Wasser's lab. "When a single elephant population decreases by three percent annually, that isn't happenstance. Ad campaigns and public service
35 announcements can only go so far. What we're trying to do is stop the killing at its source."

For Wasser and his lab, the "source" is found in hair, tissue, and dung samples retrieved from savanna and forest elephants in nature reserves across Africa. These
40 samples contain DNA, the key to unlocking exactly where poached elephants are being killed. For the last fifteen years, Wasser and collaborative researchers have amassed 1,350 distinct DNA samples from 29 countries throughout the continent. The result of such a large-scale group effort
45 is a thorough DNA population map. When a shipment of ivory is seized, a sample as small as a half-dollar disk can be analyzed and its DNA matched with similar profiles. Based on the result, the exact source of the poaching can be pinpointed.

50 CITES has played a central role in the success of Wasser's work. In 2013, the international body agreed unanimously to send all seized ivory to Wasser's lab. Following this decision, Interpol (International Criminal Police Organization) has submitted for forensic analysis
55 28 seized ivory shipments, weighing half a ton each. Over half of seized ivory is of this volume or even larger, apprehended all over the earth.

Wasser's analysis has also revealed evolving patterns in poaching. Until 2006, most illegal ivory was sourced
60 in Zambia and the Democratic Republic of the Congo, in south-central Africa. However, very little ivory has been located in Zambia since 2007. Instead, most savanna elephant ivory has come from the border of Tanzania and Mozambique, and forest elephant ivory has been sourced
65 in the forest areas of Gabon, Republic of the Congo, and the Central African Republic. Such exact sourcing methods plays an integral role in delivering justice and furthering protections for the elephant population.

Another pattern discovered through DNA mapping
70 is black market shipping routes. Poachers attempt to redirect scrutiny by sending illegal ivory through a series of complicated routes, in which illegal ivory passes through several African and Southeast Asian countries. When ivory is seized, typically in maritime ports, it
75 has in the past been difficult to ascertain its true source location. Thanks to Wasser's population map and DNA analysis, the location of the seizure no longer plays a factor in determining where the elephants were poached. As one example, a large shipment of ivory was seized in
80 Singapore, but when samples were analyzed and matched in the database, they matched the DNA profiles of elephant populations in Zambia. Equipped with these resources, international authorities were able to bring about the resignation of Zambia's director of wildlife and enforce
85 more severe sentencing on ivory smugglers in the country.

"What we're working on in concert with CITES and Interpol is to identify which countries are doing the worst harm," says Rosenberg. "Of course, we need to educate the public about where ivory is coming from. But more
90 importantly, we feel that it's necessary to expose who these offenders are. Then, their own countries can impose sanctions and cut illegal trafficking routes off at the source." Rosenberg predicts that this identification system will soon expand to Asia, where the elephant population
95 is even more threatened than in Africa.

Dr. Vincent Palys, director of the elephant division in CITES is optimistic about the future of the collaborative DNA mapping program. "Our generation is currently at risk of being the last to have elephants—real, living
100 elephants, all gone in another fifty years. DNA mapping and the participation of the local and international authorities has the potential to turn back the tide and save this species."

Entrance Ticket   Learning Target   Understanding Inferences   Inferences vs. Assumptions   ACT Practice   Sum It Up

3 ▰▰▰▰▰▰▰▰▰▰▰▰▰▰▰▰▰▰▰ **3**

11. It can reasonably be inferred from the passage that which of the following is LEAST responsible for the epidemic of African elephant poaching?

    A. Efforts to curb the demand for ivory
    B. Unmonitored domestic ivory markets
    C. Chronic underfunding for wildlife management authorities
    D. The high market value of ivory

12. It can most reasonably be inferred from the passage that the elephant DNA map created by Wasser's team includes which nation?

    F. Zimbabwe
    G. Republic of the Congo
    H. Singapore
    J. Uganda

13. It can most reasonably be inferred from the passage that a protected ecosystem in Africa is nevertheless dangerous for elephant herds primarily because it:

    A. is home to a large number and diversity of predators.
    B. is not under the jurisdiction of the U.S. Fish and Wildlife Service.
    C. has a climate that is unsuitable for them.
    D. lacks effective enforcement against elephant poaching.

14. It can most reasonably be inferred from the passage that ivory brings the highest price when it is in the form of:

    F. tusks.
    G. half-dollar-shaped disks.
    H. carved decorations.
    J. jewelry.

15. It can reasonably be inferred from the passage that international support for DNA testing of ivory has:

    A. suffered from a lack of public understanding.
    B. gained momentum in recent years.
    C. always been strong.
    D. lagged behind scientific advancements.

END OF SET THREE
STOP! DO NOT GO ON TO THE NEXT PAGE
UNTIL TOLD TO DO SO.

Entrance Ticket   Learning Target   Understanding Inferences   Inferences vs. Assumptions   ACT Practice   Sum It Up

Sum It Up

Tips and Techniques

Sounds Right: Eliminate the answers that sound wrong. Doing so may not help you eliminate the trickiest wrong answers, but it will help you get started and save time.

Scanning: Make sure you always check for support in the passage. Find the evidence and use it.

Entrance Ticket   Learning Target   Understanding Inferences   Inferences vs. Assumptions   ACT Practice   Sum It Up

82

Drawing Conclusions Part 2

CAPTION:

5.1 Entrance Ticket

Read the passage and answer the questions.

Marble Cave, the finest cave already explored in Missouri, is southeast of the center of Stone County, a short distance north of the picturesque White River.

5   Beyond the wilderness is the Marble Cave property; the entrance to the Cave is through a large sinkhole in the top of Roark Mountain. This hole is about two hundred feet long, one hundred feet wide, and thirty-five feet deep. It
10 is shaped like a great oblong bowl with sloping sides, divided irregularly near the middle. The bottom is broken out in a jagged way that is both intriguing and terrifying and provides ample support for the growth of ferns, wild roses, and
15 other vegetation with which it is abundantly decorated. About half of the descent into the basin is accomplished by scrambling down the roughly broken rocks and the balance by a broad wooden stairway ending at a narrow platform
20 that supports the locked gate.

Being the first visiting party of the season, we encountered certain disadvantages in the form of a great accumulation of wet clay and rubbish washed in by the rains since the pre-
25 vious summer. We opened the gate with considerable effort and slowly and cautiously descended the slippery, clay-banked stairs to the immense mound of debris forty-five feet below the gate to behold, at last, the grandeur of the
30 Auditorium.

The magnificence of that one chamber would give Marble Cave worldwide fame even if there were nothing more beyond. The blue-gray limestone walls have a greater charm than
35 those of an open canyon, owing to the fact that they sweep away from any given point in long, true curves to form an elliptical chamber three hundred fifty feet long by one hundred twenty-five feet wide, with the vault above showing
40 absolute perfection of arch and measuring, by the survey, from its lowest to its highest point, 195 feet. In addition to the artistic superiority of architectural form, Marble Cave's acoustic properties having been tested, and it is found to be
45 truly an auditorium. The curving walls and pure atmosphere combine to aid the voice and carry its softest tones with marvelous distinctness to every portion of the immense enclosed space.

Entrance Ticket   Learning Targets   Inferences vs. Exact Details   Identifying Incorrect Answers   ACT Practice   Sum It Up

84

5.1 Entrance Ticket

1. Details in the passage most strongly suggest which of the following about Marble Cave?
   A. The author is disgusted with the appearance of the cave's entrance.
   B. The Ozark Mountains have quiet valleys among them.
   C. Marble Cave is one of the largest caves in the Ozarks.
   D. People have been coming to see the cave for years.

2. It can be reasonably inferred from the passage that the entryway to the cave is:
   F. difficult to navigate.
   G. a safe and easy descent.
   H. neat and orderly.
   J. filled with dangerous animals.

3. In the context of the passage, the author's statement that "it is found to be truly an auditorium" (lines 44-45) most nearly means:
   A. choirs sing in the cave regularly.
   B. it is a historical venue for speeches.
   C. soft sounds can be heard with amazing clarity throughout the cave.
   D. he hopes musicians will one day perform there.

Entrance Ticket   Learning Targets   Inferences vs. Exact Details   Identifying Incorrect Answers   ACT Practice   Sum It Up

85

5.2 Learning Targets

1. Recognize questions on the ACT that ask for inferences

2. Identify good and bad inferences in ACT answer options

Self-Assessment

Circle the number that corresponds to your confidence level in your knowledge of this subject before beginning the lesson. A score of 1 means you are completely lost, and a score of 4 means you have mastered the skills. After you finish the lesson, return to the bottom of this page and circle your new confidence level to show your improvement.

Before Lesson

1   2   3   4

After Lesson

1   2   3   4

Entrance Ticket   Learning Targets   Inferences vs. Exact Details   Identifying Incorrect Answers   ACT Practice   Sum It Up

86

5.3.1 Inferences vs. Exact Details

1. Details in the passage most strongly suggest that:

   ☐ word for word   **or**   ☐ inference   **Keyword:** _____

2. When the narrator refers to "cheating the prophet," he is most likely making a statement about:

   ☐ word for word   **or**   ☐ inference   **Keyword:** _____

3. According to the author, the scientists encountered which of the following as a result of their theories?

   ☐ word for word   **or**   ☐ inference   **Keyword:** _____

4. Information in the passage indicates that which type of terrain can be found between Toronto and Ottawa?

   ☐ word for word   **or**   ☐ inference   **Keyword:** _____

5. It can be reasonably inferred from the passage that the main character most strongly desires to:

   ☐ word for word   **or**   ☐ inference   **Keyword:** _____

6. In the passage, the author indicates that he believes that the main cause for the decline in interest is:

   ☐ word for word   **or**   ☐ inference   **Keyword:** _____

Reading Tip

Scanning: The only difference between scanning for an exact detail and scanning for an inference is how you use the passage. For an inference, do not expect an exact match. Instead, scan for general supporting details from the passage.

Entrance Ticket   Learning Targets   Inferences vs. Exact Details   Identifying Incorrect Answers   ACT Practice   Sum It Up

87

5.3.2 Identifying Incorrect Answers

Mr. No Support

Mr. Opposite

Mr. Wrong Scope

Mr. Extreme

Entrance Ticket   Learning Targets   Inferences vs. Exact Details   Identifying Incorrect Answers   ACT Practice   Sum It Up

88

5.3.2 Identifying Incorrect Answers

Entrance Ticket   Learning Targets   Inferences vs. Exact Details   Identifying Incorrect Answers   ACT Practice   Sum It Up

89

5.3.2 Identifying Incorrect Answers

"Fine, my kids really want this. It's worth it. How about fifty bucks?"

Sometimes you just need to make the kids happy. Sometimes you just need to suck it up and do the right thing. But what if he wants it for himself? What if he's using the kids as bait for me to get suckered in and feel bad for him so that I give him this baseball card? It must be worth something, even if I don't know how much. In a world where everyone wants everything and everything has a price, one must have his wits about him.

1. The passage best supports which of the following statements about the father's offer of fifty bucks for the baseball card?

    A. The father knows the narrator is a good man and is trying to make a good deal.

    Type: _____

    B. The father decides the value of the card is worth more to him than he originally wished to spend.

    Explain: _____

    C. The father begins to make the kids feel bad after spending so much money on them.

    Type: _____

    D. The father assumes the narrator knows how much the baseball card is worth and is trying to use the kids as leverage.

    Type: _____

Entrance Ticket   Learning Targets   Inferences vs. Exact Details   Identifying Incorrect Answers   ACT Practice   Sum It Up

90

5.3.2 Identifying Incorrect Answers

"You know, I saw him when I was a kid. My dad and I went to a ballgame out East. It wasn't the major leagues or anything. He was pushing fifty and still hitting home runs and rounding the bases. That's dedication boys; that's how you live your life."

I try to hide my smile. I love baseball. The whole "hope springs eternal" thing? It's so romantic. And I never knew that about this fella—this ballplayer. Fifty years old and still playing the game, even for chump change, and playing with a bunch of nobodies? Running the bases? Nobody even does that anymore. But I see how these kids are looking at this dad and how this dad is telling this story. I remember my dad getting me a glove and playing catch after work. Baseball is about fatherhood, and if this is the closest he can get to his kids and the game, I'd live with being a part of it.

2. The narrator implies that what makes him happiest about selling the baseball card to the father is that:

    F. he loves baseball and will do anything to continue that passion.

    G. baseball reminds him of fatherhood and of happy childhood memories.

    H. he was able to make some money off of a card, even if it was not as much as he was expecting.

    J. he was able to hear the story of a good player who played simply because he loved the game.

    Type: _____

    Explain: _____

    Type: _____

    Type: _____

Entrance Ticket   Learning Targets   Inferences vs. Exact Details   Identifying Incorrect Answers   ACT Practice   Sum It Up

91

5.3.2 Identifying Incorrect Answers

A study was recently conducted that looked at the effects of play on the minds of young children. In recent years, elementary school teachers have begun to notice that their young students were having more and more trouble concentrating on their schoolwork, and they seemed to be more clumsy and irritable. This increase in sensory disturbances seemed to correlate with the lack of play time in the modern school structure. Researchers tested this hypothesis by looking at two kindergarten classes in similar neighborhoods. The first class followed a strict daily schedule that focused heavily on academics and left little time for free exploration, with only a brief recess after lunch. The second class had three outdoor recesses each day and also had free play time built into daily activities. The results were astounding. The teacher in the classroom that had more free play reported far fewer distressing incidents or overwrought emotions, and there was no inability on the part of the students to concentrate on their work. From this study, the researchers concluded that withholding play opportunities from children in the attempt to focus more on academics is counterproductive to the goal of helping young children acquire knowledge. They recommended that all young students be given ample access to both recess and periods of play throughout the day to best support their academic and emotional development.

3. It can be most reasonably inferred that compared to the students with less play time, the students who were given more unstructured play time:

   A. were naturally smarter.   Type: _____

   B. did not benefit from the additional play   Type: _____
       time.

   C. **were able to concentrate better on**   Explain: _____
       learning.

   D. were healthier because of recess time   Type: _____
       after lunch.

Entrance Ticket   Learning Targets   Inferences vs. Exact Details   Identifying Incorrect Answers   ACT Practice   Sum It Up

92

5.3.2 Identifying Incorrect Answers

The works of F. Scott Fitzgerald, Ernest Hemingway, and Nathanael West are all seminal works of American Modernism written from the 1920s to the 1940s. This suggests that this great era of literature was born out of one worldwide event (World War I) and was finished by another (World War II). They often are stories of reflection and include such literary techniques as stream of consciousness. F. Scott Fitzgerald's *The Great Gatsby* is about the American Dream and the downfalls of attaining it. Much of Ernest Hemingway's fiction reflects the horrors of war and the morality of youth. West's work borders on the absurd and shows the worst side of humanity. Modernism includes experimental forms of writing and storytelling and is about reassessing our own humanity. As Gertrude Stein once said, the modernists are the "Lost Generation."

4. It is most reasonable to infer from the passage that the narrator believes that Ernest Hemingway's fiction:

F. is not very reflective of his own experiences.

Type: _____

G. **was greatly influenced by the events of the times.**

Explain: _____

H. is primarily focused on the morality of young people.

Type: _____

J. is overly focused on the horrors of war.

Type: _____

Reading Tip

Process of Elimination: When you are trying to find the answer to an inference question, focus on the wrong answers, especially if you are confused. If you train yourself to find the wrong answers first, you will have a much easier time on harder questions, and you will be able to answer them more quickly.

Entrance Ticket   Learning Targets   Inferences vs. Exact Details   Identifying Incorrect Answers   ACT Practice   Sum It Up

5.4.1 Set One

Passage II

SOCIAL SCIENCE: This passage is adapted from *The History of Globalization* by Kai F. Jordan and Jason Church (©2015 by MasteryPrep).

The length of time it took to deliver a message had been a limiting factor in transatlantic communication ever since Europeans made landfall in the New World. Any relay of information between North America and Europe
5　was subject to the snaillike pace of ocean travel, along with its attendant delays. The effect was that business and political transactions on both sides of the Atlantic were hampered by long lulls in conversation.

The telegraph's debut in the late 1830s revolution-
10　ized overland communication, but water remained a barrier since it dissipated the wires' electric signal. In 1845 Charles Wheatstone hit upon the solution of coating underwater cables in gutta-percha, the adhesive juice of the *Palaquium gutta* tree. This breakthrough allowed the first
15　successful undersea cable to link Dover and Calais via the English Channel in 1851, and plans were soon underway to connect Newfoundland and Nova Scotia across the Cabot Strait.

But channels and straits were not oceans, and major
20　obstacles remained to connect two continents on opposite sides of the Atlantic. Aside from the incredible expense of manufacturing thousands of miles of conductive cable, the ocean's sheer depth complicated the engineering.

Along the entire expanse between Newfoundland
25　and Ireland (the shortest possible distance for the cable), there was a single narrow bandwidth—an undersea plateau two miles deep—that made the project seem even theoretically possible.

Samuel Morse, the telegraph pioneer, had publicly
30　advocated for the construction of a transatlantic line as early as 1840, but more than a decade had passed with no serious attempts made. Then in 1856, Cyrus West Field decided to take on the project. A prominent and vastly successful New York businessman, he had already
35　financed completion of the Newfoundland-Nova Scotia telegraph after it stalled due to bankruptcy. Though he had little knowledge of telegraphy or the deep sea, Field was savvy enough to enlist the help of experts, among them Morse, the oceanographer Matthew Maury, and British
40　engineer Charles Tilston Bright.

Even armed with such brainpower, the challenge before the newly formed Atlantic Telegraph Company was immense. At nearly 2,000 nautical miles, the cable would be by far the longest in the world. It would
45　consist of seven copper wires covered with three coats of *gutta-percha* and wound with tarred hemp inside a sheath of flexible iron strands. Heavy-duty in the literal sense, the cables weighed more than a ton per nautical mile. The enormous cost of manufacture required funding from an
50　army of investors, as well as the British and American governments, who also furnished naval warships to trail the cable across the sea. On August 5, 1857, the U.S.S. *Niagara* and the HMS *Agamemnon* finally set sail from Valentia Bay, Ireland, cable in tow.

55　But success proved elusive. The 1857 attempt was aborted when the cable snapped more than 400 miles out at sea. Undaunted, Field manufactured more cable to replace what had been lost and devised a new system of paying it out from the back of the ship. A second try in the
60　spring of 1858 also failed, but the third attempt, later that summer, proved to be the charm. On August 5, 1858, the first transatlantic telegraph cable was finally laid.

Jubilation erupted on both sides of the ocean as people realized the profound change that had occurred.
65　Queen Victoria sent a message of congratulations to President James Buchanan, who replied that the cable was "a triumph more glorious [than any] on the field of battle." The elation was short-lived though, as the cable stopped working after just three weeks. Public confidence hit a
70　new low, and Field was vilified by the press.

The Civil War's outbreak in 1861 stalled the project's renewal, but by 1865, Field had a new cable design and a single massive ship to lay its entire length. After yet another unsuccessful bid, a final attempt in July 1866
75　went smoothly, and this time the cable remained operational. At first, the high price of sending a message limited clientele to governments, corporations, and the very wealthy, but this exclusivity faded with technological advances. By 1900, fifteen transatlantic cables were in use,
80　and the process was on its way to full democratization. The cable also revolutionized stock trading between New York and London, further solidifying those cities as preeminent global financial centers.

But perhaps the cable's greatest legacy is evident in
85　the most basic tasks of 21st century life, from sending an email to receiving a cell phone call. Its success effectively laid the foundation for modern computer science, as businesses on either end quickly recognized the value of condensing frequently repeated terms into code. The
90　resulting data compression gave rise to a whole new field of study that continues to shape the digital world in which we live today.

Entrance Ticket　Learning Targets　Inferences vs. Exact Details　Identifying Incorrect Answers　ACT Practice　Sum It Up

3 ▬▬▬▬▬▬▬▬▬▬▬▬▬▬▬▬▬▬▬▬ **3**

1. It is reasonable to infer from the passage that prior to the transatlantic cable, all underwater telegraph cables were:

   A. shorter than 2,000 nautical miles.
   B. longer than 1,700 nautical miles.
   C. constructed with funding from national governments.
   D. off-limits to private enterprises.

2. The passage most strongly implies that the discovery of an undersea plateau between Newfoundland and Ireland affected the cable project by:

   F. providing a plausible path to lay the cable across the sea floor.
   G. hindering the passage of ships attempting to lay the cable.
   H. eliminating the need for submarines to lay the cable at vast depths.
   J. complicating the planning of where exactly to lay the cable.

3. The passage indicates that after the 1857 attempt to lay the cable failed, Cyrus Field felt:

   A. proud.
   B. uneasy.
   C. undeterred.
   D. defeated.

4. The passage most strongly suggests that once the 1858 cable stopped working, the public regarded the project's future with:

   F. weary optimism.
   G. mild regret.
   H. intense doubt.
   J. indifference.

5. The passage most strongly suggests that the transatlantic cable's effect on modern life is most deeply felt in terms of:

   A. its impact on computer science and data technology.
   B. London losing prominence as a global financial capital.
   C. the importance of stock markets to national economies.
   D. its encouragement of other large-scale public works.

END OF SET ONE
STOP! DO NOT GO ON TO THE NEXT PAGE
UNTIL TOLD TO DO SO.

Entrance Ticket   Learning Targets   Inferences vs. Exact Details   Identifying Incorrect Answers   ACT Practice   Sum It Up

95

5.4.2 Set Two

Passage III

HUMANITIES: This passage is adapted from the article "A Chronicle of Acoustics" by Vernon Christopher (©2015 by MasteryPrep).

Thomas Edison, the inventor of the phonograph, amazed even himself when he heard the first recording from his prototype tinfoil machine in 1877. It was his own voice reciting "Mary Had a Little Lamb," and though the
5 sound was inconsistent and tinny, he was struck by the profound novelty of hearing himself speak. The phonograph built on the work of French inventor Édouard-Léon Scott de Martinville, who had devised a technology in 1857 to transcribe recorded sounds onto paper or glass.
10 But Edison's creation was the first to play back the recorded sounds as audio, and though he didn't realize it at the time, it was the beginning of a fundamental change in the way people listened to and thought about music.

Despite the crude initial sound quality, the gener-
15 al public was captivated by recorded music. The Pacific Phonograph Company installed the first coin-operated phonograph in a San Francisco saloon in 1889, allowing patrons to select and listen to a song of their choosing for one nickel. This proto-jukebox proved hugely popular,
20 and by the mid-1890s most American cities had at least one "phonograph parlor." Inexpensive home machines followed a few years later, and with them a boom in the sales of phonograph wax cylinders (the original recording medium before wax discs).

25 Recorded music was quickly turning into a commodity, spurring a shift in the perception of its value among artists and critics. The best-selling songs were dance music, frequently performed by military bands. John Philip Sousa was one of the primary composers and
30 conductors of this style, yet he scorned recorded music as inferior to live performance. He wasn't alone in this thought. Many musicians, social theorists, and critics joined the campaign against "the menace of mechanical music," arguing that it cheapened the essential experi-
35 ence of hearing a piece of music. What had once been a unique, live performance experienced in a public place with a group was now heard privately in the home, where it was possible to listen to the same "performance" over and over.

40 The demand for records continued to snowball. On the "pro" side of the intellectual debate was the fact that music of all types could now reach a much wider audience than before. The introduction of electrical recording in 1925 also vastly improved sound quality, bringing au-
45 diences closer in some ways to the experience of hearing the music live.

But in other important ways, the heightened fidelity of the new recordings only underscored their essential difference from live performance. As Sousa and others
50 had pointed out, the recording never changed; it remained static and uncolored by live elements that often add emotion and immediacy. Perhaps less expected, though, was the way in which some recordings transcended their written music to become the "standard" versions of partic-
55 ular songs. Philosopher Andrew Kania, in his entry on "The Philosophy of Music" in the *Stanford Encyclopedia of Philosophy*, points to the Beatles as an example. "If someone asks you if you've heard 'A Day in the Life,' they will assume you know they mean the last song on
60 *Sgt. Pepper's Lonely Hearts Club Band* and not someone else's version of the song," he notes. "This is fundamentally different from classical music in which the central musical work is the composition being performed."

For all its capabilities and limitations, one thing is
65 certain: recorded music is here to stay. Today's technology allows us to carry thousands of high-fidelity songs with us wherever we go, many of which were also created using modern technology. There is now a major class of music with its roots in computers rather than acoustic
70 instruments, and its live performances consist merely of a computer playing in front of an audience. The psychological effects are, as to be expected, multifaceted. On one hand, artists are embracing technology to push the boundaries of creative expression and reach an ever-widening
75 audience. On the other, the affordable means of production and limitless supply of recorded songs can serve to saturate the marketplace and subtly devalue the listening experience.

Nevertheless, it is impossible to imagine popular
80 culture in the 20th and 21st centuries without recorded music. And certain recordings not only define eras in history but also intimate moments in our personal lives. How many of us have experienced the magic of being transported back to a specific time and place the second we
85 hear the opening bars of a particular song? Live concerts will always retain an irreplaceable experiential value, but recordings have provided them with a richly layered complement.

Entrance Ticket   Learning Targets   Inferences vs. Exact Details   Identifying Incorrect Answers   ACT Practice   Sum It Up

96

3 ▐███████████████████████████████████████▌ **3**

6. Based on the passage, why might Thomas Edison have been amazed upon hearing the recording of his own voice played back?

   F. He had always thought his voice sounded deeper than it actually did.
   G. He had never had the experience of hearing his own voice without speaking aloud.
   H. He realized immediately that his new technology would change the world.
   J. The playback was an accident, and he had not been expecting to hear anything.

7. Based on the passage, the author would most likely agree that compared to live music, recorded music offers an experience that is:

   A. distinctly different but not less important.
   B. a substandard imitation of the real thing.
   C. valuable only for its convenience.
   D. so similar as to be virtually indistinguishable.

8. The passage implies that the popularity of "phonograph parlors" in the 1890s:

   F. led to a perception of recorded music as practically worthless, since each play only cost a nickel.
   G. resulted in less work for performers of live music.
   H. encouraged the development of affordable phonographs for the home.
   J. highlighted the need for a more durable recording medium than wax cylinders.

9. It can reasonably be inferred from the passage that John Philip Sousa would most like to hear music played:

   A. on a phonograph for guests at a dinner party.
   B. as a digital recording on an MP3 player.
   C. on Edison's original tinfoil machine prototype.
   D. by a live band at a public event.

10. It can reasonably be concluded that the quotations in the fifth paragraph (lines 57-63) are taken from:

   F. John Philip Sousa's essay "The Menance of Mechanical Music."
   G. the notes of French inventor Édouard-Léon Scott de Martinville.
   H. an anonymous critic's review of The Beatles' *Sgt. Pepper's Lonely Hearts Club Band.*
   J. Andrew Kania's entry in the *Stanford Encyclopedia of Philosophy.*

END OF SET TWO
STOP! DO NOT GO ON TO THE NEXT PAGE
UNTIL TOLD TO DO SO.

Entrance Ticket   Learning Targets   Inferences vs. Exact Details   Identifying Incorrect Answers   ACT Practice   Sum It Up

5.4.3 Set Three

Passage I

PROSE FICTION: This passage is adapted from the short story "Life Before Louisiana" by Alessandro Vozza (©2015 by MasteryPrep).

When I was growing up, just over three thousand people lived in Comune di Cisternino. It was fairly crowded, but we were close with all our neighbors and knew almost everyone in the village by sight. Most people were
5 farmers, and on market days they would set up their stalls in the main piazza to sell fresh vegetables, bread, cheese, and meat. My sister and I went to the local school near the church when we did not have to work in the olive grove. Oftentimes, neighbors would bring our parents
10 ham, beans, and other goods in exchange for our olive oil, which was known throughout the Valle d'Itria.

The Vozza family had lived in Cisternino for centuries. In the 1740s two Cisternino brothers had begun harvesting olives from a grove planted by their father. Their
15 home had been a small stone *trullo* set on a hill on the outskirts of town. With each new generation the family built additions to the original cottage. Eventually, there were seven whitewashed trulli in a row, near a separate stone shed that housed the oil mill and cisterns.

20 Overall our family had reached a certain level of success, but no more so than many other families in the valley. We had beef or ham at most dinners, and our mothers always dressed us in fresh clothes for church. We gave money to the opera and for the construction of a new hos-
25 pital. But after a while my father and uncles grew more ambitious. They said the real money could only be made in Rome. There were restaurants there that would pay a high premium for superior-quality olive oil, as well as businesses that would buy lesser-grade oil for use in med-
30 icines and cosmetics. In 1930 several of the men of the family moved to Rome and set up a warehouse and shop in the Monti district.

Everyone else who stayed behind in Cisternino tended the grove and continued to sell the oil locally. We
35 all worked—me, my sister, my brothers, aunts, everybody. Even the smaller kids and my grandparents played a part during the harvest, carefully picking out leaves and stems from the olives on their way to the mill. Our *bisnonna* told us that before the aqueduct, the family had used
40 water from the cisterns to clean the olives and separate the oil from the pulp. As years went by, one generation built the larger granite mill to accommodate more fruit. Another dug the cellar beneath the shed to keep the bottled oil away from sunlight, which could rob it of its flavor.

45 Because our olive oil had a superior reputation, we worked hard year-round to keep our trees healthy. We watered, pruned, and constantly scanned the grove for ant colonies. At harvest time, we made sure to transport the picked olives to the mill right away so that the
50 fruit wouldn't have a chance to oxidize. We ground and pressed immediately and always washed our mats thoroughly with hot water between pressings.

We always harvested in mid-to-late October, but we didn't pick all the olives at once. Usually there were three
55 pressings. One reason was that our mill was too small to accommodate the whole grove, but another was that if something went wrong, the entire harvest would not be spoiled. Everyone had a job to do at every stage. First there was the picking—catching the olives in bags and carting
60 them to the mill in wagons. Then came the washing, followed by the grinding and pressing. And finally, there was bottling and counting, storing and stacking. One season my only job was to bottle the oil as it poured from the reservoir. My mind could drift, but my wrists had to stay
65 absolutely still. Another season I had to pluck the twigs and leaves from the bags as they came from the grove. Whenever Lucia did this she missed too many. Nonna said too many leaves would give the oil a sooty flavor.

I can still smell the rich aroma of our olive oil. There
70 were so many flavors in it: spicy pepper, the green earthiness of tomato leaves, and a light, banana-like sweetness behind it all. My nonna would use it in her marinara and drizzle it on top of gnocchi with parmesan, and it tasted like heaven. It satisfied the palate in a way nothing else
75 could.

It was repetitive work, but we were so proud of our finished product. Our olive oil was like a family heirloom, and it was known for its quality as far as Rome. I liked to imagine foreign dignitaries sitting down at a fancy restau-
80 rant and being served bruschetta doused with "the famous Italian olive oil"—which my family had produced and bottled by hand on our farm in Puglia.

11. According to the passage, several men of the family lived in Rome most of the time because they:

    A. wanted to open their own restaurant in the capital.
    B. made olive oil cosmetics in the Monti district.
    C. were ambitious salesmen in the Monti district.
    D. produced olive oil in the Monti district.

Entrance Ticket   Learning Targets   Inferences vs. Exact Details   Identifying Incorrect Answers   ACT Practice   Sum It Up

98

12. The passage indicates that the narrator's primary response to the aroma described in the seventh paragraph (lines 69-75) is:

   F. disappointment over a painful personal loss.
   G. warmth rising from a treasured memory.
   H. sadness that she is not still living on the family farm.
   J. satisfaction from completing a difficult task.

13. Details in the passage most strongly suggest that the people who stayed behind in the town to produce the olive oil include:

   A. women in the family.
   B. distant relatives.
   C. local vendors.
   D. neighbors.

14. The passage most strongly implies that the narrator's nonna believes in picking out leaves from the harvested olives because the leaves:

   F. should be used as fertilizer to promote future olive crops.
   G. impart an undesirable flavor to the olive oil.
   H. carry ants that could infest the olives.
   J. change the oil's flavor in a pleasant but inauthentic way.

15. It can reasonably be inferred from the passage that the author believes which of the following about the painstaking work required to harvest the olives?

   A. The careful attention to detail at every stage is the price to be paid for a superior product.
   B. Storing the oil away from sunlight is a quirk of her family's harvest tradition.
   C. Letting the olives oxidize does little to affect the quality of the oil.
   D. The use of wagons to transport the olives from the grove is necessary to yield the purest oil.

END OF SET THREE
STOP! DO NOT GO ON TO THE NEXT PAGE
UNTIL TOLD TO DO SO.

Entrance Ticket   Learning Targets   Inferences vs. Exact Details   Identifying Incorrect Answers   ACT Practice   Sum It Up

Sum It Up

Drawing Conclusions Part 2

Inference
A conclusion drawn from reasoning and available evidence; often a combination of facts

Tips and Techniques

Scanning: The only difference between scanning for an exact detail and scanning for an inference is how you use the passage. For inference questions, scan for general supporting details from the passage.

Process of Elimination: Focus on eliminating the wrong answers, especially if you are confused. If you train yourself to find the wrong answers first, you will have a much easier time on harder questions, and you will be able to answer them more quickly.

Entrance Ticket   Learning Targets   Inferences vs. Exact Details   Identifying Incorrect Answers   ACT Practice   Sum It Up

100

Intent and Purpose

CAPTION:

6.1 Entrance Ticket

Read the passage and answer the following questions.

It is universally accepted that Steve Reich and Phillip Glass are the composers responsible for giving a distinct narrative voice to the minimalist music of the 20th century. They both drew
5 from their own heritages and experiences in ways that had never been heard before. However, many musical historians agree that La Monte Young, with his unique approach to minimalism, deserves his place alongside Glass and Reich. Al-
10 though his contemporaries were more popular, La Monte Young was a pioneer in the development of drone music and performance art. He differed from others in that he used elements of *proto-flux-us* compositions to create something more akin
15 to performance art pieces. His work would later come with directions, such as "draw a straight line and follow it," or instruct listeners to build a fire, among other unusual requests. But the question that critics and audiences posed was where to
20 draw the line between music and performance art. Or did La Monte Young stumble across a new way to merge the two?

Young was a native of Bern, Idaho, but eventually moved to Los Angeles, and it was there that
25 Young would immerse himself in the jazz world. Young would go on to study composition under notable pioneers of electronic music. The genesis of his distinctive style came through his discovery of the works of John Cage. This inspiration would
30 find Young situated as a polarizing figure in the avant-garde scene of 1960s New York.

His original influence, though, came from his early days in Bern. His earliest memory of sound, he recalled, was the sound of the wind blowing
35 around his family's log cabin. Young himself considers *The Well-Tuned Piano* his masterpiece. This proved to be a catalyst in his merging of performance art and music, with the audience being surrounded by what they described as "pure and
40 intense color sensations" generated by magenta lights installed in the performance space. Young's mixture of tuning and intonation within the mechanics of the piece, as well as the performance space it occupied, created a unique experience for
45 the audience.

Narrative in music has always existed— whether it's Reich commenting on his Jewish heritage, the motion picture soundtracks of Glass, or the memories conjured up by Young that mani-
50 fest themselves in stories told completely through sound. The introduction of narrative is evident in Young's work, as it is in the works of Reich and Glass. The difference is that in Young's work, the audience finds itself with one collective foot in re-
55 ality and the other in something completely different. The installations that Young creates not only derive from a personal narrative within himself but also leave enough of a void for the audience members to fill with their own experiences and
60 emotions. Whatever space they may be occupying at that moment in time is completely dissolved by sound and light, and this cross-pollination of music and performance art gives way to something that is otherworldly.

Entrance Ticket | Learning Targets | Purpose and Main Idea | Modes of Writing | ACT Practice | Sum It Up

6.1 Entrance Ticket

1. The main purpose of the passage is to:
   A. explore the relationship between narrative and performance space in the works of three minimalist composers.
   B. examine the influence of minimalism on the New York music scene, using one composer as an example.
   C. discuss how one minimalist composer deserves more recognition for his contributions to his genre.
   D. rate the various levels of importance of three 20th century minimalist composers.

2. In the context of the passage, the main purpose of the first paragraph is to:
   F. introduce the reader to Young's style before elaborating on the influences that shaped it.
   G. relate Young's professional aspirations to his rivalries with other minimalist composers in New York.
   H. provide specific details of Young's professional success before comparing him to other composers.
   J. describe Young's relationship to his audience in order to understand why he strived for success in performance art.

3. The passage's author most likely mentions the performances of *The Well-Tuned Piano* to:
   A. provide an anecdote about a performance gone bad in an otherwise dry and technical passage.
   B. suggest that Young's combination of music and performance art was able to transport audiences.
   C. point out Young's ability to drastically change his style from one performance to the next.
   D. encourage the readers to listen to famous minimalist compositions of the 20th century.

6.2 Learning Targets

1. Identify the purpose of a detail and/or paragraphs in a passage

2. Identify the author's intent and purpose in a passage

3. Identify how an author's purpose shapes content and style

Self-Assessment

Circle the number that corresponds to your confidence level in your knowledge of this subject before beginning the lesson. A score of 1 means you are completely lost, and a score of 4 means you have mastered the skills. After you finish the lesson, return to the bottom of this page and circle your new confidence level to show your improvement.

Before Lesson

1   2   3   4

After Lesson

1   2   3   4

6.3.1 Purpose and Main Idea

Purpose: _____

_____

Main Idea: _____

_____

Example 1:

A scientist has written an article about the health hazards and environmental damage caused by a new pesticide. Identify which of the following could be the scientist's main idea and which could be the scientist's purpose in this piece:

    A.   A new pesticide is dangerous to the ecosystem.

    B.   Raising awareness of the new pesticide could trigger stronger regulations.

Example 2:

A doctor writes about her experience suffering from a chronic illness. Identify which of the following could be the doctor's main idea and which could be the doctor's purpose in this piece:

    A.   Sharing experiences of her disease will help other patients feel less lonely.

    B.   Though at first difficult, lifelong management of this disease is possible.

Example 3:

A town resident petitions the local government to build a new park in his neighborhood. Identify which of the following could be the resident's main idea and which could be the resident's purpose in this piece:

    A.   The resident hopes to secure a new park in town.

    B.   A new park would be beneficial to the community in a variety of ways.

6.3.1 Purpose and Main Idea

Example 4:

A gymnast writes a memoir about her experience in her first Olympics. Identify which of the following could be the gymnast's main idea and which could be the gymnast's purpose in this piece:

    A.   Narrating her story will help inspire younger generations to strive for their dreams.

    B.   Hard work, perseverance, and luck are essential to achieving one's goals in life.

Example 5:

A historian writes a chapter for a new textbook on the history of the Roman Empire. Identify which of the following could be the historian's main idea and which could be the historian's purpose in this piece:

    A.   The Roman Empire fell for primarily economic reasons.

    B.   The historian wishes to present a controversial alternative theory for the fall of the Roman Empire.

6.3.1 Purpose and Main Idea

Are the world's rarest creatures being killed off by illegal wildlife trade? Many people are familiar with the threat to the elephant population resulting from the skyrocketing black market dollar value of its ivory tusks. But the spotlight has recently been placed on the existence of one of the world's rarest reptiles—a semi-aquatic, nocturnal lizard native to northern Borneo. The earless monitor lizard (*Lanthanotus borneensis*) was first documented in 1877, rediscovered in 1963, and eventually disappeared from sight. That is until a group of biologists in Borneo spotted the odd, secretive reptile and snapped its picture in 2008. Intending to spark the interest of the scientific community, the biologists posted the images on social media—along with general information about its location and habitat—and within a year earless monitor lizards were for sale online.

Summary: _____

_____

Hashtag: _____

Decades ago, Indonesia, Malaysia, and Brunei enforced laws that fiercely protected earless monitor lizards. Those found guilty of poaching the lizard faced a fine of up to $8,600 and five years in prison. Unfortunately that has not been enough. Vincent Nijman, a conservation ecologist at Oxford Brookes University, estimates that at least one hundred lizards have been smuggled from the wild so far. The wildlife trade monitoring network, TRAFFIC, has documented illegal sales of the reptile in Japan, Ukraine, Germany, France, and the Czech Republic.

Summary: _____

_____

Hashtag: _____

6.3.1 Purpose and Main Idea

Because of the lack of legal enforcement within the wildlife trade, most in the industry carry out their transactions openly or utilize simple code words. To complicate matters, some unsuspecting buyers are unaware that they are a part of a covert operation. "When we started investigating this, we began to expose this really dark underbelly of online markets," says Crawford Allen of TRAFFIC. "Some of the rarest species on Earth are being traded on Facebook." Nijman is lobbying for the addition of the earless monitor lizard to international wildlife protection lists so that there will be no doubt about the trade's illegality.

Summary: _____

_____

Hashtag: _____

Experts can only estimate how many earless monitor lizards remain in the wild, but they recognize that the species is in danger. In addition to the influence of collectors who are eager to make a profit from the rare lizard's trade, much of the reptile's native habitat in Borneo has recently been destroyed by forest fires and deforestation. Without formal intervention, the earless monitor lizards could be headed toward extinction.

Summary: _____

_____

Hashtag: _____

Reading Tip

Hashtags: As you read a passage, create a "hashtag" for each paragraph. You can even write it down if you have time. This will help you navigate the passage when you need to find details to answer questions.

This page is intentionally left blank.

6.3.1 Purpose and Main Idea

Merchant and navy ships alike were constantly anchored in my town's harbor, but there was a particular vessel that still stands out in my memory—the glorious *Madonna*. Incredible!
5 I pointed at her sitting out there in the water, and I knew that one day such a vessel would be my home. I began breathing heavily, a condition I'd had since I was an infant—a condition that quelled any urge inside me to jump into the
10 ocean and glide as confidently and seamlessly as those ships did. When I got into bed and my eyes began to feel heavy, I dozed off to the sounds of more ships announcing their arrival.

During the usual morning chores, I sang
15 a few bars of a song I'd heard sailors raucously singing at the café. A sailor's song is used for a multitude of reasons: sometimes in moments of boredom on duty and other times just for fun in the cafés of port towns. I'd only ever heard them
20 sung joyously in my town, but I knew the songs could be used for much more serious purposes at sea. As I finished setting the table and cooking breakfast, my mind wandered back to the size and grandeur of that ship.

25 Walking over to the balcony, my mind immediately retreated to stories of the high seas. As I playfully leaped from one side of the balcony to the other, I suddenly began to gasp for air. The need for air immediately took over
30 any imaginary mission my mind had made up. I focused on the harbor, and soon the image of the ship sitting out there began to steady me. When I felt better, it occurred to me that whatever attachment I had to this vessel gave me an
35 inner calmness and a yearning to reach out and touch the unknown.

On race day I arrived at the dock to sign in, and the noise of the crowd deafened my ears.

Our mayor had been asked to preside over the
40 send-off speech. He praised the visiting sailors and pronounced his honest admiration for the contestants. As I hustled over to sign up, I realized that I was the very last in line, and slowly my nerves began to take over.

45 The clock struck high noon, and the contestants climbed into their skiffs. Each contestant was wearing his own elegant sailing jacket with his name embroidered on the back. My clothes were handed down from my father, who
50 had been a navy sailor during the war before he was killed in battle. His clothes felt loose on me, but nothing could have made me feel prouder than sporting my father's name. It didn't matter that we didn't share the same last name since
55 our first names were the same—Lorenzo. I stepped back and took a moment to think about who my father was at my age and wondered if he had had the same dreams as me. Somehow I knew my fate wouldn't be the same as
60 his. I saw this race as a stepping stone toward a bright future aboard larger vessels dominating the high seas.

The mayor raised the pistol and fired the starting shot. The band picked up the tempo
65 as I began breathing heavily. I turned my head quickly to face the outer harbor and focused on the towering vessel that served as my safeguard, and I regained my composure. My skiff was older than the others, but it glided beauti-
70 fully. With every stroke, I felt confident that I was starting to catch up to the more experienced sailors. I hadn't had enough experience in competitive racing to prepare myself to maintain my stamina, especially my breathing, so I quickly
75 began to tire. It was getting to be late afternoon, and the heat from the sun was beginning to

6.3.1 Purpose and Main Idea

recede. The clouds moved in and covered up the sun, but the stress of the race itself was starting to affect me. My muscles ached more
80 than they ever had in practice runs. By this time I still had to lap around the bay once more and gain headway to make it to the finish line first. I had three more skiffs to pass. Seconds felt like hours, and my bed was calling me, promising a
85 safe retreat from the soreness in my bones. As my eyes began to close, I was suddenly taken over by a second wind; I could see the finish line not ten meters away. But just near the horizon, I caught sight of that magnificent vessel weigh-
90 ing anchor, and my heart was overwhelmed. The outcome of the race suddenly became un-important compared to the feeling of knowing where I belonged—floating on the water with just a wooden vessel between me and the sea
95 I loved. I hummed a sailor song to myself and watched the *Madonna* sail off into the unknown.

6.3.1 Purpose and Main Idea

1. Why did the author include that detail?

_____

_____

2. Why did the author make that point in the paragraph?

_____

_____

3. Why did the author include that point in the passage?

_____

_____

When approaching a question about the author's intent or purpose:

   1. Consider the _____ or _____ of the passage.

   2. Identify the _____ of the paragraphs.

   3. Find the author's _____ for writing the passage.

Reading Tip

Embrace Your Inner Five-Year-Old: Ask *Why?* as in *Why was this detail included? What purpose does this detail/sentence/paragraph serve?*

6.3.2 Modes of Writing

Theme of your radio show:

_____

_____

_____

One-paragraph bit:

_____

_____

_____

_____

_____

_____

_____

_____

Mode of writing used:

_____

_____

_____

6.3.2 Modes of Writing

Example:

The main purpose of the passage is to:

A.   propose that research be continued to confirm which hibernation patterns are common to both the American and fire-bellied toad.

B.   persuade the reader that the fire-bellied toad is superior to the American toad in its adaptation to freezing temperatures.

C.   speculate on the reasons why the two toads have developed distinct specialized hibernation traits over thousands of years.

D.   describe the two toads' adaptations to their changing environments, including specialized hibernation patterns and physical attributes.

Reading Tip

Purpose: When a question asks about the purpose of a passage, consider the author's purpose for writing. Is the author trying to **entertain**, **convince**, or **inform/educate**? If you can figure out the style of writing, you can eliminate a few answers right away.

This page is intentionally left blank.

6.4.1 Set One

Passage II

SOCIAL SCIENCE: This passage is adapted from the article "The Will of the Free" by Tobias Hall (©2015 by MasteryPrep).

Daniel Dennett's eternal search for answers began after his father was killed in an unexplained plane crash. Dennett's early life and move from Beirut to Massachusetts was cast in the long shadow of a mythical,
5 unknown father figure. Dennett had come from a family of remarkable brilliance—his father was a counter-intelligence officer in the Office of Strategic Services, a predecessor of the CIA. Dennett attended Harvard University where he received a doctorate in philosophy.
10 Dennett was awarded the prestigious Erasmus prize for his exceptional contribution to society, showcasing how his work was not only important to himself but was also significant within a worldwide community.

During Dennett's first year at Winchester High
15 School, he put all his effort into a term paper on Plato and included a picture of Rodin's *The Thinker* on the cover. He humorously recalled that at the time, he hadn't really understood a word of what he had written, but writing this paper caused him to discover that he wanted to become
20 a teacher. This realization led to his first question: What would he teach? At age seventeen he had begun pursuing a mathematics degree at Wesleyan University and found himself drowning in his studies. Studying in the library late one evening, he chanced upon the text *From a*
25 *Logical Point of View,* which had been written at Harvard University by Willard Van Orman Quine. He was utterly transfixed, and by the next morning he had made up his mind to transfer to Harvard.

At the end of his college career, Dennett had begun
30 developing his own thoughts and contradicting the opinions of philosophers who came before him. By 1962 he was twenty and married and could no longer relate to the idyllic days of his youth. He was experiencing for the first time a voracious drive to refute Quine's work. His
35 youthful misguidance had now been given purpose, and he realized that he was doing exactly what he had always wanted to do. The pursuit of a valuable quarry through daunting complexities was the path he had chosen to follow, and regardless of the ambiguity of right and wrong,
40 he was coming up with His Own Answers. Now that there was no turning back, he was the one calling the shots. He defended his thesis well and had so convinced others of his points that an established professor defended a point of contention he was arguing against Quine. He saw this
45 as a remarkable achievement—an ally in an intellectual fight of epic proportions—and this affirmation inspired self-confidence.

A bit later in his academic career, there would come a mentor who would set thoughts in motion for Dennett.
50 This mentor was Gilbert Ryle, who was a major force in Oxford philosophy at the time, as well as detached from the trite and bland cliques that seemed to govern the world of academia. He taught Dennett the importance of standing against the typical Oxford philosophers whose
55 arguments consisted only of clever phrases and shallow bravado. Ryle taught Dennett to think for himself without marginalizing the opinions of others.

New influences were beginning to inspire Dennett. He began to form a relationship with science, and he
60 found that philosophers were given more flexibility in time and error, while scientists were dealt more pressure for first-time success. Although scientists had a reputation for dismissing philosophers, he found that both parties were after essentially the same answers. Dennett carries
65 on today asking these poignant questions.

1. The main purpose of the last paragraph is to:

   A. acknowledge the double standard between two fields asking similar questions.

   B. reveal that Dennett came to resent Ryle for his unyielding skepticism of science.

   C. describe a typical mentor-to-student relationship in the world of philosophical academia.

   D. catalogue the differences between scientists and philosophers when presenting research.

2. The main purpose of the passage is to:

   F. propose that by following the steps taken by Dennett, others can become philosophers as well.

   G. persuade the reader that Dennett was only able to ask questions no one could answer.

   H. speculate on how philosophers employ different methods to approach an argument.

   J. describe how Dennett developed from an inexperienced student into an established philosopher.

3 ▬▬▬▬▬▬▬▬▬▬▬▬▬▬▬▬▬▬▬▬▬ **3**

3. The main purpose of the third paragraph is to:

   A. describe a specific text written by Dennett's rival, Quine.

   B. present the process students undertake to defend their philosophical theses.

   C. provide an account of Dennett's transformation from youth to maturity.

   D. list several ways Dennett contradicted the teachings of his mentors.

4. The details describing Dennett's father in lines 6–8 are most likely included to:

   F. explain that Dennett felt an urge to follow in his father's footsteps.

   G. demonstrate the legacy of intelligence Dennett was born into.

   H. suggest that Dennett's father's military career was similar to that of Dennett's in academia.

   J. show that few philosophers relate to growing up in a military household.

5. The author capitalizes the words in line 40 most likely to signify that:

   A. Dennett believed that only his opinions were valid.

   B. these are Quine's words, not Dennett's.

   C. Dennett had begun to form theories of his own.

   D. Dennett and Quine no longer respected one another.

END OF SET ONE
STOP! DO NOT GO ON TO THE NEXT PAGE
UNTIL TOLD TO DO SO.

Entrance Ticket   Learning Targets   Purpose and Main Idea   Modes of Writing   ACT Practice   Sum It Up

6.4.2 Set Two

Passage III

HUMANITIES: This passage is adapted from *Encyclopedia Americana* by Felix Tripe (©2015 by MasteryPrep).

The *encyclopedia*, ancient Greek for *general learning*, is a word that brings to mind a comprehensive collection of information from many branches of knowledge. The encyclopedia is a relatively old creation,
5   and historians trace the existence of encyclopedias for more than 2,000 years.

In 1646 an English nobleman, Sir Thomas Browne, used the word itself to define one of his major works—*Pseudodoxia Epidemica*—which he published in the
10 midst of a scientific revolution. Johannes Aventinus used the term *encyclopaedia* as the title of his book in 1517, the first such title to appear in a major work. Printing became so readily available during the Renaissance that word of the encyclopedia's conception had spread. These books
15 were not only accessible to the wealthy church and clergy but also to the general public. These early encyclopedias became worldwide phenomena, with revised editions in continuous print until 1672. The general-purpose encyclopedia was becoming more commonly used as a
20 point of reference and was widely distributed.

Browne's *Pseudodoxia Epidemica* was a milestone for the scientific revolution of the Renaissance. Browne used his encyclopedia as a vehicle to dispute the false assumptions and superstitions that people had taken as
25 fact in the Middle Ages. Browne implemented scientific criteria to decide what he would include as factual references in his work—such as the authority of previous authors or the soundness of theoretical and empirical evidence. Today his volume would be unrecognizable
30 as an encyclopedia, but at the time it was extremely progressive—even rebellious.

It wasn't until the 18th and 19th centuries that the modern form of the encyclopedia took shape. The template for the encyclopedia we use today is traced back
35 to volumes such as *Chambers' Cyclopedia, Universal Dictionary of Arts and Sciences,* or the *Encyclopaedia Britannica.*

Before Browne's encyclopedia, there was virtually no way to mass produce and distribute books. The
40 invention of the printing press derailed the old system of scribes copying books by hand and launched the future of literacy. As popular as his *Pseudodoxia Epidemica* was, many critics professed that his work was too closely tied to mysticism. Nevertheless, this was a well-executed
45 compendium of knowledge made available to the masses for their education and for exposing false science.

During the Enlightenment, Denis Diderot remarked how vastly important it was for scholars to document knowledge for the betterment of society. He looked
50 at it as the passing down of knowledge so that future generations could be better prepared to face an uncertain future. Diderot cited duty as a reason for collecting and standardizing the transmission of information "so that the work of preceding centuries will not become useless to
55 the centuries to come, and so that our offspring, becoming better instructed, will at the same time become more virtuous and happy." Diderot understood that the work of his own generation and those who would succeed him had to act as a reference to the next, and so on. Knowledge
60 could not be exclusive; anyone anywhere needed to be able to open an encyclopedia and find the answers they sought.

This message resonated with many people, and Diderot's call to arms was heeded. By the early 1920s
65 many versions of popular encyclopedias were widely distributed. The 1950s and '60s saw the United States commercializing popular encyclopedias in installment plans that sold encyclopedia sets in volumes, lettered *A* through *Z.* Toward the end of the 20th century, encyclopedias
70 were becoming more specialized, particularly with the explosion of the Internet and its prevalence in people's homes. Online encyclopedias were suddenly available to everyone, and now online encyclopedias, such as Wikipedia, allow anyone to provide information on
75 subjects while others can contradict, correct, and edit those claims. People worldwide are learning about other cultures and sharing their own experiences, while contributing to creative dialogues as a result of these compilations of knowledge. The role of the encyclopedia
80 is still evolving, but more people than ever before can enjoy knowledge right at their fingertips or with the click of a button.

Entrance Ticket   Learning Targets   Purpose and Main Idea   Modes of Writing   ACT Practice   Sum It Up

3 ▨▨▨▨▨▨▨▨▨▨▨▨▨▨▨▨▨▨▨▨▨▨▨▨▨▨ **3**

6. The main purpose of the passage is to:

   F. identify the fallacious elements of Medieval knowledge that Sir Thomas Browne refuted in his work.
   G. list, in chronological order, each of the significant works that brought about the modern encyclopedia.
   H. discuss the evolution of the encyclopedia and the importance of widespread accessibility to knowledge.
   J. show how playwrights and poets were harmed by the conception of a uniform collection of knowledge.

7. The main purpose of the third paragraph is to:

   A. explain that playwrights had no use for a widely distributed encyclopedia.
   B. describe how Browne's encyclopedia used science to disprove misconceptions.
   C. illustrate the ways Browne used his publication to make a living.
   D. discuss the importance of mass production in the distribution of knowledge.

8. The main purpose of the final paragraph is to:

   F. provide a brief summary of the progress of the encyclopedia in the 20th century.
   G. describe how the contributors to original encyclopedias made the form what it is today.
   H. question the inaccuracies of the encyclopedia and suggest what changes could be made.
   J. examine the ways in which Diderot criticizes how people obtain information.

9. The passage quotes Diderot in lines 53–57 primarily to:

   A. point out that Diderot deserves credit for the overall success of the encyclopedia.
   B. explain the value of recording and sharing knowledge to ensure a successful future.
   C. claim that Diderot believed that the intelligence of future generations would be scarce.
   D. document Diderot's role in influencing where encyclopedias would be distributed.

10. The author's two references to the scientific revolution in lines 10 and 22 primarily serve to describe the:

   F. expanding acceptance of progressive ideas in science and knowledge.
   G. continuing desire for exploration and appreciation of literature.
   H. ongoing need to emphasize the importance of revolutions in overthrowing regimes.
   J. growing eagerness to glorify the Italian Renaissance above other movements.

END OF SET TWO
STOP! DO NOT GO ON TO THE NEXT PAGE
UNTIL TOLD TO DO SO.

Entrance Ticket   Learning Targets   Purpose and Main Idea   Modes of Writing   ACT Practice   Sum It Up

6.4.3 Set Three

Passage III

HUMANITIES: This passage is adapted from the article "In Guernica" by Leslie Antoin (©2015 by MasteryPrep).

Guernica, an oil painting by the Spanish artist Pablo Picasso (1881-1973), was, for a period, on display in New York's Museum of Modern Art. It has such a powerful effect on people that it continues to capture imaginations.
5 Embedded with symbols ranging from people, animals, and buildings under siege, it stands at roughly eleven feet tall and twenty-six feet wide and serves as a reminder about the devastation and brutality of war. It fuses the surreal with the reality of war and delivers Picasso's universal
10 message that war permeates everything. *Guernica* is perhaps one of Picasso's most famous works because it not only functions as a vehicle for a political message, but it also acts as a reminder of how art can liberate people through personal expression. At its completion the
15 painting excited the curiosity of poets and critics, who found a sort of disconcerting foreshadowing in its bleak message.

While initially commissioned by the Spanish government to paint a large mural for the World's Fair
20 in Paris, Picasso abandoned that idea once he heard of George Steer's firsthand report of the bombing of Guernica in *The New York Times.* Picasso's outrage at the situation prompted him to create a stark vision of animal and man being torn apart by the mechanization of
25 war. *Guernica* had much to do not only with the Spanish Civil War but also with Europe's preoccupation with its involvement in the Second World War. The painting had been a centerpiece of the MoMA, and it did not find its way back to Spain until much later. Picasso would not
30 allow it to be displayed in Spain until the people had a republic. This highlighted how much political discourse was attached to the work. Picasso's piece not only reflected the attachments he had with his cultural homeland, but it was also a vanguard in political art for the 20th century.

35 In the years during and following World War II, none of Picasso's work spoke with quite the political force that *Guernica* had. Picasso had stayed in Nazi-occupied France during the war, where he produced some exceptional works, such as *Still Life with Guitar* (1942). During
40 those years in France, Picasso's work was becoming increasingly internalized and personal. He had fewer exhibitions of his art during this period, since his work did not conform to the standards of the Nazis occupying the French government. Picasso continued to experiment
45 with bronze, even when bronze casting was prohibited, and he began to focus his attention on literature. He wrote numerous poems as well as two plays—*Desire Caught by the Tail* (1941) and *The Four Little Girls* (1949). These nonlinear works of literature drew on many of Picasso's

50 other interests, and for a brief period this was his main mode of expression.

Throughout his life Picasso had remained generally neutral in conflicts, with no desire to become involved, and his age had played a deciding factor in how much he
55 could offer physically; by the onset of the Spanish Civil War, Picasso was already nearing old age, so he could not participate. Left to his art, his style was evolving into what some scholars argue was more of a conscious detachment from the brutality of the war happening around him. He
60 was not only an artist who displayed his inner passions but also one who understood the dreams and fears of the masses.

The 1940s saw Picasso join the French Communist Party, and this added tension to his already strained
65 relationship with artists such as Salvador Dali and Henri Matisse. In describing how politics fit with his art, Picasso stated, "I am a Communist, and my painting is Communist painting ... But if I were a shoemaker—Royalist, or Communist, or anything else—I would not necessarily
70 hammer my shoes in a special way to show my politics." His work was still somewhat controversial, given the state of the world post-World War II, but he was able to transcend those issues and engage the expressionistic style that was unique to his talents.

75 While living out the remainder of his years in France, Picasso further transformed his style once again. He moved toward a more colorful, vivacious, adventurous mode that was unlike anything he had previously produced. Toward the end of his life, he drained his energy
80 in an attempt to amass as much work as he possibly could. This drew judgment from critics who asserted he was past his prime. But Picasso's enduring legacy and unfaltering worldwide popularity seem to imply he was simply ahead of everyone else.

11. The main purpose of the passage is to:

A. compare and contrast Picasso's life experiences in France during World War II to life in Spain.

B. depict the influence Picasso had in the popularization of the expressionist movement in France.

C. offer an explanation for Picasso's absence from military involvement during World War II.

D. discuss how Picasso's work was influenced by a world in the midst of war.

Entrance Ticket   Learning Targets   Purpose and Main Idea   Modes of Writing   ACT Practice   Sum It Up

3　　　　　　　　　　　　　　　　　　　　**3**

12. The main purpose of the fourth paragraph (lines 52–62) is to describe the:

F. transition Picasso underwent after producing *Guernica* compared to his previous work.

G. method of painting Picasso found himself employing at the time.

H. complexity of the political regime existing in Nazi-occupied France.

J. reluctance Picasso had toward becoming involved in military conflicts.

13. The primary purpose of the words in quotations marks in lines 67–70 is to:

A. indicate that the focus of Picasso's later art was exclusively anti-Spanish Civil War.

B. provide examples of reasons Picasso's work wasn't solely reliant on his belief system.

C. prove that Picasso's political work was inspired by Salvador Dali and Henri Matisse.

D. suggest that Picasso's *Guernica* was too political for the French Communist Party.

14. The author mentions Picasso's experimentation with bronze and writing literature during World War II primarily to suggest that his:

F. interest in varying art forms remained present until France was occupied in World War II.

G. time spent working with bronze and writing literature should have been spent painting.

H. fascination with other art forms gave focus to his life while in Nazi-occupied France.

J. commitment to selling art influenced him to cultivate a variety of talents for profit.

15. One main purpose of the second paragraph (lines 18–34) is to:

A. compare Picasso's work with that of other painters and sculptors of the 20th century.

B. indicate that *Guernica* explored the hopelessness and brutality Picasso associated with war.

C. describe the typical artist and political pieces that were produced in the 20th century.

D. speculate about Picasso's internal reflections and the conditions that caused the bombing of Guernica.

END OF SET THREE

STOP! DO NOT GO ON TO THE NEXT PAGE
UNTIL TOLD TO DO SO.

Entrance Ticket　Learning Targets　Purpose and Main Idea　Modes of Writing　ACT Practice　Sum It Up

Sum It Up

Intent and Purpose

Author
The writer of a piece of content, whether fiction, nonfiction, memoir, etc.

Narrator
The person who recounts the events in a story, whether a fictional character or the author of the piece

Purpose
The author's intention and reason for writing; what the author hopes the work will accomplish

Main Idea
The central idea of a text, around which all events and information are focused

Tips and Techniques

Hashtags: As you read a passage, create a "hashtag" for each paragraph. You can even write it down if you have time. This will help you navigate the passage when you need to find details to answer questions.

Embrace Your Inner Five-Year-Old: Ask *Why?* as in *Why was this detail included? What purpose does this detail/sentence/paragraph serve?*

Purpose: When a question asks about the purpose of a passage, consider the author's purpose for writing. Is the author trying to **entertain, convince,** or **inform/educate**? If you can figure out the style of writing, you can eliminate a few answers right away.

Interpret Words and Phrases Part 1

CAPTION:

7.1 Entrance Ticket

Read the passage and answer the following questions.

The Great Escape

Alex hated the detention room because it was devoid of air conditioning. It was June and incredibly hot. But Alex was mad for a multitude of other reasons. He didn't even start the food fight in the cafeteria. The teachers were indiscriminate in picking out the instigators from the crowd and were still deciding on the proper punishment; they went for everyone covered in the daily soup special. When asked who provoked the food fight, Alex said nothing. He truly didn't know.

Alex looked out the window and then at Mr. Washington. The teacher was engrossed in a fishing book. Alex looked toward the door. Maybe he could make a run for it. Was he brazen enough to do it? He wasn't known to be brave. Alex grinned.

There was only one way to find out.

1. What does *devoid* mean?

_____

2. What does *indiscriminate* mean?

_____

3. What does *provoke* mean?

_____

4. What does *engross* mean?

_____

5. What does *brazen* mean?

_____

7.2 Learning Targets

1. Distinguish figurative and literal language

2. Analyze and properly identify context

Self-Assessment

Circle the number that corresponds to your confidence level in your knowledge of this subject before beginning the lesson. A score of 1 means you are completely lost, and a score of 4 means you have mastered the skills. After you finish the lesson, return to the bottom of this page and circle your new confidence level to show your improvement.

Before Lesson

1   2   3   4

After Lesson

1   2   3   4

7.3.1 Vocabulary in Context

Use the word bank provided by your teacher to complete the sentences.

1. I _____ you to accept, please.

2. The _____ does not agree with the officially accepted religious dogma.

3. Many kids think vegetables are _____.

4. A positive self-_____ is especially important for teenagers.

5. The illness will _____ the athlete of his strength.

6. The tree _____ the light from passing through the window.

7. The innocent man made a(n)_____ to appeal for clemency.

7.3.1 Vocabulary in Context

The order *rodentia* derives its name from the Latin word *rodere*, which means *to gnaw*. This order includes rats, mice, porcupines, squirrels, and beavers and is characterized by
5 the animals' great incisors. With these giant teeth they gnaw away at the plants and woody stems they eat and use to build their homes. Though primarily vegetarians, they are not known to turn down a meaty meal, especially
10 one of fish.

These small mammals are found throughout the world, from the plains of North America to the badlands of Australia. Though the majority live on the ground, others are aquatic, and
15 some—like squirrels—live in trees. The distinguishing feature of the order *rodentia* lies in the lack of canine teeth and the presence of a large gap between the incisors and the molars. This anatomical feature allows for the incisors to be
20 slightly worn away by their facial bones, causing an extremely sharp surface—all the better to gnaw through any item that meets them.

Rabbits and hares make up the family *Leporidæ* within the order *rodentia*. One such
25 example of the family is the *Lepus cuniculus*, the wild burrowing ancestor of domesticated rabbits. These rabbits live in communities within burrows—called warrens—dug into the ground. These forms make a great nesting ground for a
30 mother rabbit, who will cover her tiny offspring with the fur she has shed. Many other species in the order *rodentia* make beds along the forest floor and conceal themselves and their young as best as possible among the leaves.

35 Aside from the *cuniculus*, all members of the *Leporidae* family are best termed *hares*, but colloquially, all are called rabbits. There are two types of hares native to Europe and Asia and

a plethora in America. Perhaps the best known
40 of these American hares is the eastern cottontail. The most important from an ecological standpoint, however, is the snowshoe hare, due to the role it plays in supporting the food cycle during the cold winter months. This species is a
45 vital source of both food and fur for humans in the northern parts of the country and Canada. When these rabbits are struck by disease or famine, the impact is greatly felt by both animal and human populations. Because hares feed on
50 bark and stems that are available year-round, they do not hibernate.

However, their cousins the pikas (*Lagomyidæ*) live above the tree line and must hibernate during the winter months. Other species live in
55 the Himalayas, where they dwell deep among the rocks, hiding away enough dried grasses and plants to sustain themselves until spring. These *conies*, as they are known in the west, are bobtailed and short eared.

1. As it is used in line 16, the word *lies* most nearly means:
   A. deceives.
   B. falsifies.
   C. exists.
   D. considers.

2. As it is used in line 29, the word *forms* most nearly means:
   F. created habitats.
   G. models of rabbit habitats.
   H. below-ground habitats.
   J. skeletons of rabbits.

7.3.1 Vocabulary in Context

3. As it is used in line 47, the phrase *struck by* most nearly means:
    - **A.** afflicted with.
    - **B.** hit strongly.
    - **C.** stumble upon something disruptive.
    - **D.** shocked.

4. As it is used in line 48, the word *felt* most nearly means:
    - **F.** touched.
    - **G.** experienced.
    - **H.** tried.
    - **J.** handled.

5. As it is used in line 57, the word *sustain* most nearly means:
    - **A.** assist.
    - **B.** defend.
    - **C.** uphold.
    - **D.** keep alive.

Reading Tip

Plug In: When the ACT asks you to determine the meaning of a word or phrase, go back to the passage and determine what you think that word or phrase means in the context. If that fails, plug in the answer choices and eliminate any that seem weird to you, then mark and move.

Entrance Ticket Learning Targets Vocabulary in Context Figurative Language ACT Practice Sum It Up

7.3.2 Figurative Language

Ancient mythology credits Hera, wife of Zeus, with creating the first lily. In Roman mythology the goddess of beauty, Venus, was said to have become so enraged by the beauty of the 5 lily that she tarnished its perfection by putting a pistil in its center. Paintings of lilies appear as early as 1580 BC, arising from the Minoan civilization in Crete that considered them sacred.

Lilies were cultivated throughout China, 10 and early European explorers prized them for their unusual beauty. The Henry Lily and the Regal Lily are two examples taken from the adventures of these explorers. The Chinese prized lilies for their decorative nature, and they 15 also utilized the bulb for a starchy food source. Though today the medicinal value of the lily is debatable, it was also used to reduce inflammation from arthritis and fever.

In biblical times, the lily represented purity, 20 ultimately becoming a emblem of the Virgin Mary. So pervasive was this connection that references to lilies appear in the Sermon on the Mount. This connection extended into modern times with the Easter Lily, or *Lilium longiflorum*, 25 a lily native to Japan. The Easter Lily migrated to America with a soldier who, struck by its beauty, brought bulbs home to Oregon after his deployment. The Easter Lily flourished in the area, which boasted a climate similar to its native 30 Japan. During World War II, the availability of the Easter Lily decreased dramatically. American nurseries of the popular species increased reciprocally. By the mid-1940s, an entire lily industry had sprung up along the West Coast.

35 This industry was helped immensely when Jan de Graaff introduced hybridization to the lily, which greatly increased its hardiness and ease of growth. De Graaff previously had success with tulip hybridization and found fame 40 with his "Enchantment" variety, a vibrant coral lily named by *Horticulture Magazine* as the most famous hybrid of all time. With the advent of de Graaff's hybrids, the lily was cemented as a staple within the American gardening world. 45 Home gardeners, once fearful of the flower's delicate nature, began incorporating lilies into their own flowerbeds.

Today, lilies remain intertwined with their ancient roots. Greek women still wear lilies in 50 their wedding crown as a symbol of purity and abundance. Likewise, lilies are often included in bridal bouquets and as decorations for communion celebrations. Conversely, lilies remain a popular funeral flower due to the idea that the 55 soul of the departed has achieved purity upon death.

1. As it is used in line 26, the word *struck* most nearly means:
   A. battered.
   B. smacked.
   C. impressed.
   D. hurt.

2. As it is used in lines 10 and 14, the word *prized* most nearly means:
   F. appreciated.
   G. counted.
   H. guarded.
   J. rated.

3. As it is used in line 5, the word *tarnished* most nearly means:
   A. to contradict.
   B. to diminish.
   C. to cause injury.
   D. to blot out.

7.3.2 Figurative Language

4. As it is used in line 40, the word *vibrant* most nearly means:
   - F. active.
   - G. energetic.
   - H. dynamic.
   - J. vivid.

5. As it is used in line 43, the word *cemented* most nearly means:
   - A. stuck together.
   - B. established.
   - C. fastened.
   - D. merged.

6. As it is used in line 29, the word *boasted* most nearly means:
   - F. gloated.
   - G. possessed.
   - H. bragged.
   - J. show-boated.

Reading Tip

Process of Elimination: If a question asks you for the meaning of *figurative* language, don't fall for the *literal* answer choice. You can double-check by asking, "Did this literally happen?" If not, eliminate the literal answer choice. These choices are there to trick you for not reading the passage!

7.3.2 Figurative Language

Welcome to *Jurassic Park*

1 Let me be <u>succinct</u>; I promise it won't be
2 long.

3 I am obsessed when it comes to dino-
4 saurs, and I don't feel <u>abashed</u> to say it. When
5 I was a kid, I watched *Jurassic Park* in theaters
6 and came home and reenacted every scene
7 with my toy dinosaurs and plastic army men; I
8 even hummed the theme song to <u>enhance</u> the
9 mood. I checked out every dinosaur book in the
10 library and dug holes in the backyard to find
11 bones. I would <u>rant</u> at the dinner table about the
12 distinctions of dinosaurs species, annoying my
13 parents. My mother appreciated my <u>zest</u>—she
14 saw my eyes <u>glow</u> with excitement any time we
15 went to the toy store.

16 In 1998, *Jurassic Park's* sequel, *The Lost*
17 *World*, came out, and I decided to be <u>noncha-</u>
18 <u>lant</u> about it. I was a teenager then; I had to
19 grow up, right? Any moment of excitement ex-
20 perienced when a trailer came on the television
21 was one of <u>brevity</u>. I couldn't let people know I

22 was still a dino-nerd. My parents found humor in
23 my futile efforts to repress my fascination. I still
24 had posters. I still watched *Jurassic Park* when
25 I was channel surfing. I unconsciously hummed
26 the theme song around the house. I eventually
27 accepted that this was part of who I was and
28 who I would continue to be.

29 Once again I stand in line at the movie the-
30 ater waiting to buy tickets to see *Jurassic World*.
31 I'm an adult now, but I still hum the theme song.
32 My dinosaur toys are packed away in a card-
33 board box, and my videotapes of the old movies
34 are nearly broken after a <u>multitude</u> of viewings;
35 my brother and I spent many nights reciting
36 every line. I remember how the first movie <u>fos-</u>
37 <u>tered</u> my imagination. It made me ask "what if"
38 more often. That's why I loved it. It wasn't the
39 dinosaurs.

40 OK, maybe it wasn't *just* the dinosaurs.

Multitude: _____

Fostered: _____

Nonchalant: _____

Abashed: _____

Rant: _____

Enhance: _____

Glow: _____

Brevity: _____

Zest: _____

Succinct: _____

Reading Tip

Knowing Is Half the Battle: Always check the context when you are answering questions about inter-preting words on the ACT. A definition may sound familiar, but that does not mean it fits the context. Pay attention to the passage instead of using your own knowledge.

Entrance Ticket Learning Targets Vocabulary in Context Figurative Language ACT Practice Sum It Up

3   3

7.4.1 Set One

Passage I

PROSE FICTION: This passage is adapted from the short story "On the Road Again" by Lauren Pope (©2015 by MasteryPrep).

As a child, summertime meant one thing to me: loading up the station wagon, making a pile of peanut butter and jelly sandwiches, filling the icebox with bottled sodas, and driving across the country to some far-off
5 destination. My grandparents laid out the agenda, and my sister Sarah and I happily set off on whatever adventure they determined would best expand our horizons.

It was on one of these summer excursions that we were passed by a tour bus carrying a musician to a perfor-
10 mance in some distant city. "I do believe that bus is carrying Marty Robbins," Grandpa told Grandma, pointing to a symbol that meant nothing to me. I looked at Sarah, confused.

"Nah, it couldn't be," Grandma returned. "He hasn't
15 toured in years."

A few miles down the road, though, we drove by a second bus. This one was emblazoned with the name Marty Robbins across the side of the shiny black coach. Grandpa tipped his hat at the driver as we drove by and
20 honked his horn with a quick *beep-beep*.

When we reached the next town, we found the two buses parked outside a truck stop diner. Grandpa pulled the station wagon up next to them. We all followed him into the diner, wondering what crazy idea he'd gotten in
25 his head this time. Grandpa walked up to an old man with a thick mustache wearing a cowboy hat. The man stood up and greeted Grandpa as though he were his cousin and shook his hand. Grandpa introduced us saying, "Now, girls, this is Marty Robbins, the best western singer there
30 ever was."

The man wrinkled his mustache and laughed. "Now that is quite the introduction," he said, and he asked us if we wanted a drink. We gladly accepted and sat down on the glistening red fabric of the booth, slinking down a bit
35 to avoid the chilly breeze from the ceiling fan above us. Grandpa asked Marty what he'd been up to, and Marty told us that he had played a sold-out show in Malden the night before.

With his eyes smiling just so and that cowboy hat
40 casting a shadow over his features, Marty looked at me and asked, "So, young lady, what kinda music do you like?" I looked down at the table shyly. "Dontcha know?" he asked. I wrapped my hand around my soda, pretending to take a drink to avoid answering, but I could feel the heat
45 of the room rising with everyone's eyes upon me. I men-
tally kicked Grandpa for seeing the buses and wondered how long it would be before we could get back on the road and put more miles between us and Marty Robbins.

I finally looked up and saw the kindest smile I'd ever
50 seen. "How'd y'all like to come out to the bus?" He stood from the table. "I've got some things I think y'all would like."

We walked out with Grandpa and Grandma to the big bus with the symbol that Grandpa had spotted. Marty
55 climbed up the steps and came out with a big photograph of himself as a young man. He scratched out "To Johnny and the girls" and asked me if we had an eight-track player in our wagon. I nodded, and he handed me a big pile of tapes. "Share 'em with your friends. I sure could
60 use a new generation of fans." I nodded again.

When we got home from our vacation, Papa asked what we'd done on our two weeks away. We showed him the picture of Marty Robbins and ran off to our room to listen to his tapes. As the first one began playing, Sarah
65 made a face. I shook my head.

My memory of that trip with Grandma and Grandpa has faded now, like an old photograph with only streaks of color popping through. Today, I listen to the poetic lines of Marty Robbins's music yodel notes that I could
70 never hope to achieve, telling stories of cowboys that hit your heart like thunder crashing in the distance. I am so taken that I am nearly speechless. Somehow between that road trip and today, I've truly learned to appreciate what Grandpa meant when he called Marty the best western
75 musician around.

---

1. As it is used in line 67, the word *faded* most nearly means:

   A. dimmed.
   B. discolored.
   C. tired.
   D. lack-luster.

2. As it is used in line 7, the word *horizons* most nearly means:

   F. boundaries.
   G. experiences.
   H. stretches.
   J. fields of vision.

---

3 **3**

3. As it is used in line 72, the word *taken* most nearly means:

A. removed.
B. appropriated.
C. entranced.
D. biased.

4. As it is used in line 31, the word *wrinkled* most nearly means:

F. disheveled.
G. roughened.
H. furrowed.
J. folded.

5. As it is used in line 40, the phrase *casting a shadow* most nearly means:

A. looming.
B. covering.
C. protruding.
D. impending.

END OF SET ONE
STOP! DO NOT GO ON TO THE NEXT PAGE
UNTIL TOLD TO DO SO.

Entrance Ticket   Learning Targets   Recognizing Emotions   Decoding Vocabulary   ACT Practice   Sum It Up

7.4.2 Set Two

Passage IV

NATURAL SCIENCE: This passage is adapted from *Lakes and Their Histories: An American Journey* by Juston Voorhies (©2015 by MasteryPrep).

The wind blows about ten miles an hour from the southwest, and the humidity blankets around thirty percent. For early spring, the temperature is warm and won't send the observers scurrying too quickly back to the

5 warmth of their lodges. Jack Bartlett, a ranger with the forest department, steps forward, wearing his characteristic wide-brimmed hat and forest-green khakis. He begins speaking in excited tones about the vast expanse of impossible blue laid out in front of the eager group.

10 "The Pathfinder," Fremont, discovered Lake Tahoe, and it was immortalized by none other than Mark Twain and John Le Conte. Originally a fishing hole for the Nevada *Washoes*—who named it "Tahoe," meaning high or clear water—and the California *Monos*, Lake Tahoe

15 became the scene of many battles, first between the Native American tribes and those who sought to remove them from the land, and later between squabbling politicians who sought to control the site's vast beauty.

These politicians clamored to use their newfound

20 land to capitalize on California's booming mining industry. However, when the miners' pans remained empty, industrial efforts turned toward logging and lumbering. The most famous effort was the "Knights of the Lash" which brought men and women from across the country

25 to the dainty, glorious, and alluring picturesqueness of the region. Though winter could bring thundering clouds of rain, hail, sleet, and snow upon the mountaintops, spring unleashed a soul-stirring beauty unmatched by any location in the country. Today the area is paradise to sports-

30 men and vacationers alike, boasting as great a variety of resorts as its surrounding wildlife.

Lake Tahoe is the largest lake at its altitude, measuring twenty-three miles long by thirteen miles broad. At 6,225 feet above sea level, the lake seems closer to

35 the sky, perfectly bleeding into the heavens in both color and purity. Looking down upon it from one of its peaks gives the impression that the sky and earth have been upturned and that the observer is somehow peering down into the sky. After Mark Twain ventured to Lake Tahoe

40 from Carson City, carrying only blankets and an axe, he encouraged his readers to take the same journey on horseback. As he turned the bend that brought the lake into view, he exclaimed, "I thought it must surely be the fairest picture the whole earth affords!"

45 Articulated or not, a similar impression comes to mind when a person first sets eyes on Lake Tahoe, and the more often one sees it, the more grand and glorious it becomes. The lake ranks among the highest caliber in terms of altitude, size, beauty, majesty, and sublimity. There is

50 no mountainous body of water on earth that is its equal. The chief charm of Lake Tahoe is in the exquisite, rare, and astonishing colors of its waters. There is no shade of blue or green that cannot be found, and the absolutely clear quality of the water enhances the beauty and perfec-

55 tion of each tone.

The depth of the water has much to do with these color effects; it varies from a few feet to over 2,000 feet deep. On a clear, wind-quiet day, the lake bottom can be distinctly seen except at the greatest depths. Rocky boul-

60 ders and moss-covered rocks dot the mostly level lakebed. A ledge creates a deep blue that hints at a drop of perhaps 1,000 feet. The sands, too, influence the colorful effects of the lake. Light-colored sands are washed down into the shallower waters by the mountain streams. These

65 vary from almost white to deep yellow, brown, and red. At night, the quiet and subtle charms of the Milky Way reflect upon the surface to create a replication of the universe most people have never seen.

Forest Ranger Bartlett pauses to compose himself

70 and straighten his hat. His eyes shine in awe, reflecting the clear blue of the lake. He motions toward it, inviting the group to share in his wonder. Slowly they make their way to the water's edge, struck by the same sense of reverence described by Twain so many years before. They

75 stand silently at the most remarkable location on Earth.

6. As it is used in line 9, the phrase *laid out* most nearly means:

F. dispersed.
G. expended.
H. displayed.
J. planned.

7. As it is used in line 44, the phrase *the fairest picture* most nearly refers to:

A. the view upon turning into the Lake Tahoe area.
B. a photograph of Lake Tahoe taken by Jack Bartlett.
C. the view of Lake Tahoe from the mountaintops.
D. the view of the mountaintops from Lake Tahoe.

8. As it is used in line 35, the word *bleeding* most nearly means:

   F. draining.
   G. cutting.
   H. blending.
   J. hemorrhaging.

9. As it is used in line 25, the phrase *alluring picturesque-ness* most nearly means:

   A. imitation beauty.
   B. inviting vividness.
   C. welcome transparency.
   D. charming beauty.

10. Which of the following words from the passage is used figuratively?

    F. *Blankets* (line 2)
    G. *Battles* (line 15)
    H. *Depth* (line 56)
    J. *Reflect* (line 67)

END OF SET TWO
STOP! DO NOT GO ON TO THE NEXT PAGE
UNTIL TOLD TO DO SO.

Entrance Ticket Learning Targets Recognizing Emotions Decoding Vocabulary ACT Practice Sum It Up

7.4.3 Set Three

Passage IV

NATURAL SCIENCE: This passage is adapted from *The Art of Perfumery* by G.W. Septimus Piesse (©1857 by Lindsay and Blakiston).

"The short narcissus and fair daffodil, Pansies to please the sight, and *Cassie* sweet to smell."
- DRYDEN'S *Virgil*.

Cassie is one of those fine odors that enters into the
5 composition of the best handkerchief bouquets. However, when smelled alone, it has an intense violet odor and is rather sickly sweet. It is procured by maceration, or softened by soaking in liquid, from the *Acacia farnesiana*. The purified fat is melted, and the flowers are thrown in
10 and left to digest for several hours. The spent flowers are removed, and fresh flowers are added eight or ten times, until sufficient richness of perfume is obtained. Flowers are added until the grease will no longer cover them as they deteriorate.

15 Once strained, the pomade is kept only hot enough to remain liquid, and all impurities disappear after standing for a few days. Finally cooled, the Cassie pomade is ready for sale. The *huile de Cassie*, or fat oil of Cassie, is prepared in a similar manner, substituting the oil of Egyp-
20 tian ben nut, olive oil, or almond oil in place of suet. Both preparations are only solutions of the true essential oil of Cassie flowers in the neutral fatty body. A similar scented pomade derived from the wattle—a plant that belongs to the same genus as the *A. farnesiana*—is grown most
25 luxuriantly in Australia. Mutton fat being cheap, and the wattle plentiful, a profitable trade may be anticipated in curing the flowers.

To prepare the extract of Cassie, six pounds of No. 24 (best quality) Cassie pomade are taken, and one gallon
30 of the best rectified spirit available is poured over it. After it has digested for three to four weeks, at a summer heat, it is fit to draw from the pomatum, and, if good, it has the beautiful green color and rich, flowery smell of a Cassie blossom. All extracts made by this process—*maceration*,
35 or, as it may be called, cold infusion—give a more natural smell of the flowers than by merely dissolving the essential oil (procured by distillation) in the spirit. It is especially useful when the odor of the flower exists in only very minute quantities, as is the case with Cassie, so it is
40 the only practical mode of proceeding.

In this and all other similar cases, the pomatum must be cut into very small pieces, similar to the process of "chopping suet," prior to its being infused in the alcohol. The action of the mixture is simply a change of place in
45 the odoriferous matter, which leaves the fat body by the superior pull, or affinity, as the chemists say, of the spirits of wine, causing it to dissolve.

The major part of the extract can be poured or drawn off the pomatum without trouble, but it still retains a por-
50 tion in the interstices, which requires time to drain away, and this must be assisted by placing the pomatum in a large funnel, supported by a bottle, in order to collect the remainder. Finally, all the pomatum, which is now called *washed pomatum*, is to be placed in a tin, and the tin must
55 be set into hot water for the purpose of melting its contents; when the pomatum becomes liquefied, any extract that is still in it rises to the surface and can be skimmed off, or when the pomatum becomes cold, it can be poured from it.

60 The washed pomatum is preserved for use in the manufacture of dressing hair, for which purpose it is exceedingly well adapted. This is because of the purity of the grease from which it was originally prepared, but more particularly because of a certain portion of odor, which it
65 still retains. If it were not used up in this way, it is advised to put it for a second infusion in spirit, and thus a weaker extract could be made serviceable for lower-priced items.

I cannot leave Cassie without recommending it highly to perfumers and druggists as a scent customized
70 for the purpose of the manufacture of essences for the handkerchief and pomades for the hair. When diluted with other odors, it imparts to the whole such a true flowery fragrance that it is the admiration of all who smell it. It has contributed much to the great sale of certain proprie-
75 tary perfumes. I caution the inexperienced, however, not to confound Cassie with cassia, which has an altogether different odor.

---

11. As it is used in line 7, the word *sickly* most nearly refers to:

   A. the unpleasant sugary smell of Cassie unaccompanied by other scents.
   B. the scent of a Cassie-based perfume.
   C. illness contracted by distillers of Cassie.
   D. a nauseated feeling that comes from smelling the Cassie flower.

12. As it is used in line 10, the word *spent* most nearly means:

   F. purchased.
   G. depleted.
   H. worn out.
   J. squandered.

3   **3**

13. As it is used in line 35, the phrase *cold infusion* most
nearly refers to:

   A. a dermal injection.
   B. a clear broth.
   C. an extraction technique.
   D. a chemical mixture.

14. As it is used in line 46, the word *affinity* most nearly
means:

   F. attraction.
   G. sympathy.
   H. fondness.
   J. rapport.

15. As it is used in line 76, the word *confound* most nearly
means:

   A. prove.
   B. overthrow.
   C. amaze.
   D. confuse.

END OF SET THREE
STOP! DO NOT GO ON TO THE NEXT PAGE
UNTIL TOLD TO DO SO.

Entrance Ticket   Learning Targets   Recognizing Emotions   Decoding Vocabulary   ACT Practice   Sum It Up

Sum It Up

Interpret Words and Phrases Part 1

Figurative
Metaphorical; using words as symbols

Literal
Using a word based on its exact definition, without metaphor or exaggeration

Context
Words that surround a certain word or phrase; clarifies the meaning

Tips and Techniques

Plug In: Try to plug the words into the passage if you are not sure which one is best or even what they might mean. Sometimes you can tell by using the words in context.

Process of Elimination: If you get stuck, eliminate answers that have literal meanings, especially if the passage seems to be using a word figuratively.

Knowing Is Half the Battle: Always look back to find the context in the passage. This will help you avoid trap answers.

Interpret Words and Phrases Part 2

CAPTION:

8.1 Entrance Ticket

Read the quote and write a brief paragraph on the topic using complete sentences. You may use examples from literature, history, movies, or your personal life.

> **Do what**
> **you can**
> **where**
> **you are**
> **with what**
> **you have.**

Entrance Ticket · Learning Targets · Literal vs. Figurative · Interpretation Based on Context · ACT Practice · Sum It Up

8.2 Learning Targets

1. Distinguish between literal and figurative language within passages

2. Use context clues to discern the meaning of individual words and phrases within passages

Self-Assessment

Circle the number that corresponds to your confidence level in your knowledge of this subject before beginning the lesson. A score of 1 means you are completely lost, and a score of 4 means you have mastered the skills. After you finish the lesson, return to the bottom of this page and circle your new confidence level to show your improvement.

Before Lesson

1   2   3   4

After Lesson

1   2   3   4

Entrance Ticket   Learning Targets   Literal vs. Figurative   Interpretation Based on Context   ACT Practice   Sum It Up

141

8.3.1 Literal vs. Figurative

For each sentence your teacher provides, write whether it is used *literally* or *figuratively*.

1. _____

2. _____

3. _____

4. _____

5. _____

6. _____

7. _____

8. _____

9. _____

10. _____

11. _____

12. _____

Entrance Ticket   Learning Targets   Literal vs. Figurative   Interpretation Based on Context   ACT Practice   Sum It Up

142

8.3.1 Literal vs. Figurative

13. _____

14. _____

15. _____

16. _____

17. _____

18. _____

19. _____

20. _____

21. _____

22. _____

23. _____

24. _____

25. _____

Entrance Ticket   Learning Targets   Literal vs. Figurative   Interpretation Based on Context   ACT Practice   Sum It Up

143

8.3.1 Literal vs. Figurative

It was a gorgeous June day in downtown Los Angeles. Numerous pigeons flew and flitted around, scavenging the bits of food on the ground for their afternoon snack. Suddenly,
5 a flash of brown plummeted from the sky and struck one of the flying pigeons in an explosion of feathers. Once it hit the pigeon, the streak resolved into a peregrine falcon, clutching its victim in its talons and carrying it away. Hun-
10 dreds of nearby pigeons, driven into a frenzy of panic by the death of their fellow scavenger, flew as quickly as possible away from the danger, none venturing more than a foot or two above the ground.

15 Often human habitation in natural areas results in disaster for wildlife. The animals' habitats are destroyed and replaced with asphalt and buildings, and as a result they—along with their prey—are forced out of their environment.
20 Those species that remain may find themselves no longer welcome in the newly constructed environment, and they may even be hunted to extinction.

Only a few species have been able to
25 adapt, coexist, and even thrive in human-controlled environments: coyotes, raccoons, rats, and pigeons are some examples. The peregrine falcon is another such species. Weighing one to three pounds and measuring 15–20 inches long,
30 the peregrine is bluish-black with a cream-colored chest. In flight, its long wings (about 30 inches in length) make the bird appear to be larger than its actual size.

In its natural habitat the peregrine falcon
35 prefers to nest among rock formations, an environment inaccessible to predators where their eggs will be safe. Many structures built by humans have artificial features that mimic the natural rock formations the falcon prefers.
40 Skyscrapers, church spires, radio towers—all of these provide the height and isolation that the birds desire in their lairs.

In Los Angeles the peregrine are somewhat famous for the daily, high-speed airshows
45 they perform for urban dwellers. Nesting atop multistory corporate buildings, the birds have claimed the city's unnatural habitat as their own. Experts believe that falcons have adapted to this type of accommodation for thousands
50 of years, once roosting in the tops of the pyramids in ancient Egypt. Since the advent of the modern city in the early 20th century, falcons have continued to make their homes atop skyscrapers—right in the centers of some of the
55 most populous metropolitan areas in the world.

Entrance Ticket   Learning Targets   Literal vs. Figurative   Interpretation Based on Context   ACT Practice   Sum It Up

144

8.3.1 Literal vs. Figurative

Reading Tip

Keep Your Pencil Moving: If you struggle with questions about figurative language, try marking the figurative language as it shows up in the passage. This strategy will better prepare you to understand each word in context and will also help you remember the passage better.

Entrance Ticket   Learning Targets   Literal vs. Figurative   Interpretation Based on Context   ACT Practice   Sum It Up

8.3.2 Interpretation Based on Context

As it is used in line 13, the words *white goods* most likely refer to:

A. white plates, bowls, and cups.
B. household linens.
C. heavy household appliances.
D. a variety of small items typically sold at yard sales.

Write down each word your teacher presents. Brainstorm as many definitions as you can think of for each word.

1. _____

   _____   _____   _____

   _____   _____   _____

   _____   _____   _____

                    _____

2. _____

   _____   _____   _____

   _____   _____   _____

   _____   _____   _____

                    _____

Entrance Ticket   Learning Targets   Literal vs. Figurative   Interpretation Based on Context   ACT Practice   Sum It Up

146

8.3.2 Interpretation Based on Context

3. _____

      _____   _____   _____

      _____   _____   _____

      _____   _____   _____

                     _____

4. _____

      _____   _____   _____

      _____   _____   _____

      _____   _____   _____

                     _____

5. _____

      _____   _____   _____

      _____   _____   _____

      _____   _____   _____

                     _____

Entrance Ticket   Learning Targets   Literal vs. Figurative   Interpretation Based on Context   ACT Practice   Sum It Up

147

8.3.2 Interpretation Based on Context

When I was eleven years old, my family moved from Detroit, where I was born, to Idaho. My mother was from Idaho, and all of her siblings had moved back there in previous years.
5 Wanting their children to get to know their aunts, uncles, and cousins better—kith and kin, as my mother called them—my parents decided to relocate our family there as well. We ended up living in a small town about eighty miles outside
10 the state capital of Boise.

My parents had an interesting encounter as we were packing up to move: while selling the white goods from our house in Detroit, they met an older man who was looking for a used
15 refrigerator. As they talked, my parents shared their plan to move to southwestern Idaho. "Really?" he said. "My father was from that area. He founded a small town called Spencerville. That's our last name." My parents had no idea
20 at the time that they would settle down in that very town.

For someone raised in an urban area like me, living in Idaho was very isolating. Containing one lonely stoplight on the highway, Spen-
25 cerville was surrounded by farms and ranches. From Spencerville, we had to drive for almost an hour to get to the nearest grocery store.

My mother converted more than half of our property into a garden. We grew a vast
30 amount of produce including tomatoes, pota- toes, beans, and radishes. The garden yielded so much food that we had to can it in mason jars or dry it in an electric air dryer to keep it from going to waste. Our efforts fed us through the
35 winter and into the spring.

The winters were cold. To catch the school bus, we would wait outside at six o'clock in the morning—in degrees below zero—shivering and stamping our feet, longing for warmth.
40 Eventually my mother spoke up at the local school board meeting and asked for the bus route to be changed, so we didn't have to wait outside so long.

---

1. As it is used in line 13, the words *white goods* most likely refer to:
   A. white plates, bowls, and cups.
   B. household linens.
   C. heavy household appliances.
   D. a variety of small items typically sold at yard sales.

Passage Clues:

_____

_____

_____

2. The passage indicates that the term *kith and kin* (line 6) refers to:
   F. people from Idaho.
   G. friends and neighbors.
   H. extended relatives outside the nuclear family.
   J. another phrase for "hearth and home."

Passage Clues:

_____

_____

_____

Entrance Ticket   Learning Targets   Literal vs. Figurative   Interpretation Based on Context   ACT Practice   Sum It Up

8.3.2 Interpretation Based on Context

3. As it is used in line 20, the phrase *settle down* most nearly refers to:
   A. ceasing rowdy behavior.
   B. living in a place for an extended period of time.
   C. stabilizing someone after a period of instability.
   D. ending a turbulent or choppy state.

Passage Clues:

_____

_____

_____

4. As it is used in line 32, the word *can* most nearly means:
   F. to fire from a job.
   G. to throw something away.
   H. to preserve food in containers.
   J. to be permitted.

Passage Clues:

_____

_____

_____

5. As it is used in line 40, the phrase *spoke up* most nearly means:
   A. communicated openly.
   B. talked loudly.
   C. shouted at a group.
   D. gave a speech from a podium.

Passage Clues:

_____

_____

_____

Reading Tip

Find the Window: Some of the answers are not immediately clear without looking for passage clues. Looking at only the lines referenced in the question may not be enough. Look before and after the line references for additional context.

Entrance Ticket   Learning Targets   Literal vs. Figurative   Interpretation Based on Context   ACT Practice   Sum It Up

3   3

8.4.1 Set One

Passage I

PROSE FICTION: This passage is adapted from the short story "Corn Topping" by Shelby Winters (©2015 by MasteryPrep).

When I was fourteen, I joined the other neighborhood teens in our rural community for a summer job of topping corn. We were hired in droves by local farmers to walk down long rows of corn, pulling the pollen tassels off
5   the tops of the ripening stalks—thus, the name "corn topping." The purpose of this task was to allow for the pollen of only certain types of corn to pollinate the field, which would yield a hybrid variety of corn.

It was grueling work. The rows were a half-mile or
10   so long, and there was a foot-deep irrigation furrow between rows. Each of us were given two rows to top, one for each of our hands. Because there was a good three feet between the two rows of corn, we had to stand with our legs widespread. Straddling the furrow, one foot on each
15   side, we would stand on the raised dirt where the corn stalks were planted. To move forward we had to rock back and forth in a slow shuffle as we attempted to keep our balance and not fall into the water.

We would start before dawn, forming huge lines at
20   the entrance to the corn field. It would take two or three hours to finish topping just two rows of corn. By then, it would be around 9:30 am, and we would take a short break. Those of us who had been around for a while knew to bring gallon jugs of partially frozen water. The
25   ice wouldn't melt until almost lunchtime, giving us cold water to drink in the summer heat.

After a second row, we would break for lunch. A peanut butter and honey sandwich in a brown bag was the most common repast. After lunch we would top one more
30   row of corn before we had to quit. The last row was the hardest; by that time, the sun had become oppressive as the full heat of the day arrived. Most of us had finished our water, and we were sluggish and tired. It always seemed like the last row of the day was twice as long as the first
35   two we had topped before lunch.

Despite the difficulty of the work, the pay was terrible. We earned $2.50 an hour, and since we worked about forty hours a week, it came to only about $100 a week. Looking back, it was a pittance, but at the time, it seemed
40   like a fortune. Over the course of the summer, a person could make as much as $700 or $800 with tireless effort.

It wasn't entirely about the money, though. Since almost all the teens in the area participated in the work, it also allowed for social interaction. As a fourteen-year-old,
45   I hadn't quite built up enough confidence to mingle with girls. This was a socially acceptable setting for boys and girls to spend time together, and more than one affair of the heart was initiated at lunchtime when couples would sit together at the picnic tables and talk.

50   This annual endeavor was almost a community tradition. The corn growers had worked out a planting schedule that allowed each of them to hire many teenagers looking for work. I sometimes wonder if the parents played a role as well; with all the teens out every day, things were a
55   lot easier on the local moms and dads.

Those days are now long gone. A few years after I left home, first some and then all of the growers began employing seasonal and migrant workers to do their corn topping. This allowed them to plant larger crops without
60   the need to coordinate the planting and topping schedules with school vacations. Ironically, a few years later, someone developed a simple machine that would accomplish the same work in a fraction of the time, so in turn, the migrant workers lost their positions as well.

65   I look back on those long lost summer days with nostalgia. The work was hard, but there was a fellowship among my peers: it was a rite of passage. Grueling manual labor, such as corn topping, taught me a lot about myself and gave me respect for hard work that has lasted to this
70   very day.

1. As it is used in line 54, the word *out* most nearly means:

  A. in disrepair.
  B. on a date.
  C. away from the house.
  D. sleeping.

2. As it is used in line 31, the word *oppressive* used here most nearly means:

  F. tyrannical.
  G. mean.
  H. unjust.
  J. overbearing.

Entrance Ticket   Learning Targets   Literal vs. Figurative   Interpretation Based on Context   ACT Practice   Sum It Up

150

3

3

3. As it is used in line 23, the phrase *been around* most nearly means:

   A. walked the perimeter.
   B. had experience on the job.
   C. were native to a geographical area.
   D. waited nearby.

4. As it is used in line 17, the word *shuffle* most nearly refers to:

   F. a rearrangement of things.
   G. a dance.
   H. an awkward way of walking.
   J. a walking stick.

5. As it is used in lines 47–48, the phrase *affair of the heart* refers to:

   A. a short-lived summer romance.
   B. a cardiovascular exercise.
   C. the cause of a couple's breakup.
   D. betrayal among friends.

END OF SET ONE
STOP! DO NOT GO ON TO THE NEXT PAGE
UNTIL TOLD TO DO SO.

Entrance Ticket   Learning Targets   Literal vs. Figurative   Interpretation Based on Context   ACT Practice   Sum It Up

Passage I

PROSE FICTION: This passage is adapted from *The Basics of Training* by Paolo C. Rupert (©2015 by MasteryPrep).

Ask anyone who has been a soldier, and he will likely tell you that one of the most memorable experiences in his military career is the first few days at basic training, when the U.S. Army turns civilians into soldiers.

5   My first day of Initial Entry Training was traumatic. We arrived in groups on buses, and we were left standing in the dark with our belongings in duffle bags until everyone had arrived at the station. Then, men in U.S. Army uniforms with distinctive "Smokey the Bear" hats came
10   out and circulated among us, ensuring that everyone who was supposed to be there had arrived. They were all sergeants. Up to this point, they had been professional, quiet, and almost pleasant in their interactions with us as they asked for our names and requested to see our orders. Once
15   everyone was accounted for, a dramatic change occurred to their misleading personas.

Suddenly yelling at the top of their lungs, the drill instructors began commenting on the personal, moral, and physical shortcomings of their hapless recruits. Addition-
20   ally they began barking out a series of intricate commands to which they expected instant and perfect obedience. Any deviation from instructions resulted in the offender completing sets of ten, twenty, or—for egregious mistakes— thirty push-ups. The treatment was even-handed; no one,
25   no matter how carefully they tried to obey, or how meticulously they followed instructions, escaped doing push-ups until their arms burned from exertion.

In retrospect it is clear that the drill instructors deliberately made the orders as confusing and difficult as
30   possible so they would have excuses to reprimand every recruit. If a particular recruit managed to avoid making an error, the drill instructors made the orders even more difficult, or they gave less and less time to accomplish the tasks until that recruit did fail, at which point the sergeant
35   would require the usual penance of repeated push-ups. The purpose of this calculatedly brutal behavior was twofold. First, it began breaking down the habits and thought patterns that had defined the recruits' civilian life. Second, it quickly acclimated the recruits to the punishingly diffi-
40   cult physical training schedule we would be following for the foreseeable future.

Next, we were placed in our training companies. We would spend the next sixteen weeks doing everything with the men in our unit: sleeping (never enough), eating
45   (less than we needed), marching (entirely too much), running (everywhere we didn't march), and training. Immediately, we began running in companies all over the base

to get our training materials, uniforms and the attached insignia to quickly identify us as infantry, as well as other
50   incidentals of military life.

At about 3 a.m., we were finally permitted to collapse into our bunks. We lived in huge open-bay barracks that dated back to World War II. We had double-decker bunk beds and absolutely no privacy. The entire barracks
55   was one giant, open room. Despite the primitive accommodations, I fell asleep instantly.

Less than three hours later, our drill instructors came through the barracks, screaming that it was time for us to get up. They gave us ten minutes to change into our
60   uniforms and report to the front of the barracks—faces fully shaved. On that first morning, none of us knew what we were doing, so we were all late. We spent the next forty-five minutes doing push-ups as a company due to our inability to follow simple orders. The drill instructors
65   said they hoped to encourage us to manage our time more efficiently in the future. It was weeks before we managed to get ready and out into formation in under ten minutes.

One of the most significant techniques that the military uses to encourage a unit to work as a group is mass
70   punishment. For example, if one of the members of our barracks was late to morning formation, everyone in the barracks was punished with a lengthy session of push-ups. This had two results. One was that every soldier made it his business to ensure that the others were ready to go. If a
75   soldier struggled, he could count on other members of the unit to help him. The other result was the "dark mirror" a recruit would face if he showed an unwillingness to do his part for the unit. Forced to acknowledge his wrongdoing, the member would often be forced to recognize his
80   egotism—not by the sergeants but by his fellow recruits.

6. As it is used in lines 42 and 47, the word *companies* most nearly means:

    F. military units or groups of soldiers.
    G. companionship among several people.
    H. men who assist drill sargeants during training.
    J. business enterprises.

Entrance Ticket   Learning Targets   Literal vs. Figurative   Interpretation Based on Context   ACT Practice   Sum It Up

152

7. The passage indicates that term *misleading personas* (line 16) refers to the:

    A. uniforms worn by the narrator's drill sergeants.
    B. narrator's acceptance into the military.
    C. feigned timidity displayed by the drill sergeants.
    D. drill sergeants who brought the company to the wrong barracks.

8. It can be reasonably inferred that the phrase *"dark mirror"* in line 76 most nearly refers to:

    F. apparatus used by recruits to assist them in shaving.
    G. a slang term for punishment by military leaders.
    H. the acknowledgement of one's flaws.
    J. the realization that one does not belong in the military.

9. As it is used in lines 24, the phrase *even-handed* most nearly means:

    A. the ability to use both hands equally well.
    B. quiet and pleasant.
    C. fair and detached.
    D. given equally to all.

10. As it is used in line 49, the term *insignia* most nearly refers to which of the following?

    F. Badges or distinguishing marks
    G. Signatures in the form of fingerprints
    H. Distinctive types of headwear
    J. Identifying metal tags worn around the neck

END OF SET TWO
STOP! DO NOT GO ON TO THE NEXT PAGE
UNTIL TOLD TO DO SO.

Entrance Ticket   Learning Targets   Literal vs. Figurative   Interpretation Based on Context   ACT Practice   Sum It Up

3   3

8.4.3 Set Three

Passage II

SOCIAL SCIENCE: This passage is adapted from the article "Deadlocked" by Simone Davis (©2015 by MasteryPrep).

The argument can be made that World War II was essentially a clash of competing technologies. Many claim that Germany, one of the Axis powers, had the most advanced technology for weapon development of any of
5 the belligerents participating in the war. The country's focus was on the improvement of traditional combatants in wartime: aircraft, ships, and personal weaponry.

In the air, Germany was the first country to produce the jet fighter: the Messerschmitt Me-262. Heavily armed
10 and able to sustain a top speed of over 100 mph faster than the most efficient Allied fighter at the time, the P-51 Mustang, Germany's jet fighter, proved to be unbeatable by U.S. and British technology. While Germany developed several other highly advanced aircraft, none were used in
15 great number.

Germany was also the first country to develop a long-range ballistic missile: the V-2 rocket. The work of a team led by Dr. Wernher von Braun, the V-2 had a crippling effect on London and other British cities as
20 well as military targets in Europe once the Allied forces invaded.

Furthermore, Germany expected its fleet of submarines, known as U-boats, to defeat England by sinking the merchant ships carrying supplies to the country. In the
25 early stages of the war, German militants were remarkably successful in these attempts, but toward the end of the war, most of the German U-boats were sunk by Allied navies. Just prior to World War II's end, Germany developed a radically new type of U-boat that could have rev-
30 olutionized submarine warfare had it been implemented. The new model employed electric engines that made the submarine almost completely silent and difficult to track.

Even in the area of infantry weaponry, Germany made huge advances during World War II. While most of
35 the belligerents used archaic bolt-action rifles like those used in World War I, the German Army, the *Wehrmacht*, commissioned a study to explore potential advancements in the weapons carried by foot soldiers. After several attempts, Germany produced a new infantry weapon called
40 the StG 44, short for *sturmgewehr*—or "storm rifle." The StG 44 ammunition cartridge was smaller, lighter in weight, and detachable, allowing soldiers to carry more ammunition and quickly reload in combat.

The StG 44 was a weapon far ahead of its time.
45 The principles that led to its development have guided the development of almost every infantry weapon in the world since World War II. While the Allies concentrated on other areas of research and development at the time of World War II, Germany held the technological edge in
50 many areas of weapon development.

Prior to the war, however, Britain secured a copy of the Enigma machine that was used by Germany to encode the messages they transmitted in some of their most important communications. A team of British scientists, in-
55 cluding the computer scientist Alan Turing, built one of the world's first computers at Bletchley Park in England. This enabled Britain to decode German communications that were encoded using Enigma machines almost as fast as Germany could encode them. This gave Britain an
60 almost insurmountable advantage during World War II. Often the Allies knew of German battle plans before the information had reached local German commanders.

Moreover, Britain, concerned about the buildup of German airpower prior to World War II, conducted re-
65 search and development of the radar system capable of detecting aircraft before it reached its target. Because of this pre-war research, Britain was years ahead in radar technology when the war began in 1939. This lead worked to Britain's advantage in the Battle of Britain, during
70 which Germany flew tens of thousands of missions to bomb London and other British cities. Fighter pilots of the Royal Air Force used radar to determine the German bombers' locations long before they arrived in England, and they were thus able to inflict crippling losses on
75 German pilots and aircrews.

The final, most powerful technology developed by the Allies in World War II was the atomic bomb. In great secrecy, at a cost of several billion dollars, scientists from the U.S. and Great Britain unlocked the principles of
80 atomic fission to develop a weapon that used radioactive materials to create a nuclear reaction. This weapon was of such destructive power that a single bomb could inflict as much damage as a single conventional bombing raid involving hundreds of bombers and thousands of tons of
85 conventional explosives. The launch of the atomic bomb against Japan led to the end of World War II.

Entrance Ticket   Learning Targets   Literal vs. Figurative   Interpretation Based on Context   ACT Practice   Sum It Up

154

3 　　　　　　　　　　　　　　　　　　　 **3**

11. As it is used in line 51, the word *copy* most nearly means:

A. reproduction.
B. close imitation.
C. paper document.
D. adaptation.

12. In the context of the fourth paragraph, the statement in lines 28–30 most nearly means that:

F. the German U-boat was radically successful against Allied forces.
G. the redesigned German U-boat, though sophisticated, was not used.
H. most submarines used during WWII were almost completely silent.
J. the author believes World War II ended prematurely.

13. In the context of the sixth paragraph, the statement in line 44 most nearly means that the StG 44:

A. was too advanced for practical use.
B. was not available at the beginning of World War II.
C. had semi-automatic and automatic fire modes.
D. was used as the basis for the design of modern weapons.

14. The passage's repetitive use of the metaphor *crippling* in line 19 and line 74 conveys:

F. a devastating effect.
G. a physical handicap.
H. a disadvantage in wartime.
J. a minor setback.

15. Based on the passage, the author's phrase "Even in the area of infantry weaponry" in line 33 is used to convey:

A. the assertion that Germany concentrated on a single area of research.
B. the author's belief that Germany was the superior power in World War II.
C. further emphasis on Germany's advanced technology in weapon development.
D. the argument that Germany could have invented the atomic bomb.

END OF SET THREE
STOP! DO NOT GO ON TO THE NEXT PAGE
UNTIL TOLD TO DO SO.

Entrance Ticket　　Learning Targets　　Literal vs. Figurative　　Interpretation Based on Context　　ACT Practice　　Sum It Up

Sum It Up

Interpret Words and Phrases Part 2

Figurative
Metaphorical; a statement not intended to be taken literally

Literal
A statement meant to be understood in its basic sense, without metaphor

Context
The clues and circumstances that precede and follow a word or phrase and that help clarify its meaning

Tips and Techniques

Keep Your Pencil Moving: If you struggle with questions about figurative language, try marking the figurative language as it shows up in the passage. This strategy will better prepare you to understand each word in context and will help you remember the passage better as well.

Find the Window: Some of the answers are not immediately clear without looking for passage clues. Looking at only the lines referenced in the question may not be enough. Look before and after the line references for additional context.

Entrance Ticket   Learning Targets   Literal vs. Figurative   Interpretation Based on Context   ACT Practice   Sum It Up

156

Analyze Word and Phrase Choices

CAPTION:

9.1 Entrance Ticket

Write a paragraph (5-7 sentences) explaining the cartoon.

"I have two ears. One helps me hear what you say, and the other helps me hear what you mean."

9.2 Learning Targets

1. Understand author's tone and meaning based on word choice and phrasing

2. Use context clues to analyze author's meaning

Self-Assessment

Circle the number that corresponds to your confidence level in your knowledge of this subject before beginning the lesson. A score of 1 means you are completely lost, and a score of 4 means you have mastered the skills. After you finish the lesson, return to the bottom of this page and circle your new confidence level to show your improvement.

Before Lesson

1   2   3   4

After Lesson

1   2   3   4

9.3.1 Idioms in Context

"Gina, this is not what it means to cut corners."

9.3.1 Idioms in Context

1. *Best thing since sliced bread*

   Before Example: _____

   After Example: _____

2. *Bob's your uncle*

   Before Example: _____

   After Example: _____

3. *Cat got your tongue?*

   Before Example: _____

   _____

   After Example: _____

   _____

4. *Devil's advocate*

   Before Example: _____

   After Example: _____

5. *Eat crow*

   Before Example: _____

   After Example: _____

6. *Egg on my face*

   Before Example: _____

   After Example: _____

9.3.1 Idioms in Context

1. My grandmother's rocking chair was the meter of my childhood. During times of trouble she rocked back and forth with a quick and nervous agitation. But on happier days she would rock peacefully back and forth, and the chair would produce its regular, comforting squeak.

   _____

2. It was during the 1950s that Elvis Presley's singing career took off. He set fire to his hometown of Memphis, Tennessee, with his mix of musical influences and provocative performances.

   _____

3. When I go to sleep, I close my body's eyes for rest and open my dream's eyes for adventure. In the night, I travel to far away lands and meet the most peculiar and fascinating characters.

   _____

4. Ralph Abernathy was a close friend of Dr. Martin Luther King Jr. The two quickly became pioneers of the Civil Rights Movement and together battled against the oppression and prejudice that ran rampant across the nation.

   _____

9.3.2 Decoding Using Context Clues

It might sound inconsiderate, but I don't care if anyone else is going to be there when I go. I'm looking forward solely to the change in scenery. Out on the farm, my senses are recalibrated to their new surroundings. Gone are the culture, fashion, and anxious pace of the city. There are no longer a million new ideas waiting to be examined, celebrated, or criticized. Instead there is simply light, shade, and a breeze
5   coming over the meadow. Time, which has ultimate significance in the world of deadlines and planning and accomplishment, can evaporate here. I sit by a stream and close my eyes, and suddenly the idea that I've been here forever and will always be here seems not only possible but obvious. It's as if a silent voice is reassuring me, "All is one." Of course, it does only last a moment, but the effect reverberates in my soul for much longer.

1. ☐ ☐   The narrator has lived on the farm her entire life, which feels like forever.
  yes   **no**

  ☐ ☐   When the narrator is on the farm, it feels like time stops and all is peaceful.
  yes   **no**

At the time of its release, James Cameron's *Titanic* was the most expensive movie ever made, with a final price tag exceeding $200 million. Crews built a full-scale model of the original ship to be sunk inside a seventeen-million-gallon tank (which was also custom built for the production). In addition, Cameron insisted that every prop on the ship be made from scratch, since the *RMS Titanic* was brand new at the
5   time of its sinking. The rooms, carpeting, individual pieces of furniture, decorations, wall paneling, cutlery, and crockery, each with the White Star Line crest, were among the features that were true to the original.

The filming schedule, which was originally slated to last 138 days, eventually grew to 160 days as many cast members came down with colds, flu, or kidney infections after spending hours in the cold water. Executives at 20th Century Fox—which was bankrolling the film—began to think that they might
10   have bitten off more than they could chew. They knew Cameron had a reputation as a perfectionist, but the fantastic success of his earlier films led the producers to greenlight his proposal without the standard level of scrutiny.

2.   The statement that the 20th Century Fox executives "began to think that they might have bitten off more than they could chew" (lines 9–10) most strongly suggests that at this point in the production, 20th Century Fox executives were:
  F.   determined.
  G.   stoic.
  H.   excited.
  J.   anxious.

ACT® Mastery Reading

9.3.2 Decoding Using Context Clues

The breaking of the sound barrier was an aeronautical achievement that changed the nature of air travel. This feat was considered difficult because the round nose of the plane approaching the speed of sound created shock waves that caused violent instability in the long wings of the aircraft. This often caused the pilot to lose control of the aircraft and die in the resulting crash. This particular problem,
5 however, was remedied by a simple fix. In 1942 the United Kingdom's Ministry of Aviation created the Miles M.52, which had a cone-shaped, pointed nose and a shorter wingspan. Combined with the conical nose—which was significantly more aerodynamic—the clipped wings were short enough to avoid what few shock waves the approach created. This plane became the prototype for the Bell X-1, in which Air Force Captain Chuck Yeager officially broke the sound barrier less than five years later.

3. Based on the passage, how should the assertion that the problem was "remedied by a simple fix" (line 5) be read?
   A. Ironically: the problem was not with the aircraft but with inexperienced pilots.
   B. Ironically: the engineers had overlooked a simple error in calculation.
   C. Literally: the solution was an adjustment to the design of the aircraft.
   D. Sarcastically: the problem persisted for decades after the creation of the Miles M.52.

Reading Tip

Use Context Clues: When a question says *most nearly means that*, the ACT will require you to use context clues to find the correct answer. Do not use your first instinct; instead look for your answer in the surrounding paragraph. Finally, remember to use elimination whenever you can.

9.3.2 Decoding Using Context Clues

C. Vann Woodward and Howard Zinn both made acclaimed contributions to American historical writing as a result of their distinct social and political perspectives. The reason is understandable: through their writing, they have opened up the past for reexamination so that younger generations can find themselves participating in events that have already taken place. David McCullough, a contemporary of both,
5 has enjoyed even more widespread fame through his distinct style of storytelling. Where Zinn and Woodward studied movements, McCullough studied people: his books delve deep into the psyches of important figures to illustrate historical events within an intensely personal context. This approach has lent itself well to adaptation into movies and television, enticing renowned actors to sink their teeth into the roles so richly and humanely described in McCullough's books. But are these characters really as true to life as their
10 author insists? Or are they, like an actor's performance, a mix of fact, fiction, and interpretation?

1. Based on the passage, how should the statement that McCullough "studied people" (line 6) be read?
   A. Literally: he analyzes important people in private counseling sessions.
   B. Literally: individual people are the subjects of his historical books.
   C. Ironically: the movements and events in his books are more significant than the people.
   D. Sarcastically: to the author, personal narratives are a ridiculous context through which to study history.

Jeffrey James "J.J." Abrams is widely thought of today as one of the most successful writer-directors in the movie business. Known primarily for action, drama, and science fiction films, he is also a prolific television producer-director, having created the series *Felicity*, *Lost*, and *Alias*. With the growing popularity of science fiction, Abrams has found a niche for his talents. He can boast of the creation of the newest
5 installments in the *Star Trek* franchise with *Star Trek* (2009) and *Star Trek Into Darkness* (2013). With these films, Abrams created a completely reenvisioned saga. His sci-fi résumé is only getting more impressive, as he is currently working on the newest episode of the *Star Wars* sequel trilogy, *Star Wars: The Force Awakens*, in which Harrison Ford, Mark Hamill, and Carrie Fisher return to reprise their roles from the original trilogy.

2. In describing Abrams's most recent *Star Trek* installment as "reenvisioned" (line 6), the author is most directly referring to the fact that:
   F. the plots of the resulting films were too far removed from the original universe to be recognizable to original *Star Trek* fans.
   G. Abrams replicated the plot, props, and characters from the classic *Star Trek* universe and passed off the result as his own invention.
   H. Abrams created a remake of the classic universe in a way that presented familiar elements in a contemporary style.
   J. modern audiences are uninterested in science fiction, so directors often have to change everything within a production but its title.

3   3

9.4.1 Set One

Passage I

PROSE FICTION: This passage is adapted from the essay "Some Nonsense About a Dog" by Harry Esty Dounce, which appeared in Christopher Morley's *Modern Essays* in 1921.

The day he came was a beautiful, bright, cool one in August. A touring car brought him. They put him down on our corner, meaning to lose him, but he crawled under the car, and they had to prod him out and throw stones before
5 they could drive on. I carried him over the railroad tracks. That night he got chop bones, and my mother got a sensible homily on the unwisdom of feeding strays, so he was left outdoors. He slept on the mat. The second morning we thought he had gone. The third he was back, wagging
10 approval of us and intent to stay, which seemed to leave no choice but to take him in. We had fun over names: "Jellywaggles," "Rags," or "Toby." Finally we called him "Nibbie," and soon his tail would answer to it.

Cleaned up—scrubbed, the insoluble matted locks
15 clipped from his coat, his trampish collar replaced with a new one bearing a license tag—he was far from being unpresentable. A vet once opined that for a mongrel he was a good dog. Always, depending on the moment's mood, he was either terrier or spaniel, the snap and scrap and perk
20 of the one alternating with the gentle snuggling indolence of the other.

As terrier he would dig furiously by the hour after a field mouse; as spaniel he would "read" the breeze with the best nose among the dog folk of our neighborhood
25 or follow a trail quite well. I know there was retrieving blood. A year ago in May he caught and brought me, not doing the least injury, an oriole that probably had flown against a wire and was struggling disabled in the grass.

Nibbie was shabby-genteel black, sunburnt as to the
30 mustache, grizzled as to the raggy fringe on his haunches. He had a white stock and shirt-frill and a white fore-paw. The brown eyes full of heart were the best point. His body coat was rough Scottish worsted, the little black pate was cotton-soft like shoddy, and the big black ears were gen-
35 uine spaniel silk. As a terrier he held them up smartly and carried a plumy fishhook of a tail; as a spaniel the ears drooped and the tail swung meekly as if in apology for never having been clipped. The other day when we had to say goodbye to him, each of us cut one silky tuft from an
40 ear, very much as we had so often when he'd been among the burdocks in the field where the garden is.

In flea time it seemed hardly possible that a dog of his size could sustain his population. We finally found a true flea bane, but deserted one day, he was populous
45 again the next. They don't relish every human—me they did; I used to storm at him for it, and he used to, between

spasms of scratching, listen admiringly and wag. We think he supposed his tormentors were winged insects, for he sought refuge in dark clothes-closets where a flying imp
50 wouldn't logically come.

He was willful, insistent on landing in laps when their owners wanted to read. He *would* make advances to visitors who were polite about him. He *would* get up on the living room table, why and how, heaven knows, find-
55 ing his opportunity when we were out of the house, and taking care to be upstairs on a bed by the time we had the front door open; I used to slip up to the porch and catch through a window the diving flourish of his sinful tail.

One of his faults must have been a neurosis, really.
60 He led a hard life before we took him in, as witnessed in the lame hind leg that made him sit up side-saddle fashion and two such scars on his back as boiling hot grease might have made. And something especially cruel had been done to him when asleep; for if you bent over him
65 napping or in his bed, he would half rouse and growl and sometimes snap blindly.

He was spoiled. That was our doing. We babied him abominably—he was, for two years, the only subject we had for such malpractice. He had conscience enough to be
70 sly. I remember the summer evening we stepped outside for just an instant and came back to find a curious groove across the butter on the dining table and an ever-so-innocent Nibbie in a chair in the next room.

It was lucky that the big dogs in our neighborhood
75 were patient. And he never would learn about automobiles. He usually tried to tackle them head on, often stopping cars with merciful drivers. When the car wouldn't stop, luck would save him by a fraction of an inch. I couldn't spank that out of him either. We had really been expecting
80 what finally happened for two years.

That's about all. Too much, I am afraid. A decent fate made it quick the other night, and clean and close at hand, in fact, on the same street corner where once a car had left the small scapegrace for us. We tell ourselves we
85 couldn't have had him forever in any event—that some day, for the junior member's sake, we shall get another dog. We keep telling ourselves these things and talking with animation on other topics. The muzzle, the leash, and the drinking dish are hidden, the last muddy paw track
90 swept up, the nose smudges washed off the favorite front window pane.

But the house is full of a little snoofing, wagging, loving ghost. I know how the boy Thoreau felt about a hereafter with dogs barred. I want to think that some-
95 where, some time, I will be coming home again, and that when the door opens Nibbie will be on hand to caper welcome.

3   **3**

1. Based on the passage, when the narrator states that Nibbie "had conscience enough to be sly" (lines 69–70), he most likely means that Nibbie:

   A. kept his mischief to a minimum while the family was near.
   B. hid all the destroyed toys and shoes from the family's view.
   C. was always well-behaved when the family was away from home.
   D. jumped into the laps of visitors who paid him any attention.

2. In describing Nibbie's problem with fleas and the doubt that Nibbie could "sustain his population" (line 43), the narrator is most directly referring to the fact that:

   F. the fleas living on Nibbie made him afraid to leave the clothes-closet to eat his dinner.
   G. Nibbie wagged his tail at the family but snapped blindly at fleas when left alone.
   H. no other dog in the neighborhood had as many fleas as Nibbie had that season.
   J. the large number of fleas living on Nibbie was incongruous to his small size.

3. In the context of the passage, the narrator's statement that he and his family had anticipated what eventually happened to Nibbie for two years (lines 79–80) primarily emphasizes that:

   A. the narrator's family's was able to predict the outcome of everyday events.
   B. the family was not surprised that Nibbie's reckless behavior led him to being struck by a car.
   C. the narrator's belief in fate saved Nibbie from neighborhood dangers.
   D. Nibbie's previous owners hoped he would run out into the street.

4. When the author says that Nibbie's first owners let him out "meaning to lose him" (line 3), he is most likely making the point that:

   F. the first owners were careless and could not keep track of him.
   G. Nibbie's owners were abandoning him.
   H. Nibbie wandered off and got lost.
   J. the author lost Nibbie under the car.

5. Based on the passage, when the author refers to Nibbie as having "retrieving blood" (lines 25–26), he most likely meant that Nibbie:

   A. was a ferocious hunter that brought back his kills to the narrator.
   B. had a health problem involving his blood vessels.
   C. sustained a gruesome injury while playing fetch.
   D. displayed characteristics of a particular breed of dog.

END OF SET ONE
STOP! DO NOT GO ON TO THE NEXT PAGE
UNTIL TOLD TO DO SO.

Entrance Ticket   Learning Targets   Idioms in Context   Decoding Using Context Clues   ACT Practice   Sum It Up

3　　　　　　　　　　　　　　　　3

9.4.2 Set Two

Passage IV

NATURAL SCIENCE: This passage is adapted from *Getting Acquainted with the Trees* by J. Horace McFarland (©1914 by The Macmillan Company).

The old saw has it, "Great oaks from little acorns grow," and all of us who remember the saying have thus some idea of what the beginning of an oak is. But what of the beginning of the acorn? In a general way,
5　one inferentially supposes that there must be a flower somewhere in the life history of the towering white oak that has defied the storms of centuries and seems a type of everything sturdy and strong and masculine; but what sort of a flower could one imagine as the source of so much
10　majesty? We know of the great magnolias, with large, unmistakable blooms befitting the richness of the foliage that follows them. We see, and some of us admire, the exquisitely delicate blossoms of that splendid American tree, the tulip or whitewood. We inhale with delight the
15　fragrance that makes notable the time when the common locust sends forth its white racemes of loveliness. But we miss, many of us, the flowering of the oaks in early spring, and we do not realize that this family of trees, most notable for rugged strength, has its bloom of beginning at
20　the other end of the scale, in flowers of delicate coloring and rather diminutive size.

The reason I missed appreciating the flowers of the oak—they are quite new to me—for some years of tree admiration was because of the distracting accompaniment
25　the tree gives to the blooms. Some trees—most of the maples, for instance—send out their flowers boldly ahead of the foliage, and it is thus easy to see what is happening above your head as you stroll along drinking in the spring's nectar of spicy air. Others, again, have such
30　showy blooms that the mass of foliage only accentuates their attractiveness, and it is not possible to miss them.

But the oak is different; it is as modest as it is strong, and its bloom is nearly surrounded by the opening leaves in most seasons and in most of the species I am just
35　beginning to be acquainted with. Then, too, these opening leaves are of such indescribable colors—if the delicate chromatic tints they reflect to the eye may be so strongly named—that they harmonize, and do not contrast, with the flowers. It is with them almost as with a fearless
40　chipmunk whose acquaintance I cultivated one summer— he was cheerful with stripes of soft color, yet he so fitted any surroundings he chose to be in that when he was quiet he simply disappeared! The oak's flowers and its exquisite unfolding of young foliage combine in one effect, and it
45　is an effect so beautiful that one easily fails to separate its parts or to see which of the mass of soft pink, gray, yellow, and green is bloom and which of it is leafage.

The white oak leaf is the most familiar and characteristic, perhaps, of the family, but other species,
50　close to the white oak in habit, show foliage of a very different appearance. The live oak, by the way, has a leaf very little like the typical oak—it is elliptical in shape and smooth in outline. The curious parasitic moss that so frequently covers the tree obscures the really handsome
55　foliage. The English oak, grand tree that it is, grows well in America, as everything English should by right, and there are fine trees of this *Quercus Robur* on Long Island. The acorns are of unusual elegance, as the photograph that shows them will prove.

60　The red oak, the black oak, the scarlet oak—all splendid forest trees of the Northeast—are in the group of confusion that can be readily separated only by the timber-cruiser, who knows every tree in the forest for its economic value, or by the botanist, with his paperback
65　Gray's Manual in hand. I confess to bewilderment in five minutes after the differences have been explained to me, and I enjoyed, not long ago, the confusion of a skillful nurseryman who was endeavoring to show me his young trees of red oak that the label proved to be scarlet! But
70　the splendidly effective trees themselves can be fully appreciated, and the distinctions will appear as one studies carefully the features of these living gifts of nature's greenness. The trees wait on one, and once the habit of appreciation and investigation is formed, each walk afield,
75　in forest or park, leads to the acquirement of some new bit of tree lore, which becomes more precious and delightful as it is passed on and commented upon in association with some other member of the happily growing fraternity of nature-lovers.

80　These oak notes are not intended to be complete but only to suggest some points for investigation and appreciation to my fellows in the brotherhood. I have never walked between Trenton and New York, and therefore, never made the desired acquaintance with the scrub oaks
85　along the way. Nor have I dipped as fully into the oak treasures of the Arnold Arboretum as I want to some day. But my camera is yet available, and the trees are waiting; the tree love is growing, and the tree friends are inviting, and together we will add to the oak knowledge and to that
90　thankfulness for life and love and friends that the trees do most constantly cause to flourish.

Entrance Ticket　Learning Targets　Idioms in Context　Decoding Using Context Clues　ACT Practice　Sum It Up

3 　　　　　　　　　　　　　　　　　　　　　 **3**

6. Based on the passage, when the author mentions that only a "timber-cruiser" (line 63) can distinguish various species of oak tree, he is most likely referring to:

   F. the casual lovers of nature who use a guidebook for reference.
   G. the botanists and scientists who have extensive knowledge of trees.
   H. the individuals who assess the worth of trees for profit.
   J. the nurserymen who must assign names to and label young trees.

7. In describing the "desired acquaintance" (line 84) of the scrub oaks between Trenton and New York, the author is most directly referring to the fact that:

   A. he is tired of visiting forests and would prefer to buy his own trees from a nursery.
   B. he has never encountered the trees in this area but is eager to increase his knowledge.
   C. he prefers the Arnold Arboretum to the scrub oaks found in Trenton and New York.
   D. these were the sites that drew him to studying oak trees early in his life.

8. In the context of the passage, the author's description of other trees' large or fragrant blooms that are impossible to miss (lines 10-16) primarily emphasizes:

   F. that other trees' blooms blend in with their foliage more so than the oak.
   G. their contrast to oak blooms, which are often overlooked.
   H. the author's preference for maple and whitewood trees over oak trees.
   J. that other trees tend to develop blossoms at the same time as foliage.

9. In lines 73–79, the narrator most strongly stresses:

   A. the rewards of being curious about tree lore and sharing knowledge with other nature-lovers.
   B. the benefits of joining the expanding numbers of nature-lovers known throughout the world for their generosity.
   C. that in order to join the fraternity of nature-lovers, one must learn everything possible about tree lore.
   D. that he would rather be accompanied on walks by experienced nature lovers than walk in solitude.

10. In the context of the passage, the author's description of a chipmunk in lines 39–43 primarily makes the point that:

    F. the outdoors are not just for tree enthusiasts but for nature-lovers of all kinds.
    G. just like the chipmunk, the oak tree's foliage is able to blend in with its surroundings.
    H. the chipmunk's glaring colors contrast with its surroundings, unlike the modest oak tree.
    J. people are surrounded by nature and sometimes encounter wildlife in unexpected places.

END OF SET TWO
STOP! DO NOT GO ON TO THE NEXT PAGE
UNTIL TOLD TO DO SO.

Entrance Ticket　Learning Targets　Idioms in Context　Decoding Using Context Clues　ACT Practice　Sum It Up

3   3

9.4.3 Set Three

Passage III

HUMANITIES: This passage is adapted from *A Mirror of Motion* by Georges Beringer (©2015 by MasteryPrep).

Movies have been called *the art form of the 20th century*. While technology developed in the 19th century popularized the novelty of moving pictures, it was in the 20th century that the very fabric of life all over the
5 world became a pattern for and a reflection of the movies. Cinema both reflects and influences the tastes, values, and fashion of its audience—hence, a mirror of motion. In turn, the movie–audience relationship affects product sales as well.

10 Many film critics and philosophical historians, such as A.S. Ferguson in *Plato's Smile of Light*, see movies as an ironic embodiment of Plato's cave allegory, wherein a group of prisoners believes that the shadows passing before them on the cave wall are not projections but reality.
15 When equating cinema to the way rulers manipulate the human population, the image of a movie house and its spectators is unmistakable. But the "rulers" of these modern reflections projected onto a movie screen are studios and marketing executives reflecting the fantastical
20 desires of the audience to sell merchandise. While few paying customers actually believe that what they see is real, they do identify with the characters on-screen, often viewing them as role models. This results in repeated viewings and merchandise sales in the likeness of their
25 favorite characters.

Early in the 20th century, audience reactions took the film industry and manufacturers by surprise. The demand for men's undershirts all but disappeared after film star Clark Gable refused to wear one in *It Happened One Night*
30 (1934) and started a whole generation of young males going bare-chested under their outer garments. Marlon Brando brought back the undershirt's popularity in *A Streetcar Named Desire* (1951), notably wearing it alone, without an overshirt. From a film's inception, movie tie-
35 ins and merchandise are the most sought-after secondary market; a hit movie—particularly geared toward children or young adults—can yield far more profit than ticket sales. The *Star Wars* saga made its producer/director/ writer George Lucas a wealthy man—not from ticket
40 sales, but from countless themed toys, posters, action figures, video games, apparel, and other memorabilia.

But this moving mirror of manners and marketing sprang from origins much more humble than the movie industry as we know it today. The earliest form of cinema
45 was a simple lens attached to one side of a wooden box. For centuries, glass makers had known that in a dark room, simple sunlight could be projected through a glass lens onto a flat vertical surface. The image would always
50 be inverted. But when the light was reflected by a mirror and through a glass prism, one could circle around it and see the everyday world projected into the room. By the early 1800s, entrepreneurs were projecting images from glass slides onto white sheets in tents and storefronts all over Europe and the Americas.

55 The popularity of this *laterna magica* led to the desire to show photographic images of people, animals, and the world in motion—a technological reinvention of human sight. The first moving images were produced in the 1830s by using a series of revolving drums, mirrors,
60 and disks. Invented independently in Austria, Belgium, and Britain, they were true recorded photographs that— when viewed from above while spinning—exploited a defect in the retina of the human eye in which afterimages would remain in view, creating the illusion that still images
65 appeared to move by themselves. The most famous of these was the Englishman William Horner's wondrous Zoetrope machine. *Zoetrope* was taken from the Greek words meaning *life turning*. The word *cinema*, from the Greek word for *movement*, was coined by French film
70 pioneers the Lumière brothers for their cinematograph, which presented these seemingly moving photographs. Simultaneously, French stage magician George Méliès was exploring fantastical visionary worlds by exploiting the illusions of such special-effect techniques as double
75 exposure, jump cutting, and stop motion.

During the pre-World War I decades, technological improvements led to new techniques of writing, scripting, and editing films and increasing ticket sales by advertising popular performers, which gave rise to the
80 Hollywood Star System. Aspiring movie stars flocked to Hollywood looking for their big break, but many found it was not worth the price. As various independent companies consolidated and merged for financial gain, studios streamlined and industrialized the production
85 and marketing of movies like an assembly line. The film industry continued to prioritize monetary gain over artistic expression, becoming one of the most profitable industries in the United States. Even through the Great Depression, film companies garnered profits by servicing
90 the fantasies of wealth and happiness. Today, for better or worse, cinema—along with its counterpart, television— seems to maintain that grip on those of us who desire a small escape from everyday realities.

Entrance Ticket   Learning Targets   Idioms in Context   Decoding Using Context Clues   ACT Practice   Sum It Up

3

3

11. Based on the passage, when the author calls film "a mirror of motion" (line 7), he most likely means that movies:

   A. portray visions of life that do not reflect actual events.
   B. use reflecting screens to advertise their products.
   C. reflect the values of the audience and inspire reciprocal responses.
   D. have little to no lasting effect on the culture of those who watch them.

12. When describing the origins of cinema as "humble" (line 43), the author is most directly referring to the fact that:

   F. despite cinema's mass market appeal, it arose from a simple device made from a wooden box.
   G. cinema was created so that working-class families could enjoy relaxing outings together.
   H. the Lumière brothers sold their first batch of cinematographs in an attempt to make a living.
   J. film executives and producers have become increasingly focused on monetary gain.

13. In the context of the passage, the author equates Plato's cave allegory to modern cinema audiences (lines 10–17) primarily to emphasize:

   A. the physical similarities between shadows on a wall and reflections of light on a movie screen.
   B. that the distortion of true reality is present in both the cave and the movie house.
   C. that modern movie houses were inspired by Plato's ideas about reality and perception.
   D. that the author hopes readers will be persuaded by Ferguson's unpopular theory.

14. Based on the passage, how should the assertion that images of the world in motion led to a "technological reinvention of human sight" (lines 57–58) be read?

   F. Literally: technology changes the way human eyes transmit images to the brain.
   G. Critically: the author is skeptical of the ways technology changes preexisting ideas.
   H. Figuratively: people began to perceive the world in a new way through the spread of moving pictures.
   J. Sarcastically: the invention of cinema failed to change people's perception of the world around them.

15. The statement "many found it was not worth the price" (line 81–82) strongly suggests that becoming a Hollywood star was:

   A. worthwhile.
   B. challenging.
   C. advantageous.
   D. uncomplicated.

END OF SET THREE
STOP! DO NOT GO ON TO THE NEXT PAGE
UNTIL TOLD TO DO SO.

Entrance Ticket   Learning Targets   Idioms in Context   Decoding Using Context Clues   ACT Practice   Sum It Up

Sum It Up

Analyze Word and Phrase Choices

Idiom
A word or phrase that means something different from its literal meaning

Tips and Techniques

Use Context Clues: When a question says *most nearly means that*, the ACT will require you to use context clues to find the correct answer. Do not use your first instinct; instead look for your answer in the surrounding paragraph. Finally, remember to use elimination whenever you can.

Supporting Claims

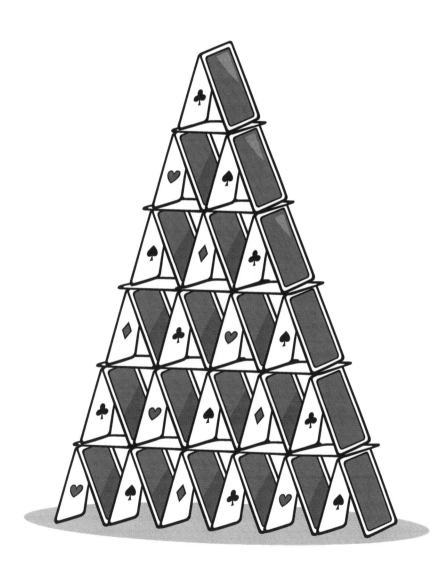

CAPTION:

10.1 Entrance Ticket

Read the passage and answer the questions.

The speed of light in a vacuum—186,292 miles per second—is a universal physical constant, denoted by the constant c. In his special theory of relativity, Albert Einstein posited that
5 c is the maximum speed at which any physical object or electromagnetic or gravity wave can travel in a vacuum, a space entirely devoid of matter. While light traveling through a vacuum has a constant speed, light traveling through
10 physical materials, such as water, glass, or lead, moves more slowly.

A curious phenomenon called Cherenkov radiation is a type of electromagnetic radiation that occurs when a charged particle passes
15 through a material at a speed greater than light would be able to pass through the same medium. When this happens the charged particle disrupts the local electromagnetic field as it passes through. Because the particle moves
20 so quickly, the disruption of the field acts like a shockwave that follows the path of the particle through the material. The resulting energy is electromagnetic radiation—most commonly recognized as the distinctive blue glow that is
25 associated with radioactive materials. In fact most of the processes that produce Cherenkov radiation are associated with nuclear reactions and radioactive materials, such as the radioactive decay of uranium, which emits fast-moving
30 charged particles.

As an example think of a supersonic aircraft and the sonic boom that follows. If the aircraft is like a charged particle speeding through a material, then the sound of the sonic boom is
35 like the glow of Cherenkov radiation. The sonic boom can only travel at the speed of sound, so it always lags behind the aircraft.

Likewise, Cherenkov radiation always follows the flight of the particle that created
40 it, since the particle is moving faster than the speed of light. Of special note, however, is that though Cherenkov radiation travels through material more quickly than light, it does not violate Einstein's special theory of relativity. Cherenkov
45 radiation still travels more slowly than c—the speed of light in a vacuum.

Entrance Ticket   Learning Targets   Claims and Evidence   ACT Practice   Sum It Up

10.1 Entrance Ticket

1. Which of the following examples is used to support the claim that the speed of light is the maximum speed at which matter can move through a vacuum?
   A. Although Cherenkov radiation travels more quickly than light itself, it still travels more slowly than the speed of light.
   B. Einstein identified c as the universal maximum speed that any object or wave can travel in a space devoid of matter.
   C. The radioactive decay of uranium emits the curious blue glow associated with the production of Cherenkov radiation.
   D. Einstein discovered that supersonic aircraft produce a sonic boom that travels at the speed of sound and lags behind the aircraft.

2. Which paragraph does the above example belong to?
   F. Paragraph 1
   G. Paragraph 2
   H. Paragraph 3
   J. Paragraph 4

3. The author supports his claim that "c is the maximum speed at which any physical object or electromagnetic or gravity wave can travel in a vacuum" (lines 5–7) primarily by:
   A. explaining how a charged particle can move faster than sound in certain materials.
   B. providing examples of materials through which light moves more slowly.
   C. indicating that this principle was proven by Albert Einstein.
   D. illustrating that Cherenkov radiation emits a distinctive blue glow.

10.2 Learning Targets

1. Identify and relate claims with appropriate examples and answer choices

2. Identify and relate examples with appropriate claims using several different strategies

Self-Assessment

Circle the number that corresponds to your confidence level in your knowledge of this subject before beginning the lesson. A score of 1 means you are completely lost, and a score of 4 means you have mastered the skills. After you finish the lesson, return to the bottom of this page and circle your new confidence level to show your improvement.

Before Lesson

| 1 | 2 | 3 | 4 |

After Lesson

| 1 | 2 | 3 | 4 |

10.3.1 Claims and Evidence

1. Which of the following does the passage's author cite as the reason that Cherenkov radiation always lags behind the high-speed particle responsible for it?
   A. The particle moves more quickly than the speed of light.
   B. The radiation produced is in the ultraviolet/blue visible spectrum.
   C. The speed of light in a vacuum is a universal constant.
   D. Cherenkov radiation travels more slowly than c.

2. The reference to the supersonic aircraft and sonic boom most directly supports which of the following points made in the passage?
   F. Light waves in a vacuum travel at a maximum speed denoted by the universal constant c.
   G. Fast-moving charged particles disrupt the local electromagnetic fields.
   H. Charged particles move more quickly through certain materials than the radiation that follows.
   J. Einstein's special theory of relativity disproves the concept of a sonic boom.

How are these two question types different?

_____

_____

_____

_____

How are they similar?

_____

_____

_____

_____

10.3.1 Claims and Evidence

When describing traditional Japanese clothing, many refer to the *kimono*, the classic silken garb of Japanese women. The elaborate kimono worn by upper-class women on formal
5 occasions, in particular, often symbolizes what many think of as "Old Japan." Yet the kimono as it is known today evolved through a long series of refinements before it reached its modern form. Although the kimono is still considered
10 the standard in Japanese formal attire, clothing worn by Japanese women of the upper classes in the classical Heian and the medieval Muromachi and Kamakura periods was very different from the class-spanning kimono of today.

15 In the Heian period (794–1185), it was fashionable to dress in as many as twenty-five layered robes of very thin material, the hue of each layer blending with the layers above. The robes were fastened with a thin belt around the
20 waist, and underneath, the women wore a wide-legged trouser known as a *hakama.* During the Kamakura (1185–1333) and Muromachi (1337–1563) periods, the style was simplified. The *kosode*—a thin thigh-length robe made of
25 simple, white fabric and worn as an undergarment for the Heian costumes—was lengthened to the ankle and became the standard form of dress for all classes of Japanese women, not just the elite. The kosode had narrow sleeves
30 and was fastened by a thin strip of fabric, or *obi.* It was not until the Edo period (1603–1868) that the kimono began to resemble its present form. Women began to look for more variety in their clothing, which led to the use of colorful
35 patterns with varied themes.

The late Edo period (1720–1868) saw the advent of the professional female entertainers known as *geisha*. Highly trained in the traditionally female arts of poetry, dance, and
40 song, geisha were perceived as culturally superior. The competition between geisha to create the most elegant outfits led to the use of fabric with increasingly sophisticated dye patterns to match the wearer's status. To add elegance,
45 the obi evolved from a simple, thin fabric belt to a wide sash that was wrapped around the waist five times and fastened with a silken cord. The kosode's sleeves were widened until they almost touched the ground, making the kimono
50 more stylish.

By the late 18th century, the kimono had reached its final form, becoming the everyday wear of all classes of Japanese women. Even the poorest woman had a "dress kimono" made
55 of silk and dyed in elaborate patterns—even if her everyday wear was white or black and made of hemp.

Entrance Ticket   Learning Targets   Claims and Evidence   ACT Practice   Sum It Up

10.3.1 Claims and Evidence

1. Lines 38–44 primarily serve to illustrate the point made in the third paragraph (lines 36–50) that in the Edo period, the geisha profession was:
   A. scorned.
   B. esteemed.
   C. diverse.
   D. demanding.

2. Based on the passage, the author most strongly supports which of the following about the development of the modern kimono?
   F. The hakama, the obi, and the kosode have remained almost unchanged since the Heian period.
   G. The wealthy classes played an important role in the development of the modern Japanese kimono.
   H. It evolved over several hundred years and reached its current form in the 18th century.
   J. It was worn only by geisha until the late Edo period, when more women could afford the expensive silk.

3. For the passage's author, lines 31–35 mainly serve to support her earlier point that:
   A. the kimono of today is not representative of "Old Japan."
   B. the women in the Heian period wore layers of clothing.
   C. the cultural superiority of the geisha allowed them to obtain expensive fabrics.
   D. the kimono was always black and white prior to the Edo period.

4. The reference to the appearance of geisha as entertainers directly supports which of the following points made in the passage?
   F. The types of clothing worn by upper-class women of the Heian period was very conservative.
   G. The kimono is one of the most recognized symbols of traditional Japanese culture.
   H. Even poor women often owned a good "dress kimono" decorated in elaborate patterns and made from silk.
   J. The modern version of the kimono was greatly influenced by the prominence of geisha.

Reading Tip

Decoding: If the question includes words like *supports which of the following* or *serves to illustrate which*, then you know that the question is giving an example and you need to match it to a claim.

10.4.1 Set One

Passage II

SOCIAL SCIENCE: This passage is adapted from *Religious Histories* by Arthur Ketill (©2015 by MasteryPrep).

The first evidence of Christianity in England originates from the late second century A.D., when the population of Roman Britain was highly diverse and included merchants and soldiers from all over the empire. At the
[5] time England and Wales were ruled by the Romans, who were not tolerant of Christianity, and persecution was widespread. St. Alban, the first British Christian martyr, was executed in 304. Emperor Constantine later granted Christians the freedom to worship, and by the fourth cen-
[10] tury—following the departure of the Romans from Britain in 410—Christianity became widespread in England.

Following the end of Roman rule in Britain, Christianity continued to thrive in Wales. The Welsh Church was essentially a monastic sect with the underlying belief
[15] that the ideal path to holiness is to retire from the world and live in a community dedicated to prayer alone. During this time, Wales consisted of groups of tribesmen following powerful secular chieftains. The Church in Wales followed a similar structure; the great monasteries func-
[20] tioned as a spiritual clan in which the abbot was the chieftain, the clergy represented the heads of the families, and the monks were the tribesmen. Their churches were built on land owned by the various orders.

Christianity had also begun to spread to Ireland and
[25] Scotland; Ninian, the foreign-educated son of a British chief, established a community at Whithorn in Scotland. Later, Bishop Patrick of the Irish, also highly educated in Europe, went on to establish an independent branch of the church at Armagh in Northern Ireland. Finally, the Celtic
[30] Church was formed. This was the result of the missionary work of these British clerics and their followers, with no influence from Rome.

Hard times fell upon the Church with the Anglo-Saxon invasion of Britain between the fourth and
[35] sixth centuries. Most of the formal Church was destroyed and replaced with a form of polytheism, the worship of many gods. Ultimately the Anglo-Saxon invasions did not destroy Christianity but drove it abroad, where the churches in Cornwall, Ireland, and Scotland formed a sin-
[40] gle religious group, bound together by frequent contact and exchanges of clergy.

The reintroduction of Christianity in Britain is largely credited to the Gregorian Mission. In 596, Pope Gregory the Great appointed Augustine, a monk practicing in
[45] Rome, to convert Britain's Anglo-Saxons. Augustine led the mission to the province of Kent and was appointed the first Archbishop of Canterbury. Further missionaries were sent from Rome in 602, and in 604 Augustine founded two additional bishoprics in Britain.

[50] For the next fifty years, the British Church, representing the old Celtic branch, and the Continental Church, which represented the new organization Augustine had implemented in Rome, existed independently of each other. Pope Gregory had hoped that Augustine would con-
[55] vert all of England to Christianity, but Augustine failed to extend his authority beyond Kent and Essex. Augustine and the Celtic British bishops argued heatedly over such issues as the date on which to celebrate Easter, the manner of baptism, and the manner of vows that a man must take
[60] upon entering a monastery.

The conversion of Saxon England was a process that spanned the seventh century. In 669 Theodore of Tarsus was appointed the eighth Archbishop of Canterbury, charged with organizing the English Church. Although
[65] Augustine, who created its ecclesial structure, is regarded as the father of the Church of England, Theodore of Tarsus is perhaps equally significant. Theodore initiated reforms concerning the proper celebration of Easter, episcopal authority, marriage, and other matters that had caused disso-
[70] nance within the Church. It was Theodore of Tarsus who initiated the division of dioceses in England into smaller sections. Today, though many more dioceses have been created, the boundaries created by Theodore of Tarsus are still recognizable on the map of the British Isles.

1. To support his assertion about the success of the Christian sect in Wales, the passage's author points out that:

   A. the structure of the sect closely mirrored the preexisting secular society.
   B. the powerful secular chieftains were unable to put up resistance to the Church.
   C. the Saxons successfully established the first monasteries in Wales.
   D. the monasteries of Wales provided protection from the Romans.

Entrance Ticket　Learning Targets　Claims and Evidence　ACT Practice　Sum It Up

3   **3**

2. The author's claim that "Theodore of Tarsus is perhaps equally significant" (lines 66–67) is best supported and illustrated by his:

  F. account of the Anglo-Saxon invasion of England (lines 33–41).
  G. reference to the diocesan boundaries and reforms still recognized today (lines 67–74).
  H. comments about the spread of the Church to Scotland and Ireland (lines 24–32).
  J. comparison of the parallel secular and Christian structures in Wales (lines 12–23).

3. Based on the passage, the outcome of the Anglo-Saxon invasion most strongly supports which of the following about the history of the Church in Britain?

  A. The Church was divided into multiple dioceses that kept in constant contact and were united against the Anglo-Saxons.
  B. Augustine was appointed as the first Archbishop of Canterbury and converted hundreds of Anglo-Saxons.
  C. Christianity in Britain was replaced by polytheism for a time, while a unified Church flourished abroad.
  D. The spread of monastic churches in Wales led to the conversion of Cornwall, while the British Church remained intact.

4. Lines 54–56 primarily serve to illustrate the point made in the sixth paragraph (lines 50–60) that the conversion missions in Britain carried out by Augustine were:

  F. widespread.
  G. immediately successful.
  H. cause for war between British clans.
  J. largely ineffectual.

5. Which of the following is a detail used in the passage to support the claim that Augustine was at the forefront of the Gregorian Mission?

  A. Augustine is widely regarded as the founder of the English Church.
  B. The reintroduction of Christianity in Britain is largely credited to the cooperation of Rome and Canterbury.
  C. Augustine led the mission from Rome to Britain and was appointed the first Archbishop of Canterbury.
  D. The Celtic Church was formed through the joint efforts of Rome and the English Church.

END OF SET ONE
STOP! DO NOT GO ON TO THE NEXT PAGE
UNTIL TOLD TO DO SO.

Entrance Ticket   Learning Targets   Claims and Evidence   ACT Practice   Sum It Up

10.4.2 Set Two

Passage II

SOCIAL SCIENCE: This passage is adapted from *Aerial Warfare and Strategy Since 1900* by David Harr (©2015 by MasteryPrep).

On Sunday, December 7, 1941, the Imperial Japanese Navy attacked the United States naval base at Pearl Harbor, the main base of the U.S. Pacific Fleet. When the attack was over, all eight U.S. battleships, three cruisers, and three destroyers in use had been sunk or damaged. In addition 188 U.S. grounded aircraft were destroyed.

A few hours later Japanese air units attacked Clark Field, the main U.S. Army Air Force base in the South Pacific. The Japanese bombers found the American planes parked in neat rows on the ground, an easy target. The morning raid by the Japanese resulted in the destruction of half of the American aircraft at Clark Field.

These attacks were only the first in a seemingly unending string of victories by Japanese military forces in the Pacific during the early part of 1942. By March Japan had secured Singapore and the oil-rich Dutch Indies. In May the last American forces in the Philippines surrendered to the Japanese, resulting in the capture of 90,000 American troops.

By the end of May 1942, Japan controlled an area of the Pacific extending almost 3,000 miles from the home islands and threatened both Hawaii and Australia. American forces were desperate to put an end to Japan's victories.

In the middle of one of the most desolate regions of the Pacific Ocean—about halfway between Hawaii and the next-nearest island—lies Midway Atoll. Since it is the only land for thousands of miles in any direction, it is ideally located to act as a base for military operations further west, including attacks on Hawaii and the west coast of the United States. The Japanese focused on securing Midway Atoll for use as a staging area and refueling station for future military operations.

The Japanese decided to launch an attack on Midway to secure it as a base and to draw out the U.S. Navy aircraft carriers, which the Japanese were desperate to destroy. They viewed the American carriers as the biggest obstacle to their complete domination of the Pacific from Japan to the west coast of the United States.

In June 1942, the Japanese launched their attack against the island. Unfortunately for the Japanese, U.S. Army Intelligence had cracked their enemy's codes in order to monitor Japanese communications. Thus, the U.S. Navy was informed of the attack before it happened and set out its entire available force of aircraft carriers to meet the Japanese.

The Battle of Midway commenced on June 3, 1942, with heavy air strikes from the Japanese aircraft carriers on the base at Midway Island. As Japan's planes were returning, however, an American scout plane located the task force. The U.S. immediately launched every plane at its disposal to attack the Japanese carriers.

Unfortunately the American bombers sent after the Japanese task force were largely ineffective. The first group to reach the Japanese carriers were torpedo bombers from the aircraft carrier *Hornet*. The Americans' low-flying, slow-moving planes were easily shot down by the Japanese combat air patrol of Zeros. The Zero was the most advanced naval fighter at that point in the war, and it easily outclassed most of the American fighters that flew against it. Next the U.S. launched attacks from *Enterprise* and *Yorktown,* and those planes were shot down as easily as their comrades'. When initial attacks were complete, only six of forty-five U.S. torpedo bombers returned from the mission. Moreover, of the several U.S. torpedo bombers that managed to hit their targets, none had torpedoes that actually detonated.

Fortunately for the U.S., its squad of dive bombers located the Japanese task force. As Japan's Zeros descended to nearly sea level to complete their attack on the U.S. torpedo bombers, the U.S. dive bombers— flying at 25,000 feet—were able to launch their attacks from above. Once the U.S. dive bombers had finished their strikes, three of the four Japanese carriers had been destroyed. The Americans utilized the opportunity to mount an additional strike before dark, sinking the remaining Japanese carrier. In addition, Japan lost hundreds of its aircraft.

The Battle of Midway is widely regarded as the turning point of World War II in the Pacific Theater. The Japanese never recovered from the loss of their four carriers and the experienced air crews, and Midway marked the last time that the Japanese mounted offensive operations in the Pacific. From that point on they fought a defensive war.

3

6. For the passage's author, lines 20–24 mainly serve to support his earlier point that:

   F. the string of victories by the Japanese military made them a dominant force.
   G. the Japanese were desperate to put an end to American victories.
   H. nearly 100,000 American troops had surrendered to Japan in the Philippines.
   J. the attacks on Pearl Harbor and Clark Field caught the Americans by surprise.

7. The reference to the Midway Atoll most directly supports which of the following points made in the passage?

   A. Clark Field was the only other U.S. Army Air Force base in the South Pacific.
   B. The Japanese were desperate to destroy U.S. aircraft carriers.
   C. Midway made an ideal base and refueling station for naval operations in the Pacific.
   D. Japan controlled a huge area of the Pacific and was a threat to both Hawaii and Australia.

8. According to the passage, the narrator suggests that the success of the U.S. dive bombing attacks on Japan's Zero naval fighters hinged on:

   F. the poor performance of the torpedoes launched previously by U.S. torpedo bombers.
   G. the Japanese Zero naval fighters' inability to defeat American aircraft.
   H. information that U.S. intelligence was able to obtain regarding Japan's plan of attack.
   J. the sea-level location of the Zeros that allowed the U.S. to stack from above.

9. Which of the following does the author cite as evidence that the Battle of Midway was a turning point for WWII?

   A. This battle was Japan's last offensive strike in the Pacific.
   B. The U.S. took over Midway Atoll for use as a base.
   C. Only six U.S. torpedo bombers remained intact.
   D. This battle marked the end of Japan's participation in the war.

10. The author supports his claim that "the American bombers sent after the Japanese task force were largely ineffective" (lines 53–54) primarily by:

   F. comparing the experience and skill levels of Japanese and American air crews.
   G. describing how the Japanese carriers launched heavy attacks against the airbase on Midway Atoll.
   H. explaining that the Japanese had intercepted the U.S. task force and launched a defensive strike.
   J. revealing that many torpedoes were faulty and that the Zero outranked the American aircraft.

END OF SET TWO

STOP! DO NOT GO ON TO THE NEXT PAGE
UNTIL TOLD TO DO SO.

Entrance Ticket   Learning Targets   Claims and Evidence   ACT Practice   Sum It Up

10.4.3 Set Three

Passage IV

NATURAL SCIENCE: This passage is adapted from *The Future's Machines* by Yelena Corvene (©2015 by MasteryPrep).

During the mid-to-late 20th century, computer central processing unit (CPU) speeds improved at an average rate of fifty-two percent per year. For 30 years the fundamental contributor to increasing system performance was
[5] the rising speed of the CPU. This was primarily done by increasing the microprocessor's frequency, which is measured in hertz. To illustrate, the first microprocessors ran at frequencies close to 1 Megahertz (MHz), or 1,000,000 Hertz, while modern microprocessors run at frequencies
[10] exceeding 3 Gigahertz (GHz), or 3,000,000,000 Hertz. These early jumps in speed led many programmers to believe that they could increase the speed of their programs simply by waiting a few months or years for a faster circuit, or "chip," to become available. However, they quick-
[15] ly learned that as the frequency of the microprocessor is increased, the power consumption significantly increases as well. This increase in power consumption was initially managed through the miniaturization of transistors.

In 2000 the microprocessor industry ran into what
[20] is known as a "power wall"—the point at which it is no longer possible to offset power consumption and heat production through transistor miniaturization. To overcome this power wall, CPU manufacturers determined that it was possible to replicate a CPU multiple times on a single
[25] chip while keeping the power consumption stable. This discovery marked the end of single chip processors and the beginning of multi-core processors: single chips containing two or more CPUs.

From this point on, the world of application pro-
[30] gramming was drastically altered. Intel and other CPU manufacturers used multi-core processors to increase CPU capacity and increase speed. By 2015 the Intel processor ran on speeds up to 3.6 GHz, compared to its speed of 1.7 GHz in 2001. The change in focus from single-processor
[35] performance to multi-core performance for CPUs marked a fundamental paradigm shift for all computer application programmers. Multi-core programming had been primarily utilized by scientific computing specialists; now it could be used as the primary method for all application
[40] programmers in order to improve software performance. This presented some difficulty within the computer science industry, however, as multi-core programming is more difficult than single-threaded programming.

As multi-core programming evolved, a revolution
[45] occurred within the computer graphics community—particularly among high-end game developers. Game pro-grammers spent enormous amounts of time improving graphics and maximizing the performance of their games by utilizing increasingly sophisticated physics. However,
[50] there would be a consequence: suddenly even the most powerful consumer CPU couldn't efficiently process these new, highly sophisticated graphics. To alleviate the problem, accelerated video game cards were created, but game developers found the software interface inflexible
[55] and sought a better solution.

In 2001 the Xbox gaming console was released with Nvidia GeForce 3 video architecture. Unlike previous video game cards, the GeForce 3 was a piece of programmable graphics hardware called a "graphics processing
[60] unit" (GPU). Since its release, each generation of GPUs has increased in speed and memory, thus significantly improving game quality.

The high-performance computing (HPC) community took notice of the new GPU platform. They began to
[65] explore the possibility of using GPUs for numerical work unrelated to computer graphics, a task typically done with highly expensive supercomputers. For a fraction of the cost, experts noted, it was now possible to obtain hardware that could rival the numerical processing power of a
[70] million-dollar supercomputer. Likewise, the conversion of numerical programs to operate on GPUs took place, and the "general-purpose computing on graphics processing units" (GPGPU) movement was born. Today the GPGPU and HPC communities are vibrant and active partners in
[75] numerical and scientific computing.

11. According to the passage, the endeavor to replace single-chip processors with multi-core processors was caused by:

A. the reduction of the size of transistors.
B. the scarcity of increasingly faster circuits.
C. the general-purpose computing on graphics processing units movement.
D. a power wall experienced by the microprocessor industry.

3 ================================ **3**

12. The author's statement that "the world of application programming was drastically altered" (lines 29–30) is best supported and illustrated by her:

    F. explanation of the GPGPU movement that began to replace expensive supercomputers (lines 63–75).

    G. description of the switch from single-threaded to multi-core programming (lines 34–43).

    H. account of manufacturers' attempts to overcome the power wall faced by the microprocessor industry (lines 19–28).

    J. comments on programs that boasted higher speeds, as well as increased power consumption (lines 11–18).

13. Lines 73–75 primarily serve to illustrate the point made in the sixth paragraph (lines 63–75) that the relationship forged between the high-performance computing (HPC) community and the gaming community using graphics processing units (GPU) was:

    A. mutually beneficial.

    B. expensive.

    C. ultimately a failure.

    D. hypothetical.

14. The passage most strongly supports which of the following about high-end game development?

    F. CPUs make it possible for consumers to process the most innovative computer game graphics.

    G. As graphics became more sophisticated, technology available to consumers also advanced.

    H. Experts noted that it was possible to perform general-purpose computing on graphics processing units.

    J. By 2001 video architecture like that in the Xbox gaming console had become obsolete.

15. How does the author directly support the claim that CPU speeds increased at a rate of fifty-two percent per year?

    A. By showing the speed increases of CPUs over time

    B. By explaining the operation of the microprocessor

    C. By illustrating the rapid increase in chip production

    D. By describing the development of multi-core processors

END OF SET THREE
STOP! DO NOT GO ON TO THE NEXT PAGE
UNTIL TOLD TO DO SO.

Entrance Ticket   Learning Targets   Claims and Evidence   ACT Practice   Sum It Up

Sum It Up

Supporting Claims

Introduction
Includes the topic sentence with the main idea

Body Paragraph
Presents a different point that relates to the main idea; gives examples and provides evidence

Conclusion
Refers back to the main idea and draws connections from the body paragraphs

Tips and Techniques

Decoding: If the question includes words like *supports which of the following* or *serves to illustrate which*, then you know that the question is giving an example and you need to match it to a claim.

Relate to Passage as a Whole

CAPTION:

11.1 Entrance Ticket

Choose one:

- Write a paragraph describing a time when something you said was taken out of context. You can make up a short story if you do not have this experience.

- Write a paragraph describing a time when you needed to know the whole story about something.

_____

_____

_____

_____

_____

_____

_____

_____

_____

_____

_____

_____

_____

_____

_____

11.2 Learning Targets

1. Recognize the meaning of a detail in relation to the context of the passage as a whole

2. Determine the purpose of a detail in relation to the context of the passage as a whole

Self-Assessment

Circle the number that corresponds to your confidence level in your knowledge of this subject before beginning the lesson. A score of 1 means you are completely lost, and a score of 4 means you have mastered the skills. After you finish the lesson, return to the bottom of this page and circle your new confidence level to show your improvement.

Before Lesson

1   2   3   4

After Lesson

1   2   3   4

Entrance Ticket   Learning Targets   Using Context   The Big Picture   ACT Practice   Sum It Up

11.3.1 Using Context

Example 1:

- **A.** Uniforms teach students how to dress professionally in the future.
- **B.** Uniforms are very common across the country.
- **C.** Uniforms and dress codes can be found in almost every job.
- **D.** Schools can regulate what their students must wear.

Example 2:

- **F.** Team sports force children to build communication skills.
- **G.** Most players do not end up playing professionally, but some do go on to coach.
- **H.** College athletes are sometimes the best students in their classes.
- **J.** It takes a strong work ethic to play sports.

Example 3:

- **A.** Getting a college education can open doors to hundreds of careers.
- **B.** Traveling the world can itself be a worthwhile education.
- **C.** Growing up without parents can be difficult.
- **D.** Going away to college can help create a sense of individualism.

11.3.1 Using Context

I'm not eager to face the predawn wind chill, but I need to get the bakery up and running. I didn't sleep well, and I'm feeling sluggish. I shower, reluctantly put on my winter gear, and
5 head out the door.

All the way there, I'm hoping my efforts won't go to waste. Certainly there will be a few brave souls who face the storm to get their hands on freshly baked bread.

10 After several hours of prepping and baking, I open the bakery and wait. Business is slow. Mostly I sit and watch the snow fall—and the clock that barely moves.

Just before closing, a woman comes in.
15 She's eager, breathless—way too enthusiastic to be stopping in for Italian loaves or a sweet indulgence. She stomps the snow off her boots and takes off her hat. "The sign in your window says you have windmill cookies; is that correct?"
20 she says, pointing to the menu board.

"Yes," I say, "but those require a special order, and I don't have any made." Most people don't even know what windmill cookies are. I keep thinking I should remove them from the
25 menu, but they remind me of my aunt. She always had them for us when we would visit.

She lets out a desperate sigh and says, "Please, is there any way you could make me some? I'm willing to pay." At first I get excited,
30 calculating the loss in sales that I could recoup with one overpriced order. But then I remember what a pain they are to make. "I wasn't prepared for a custom order," I reply.

"I hate to bother you, but it would mean a
35 lot. How much can I offer you?"

The woman is almost begging me. Now perhaps I don't understand the appeal of windmill cookies (which I do), but I realize I am with a desperate woman. She also doesn't look like
40 the type of person who would offer to throw a wad of cash at something she wanted "just because."

"I'll make them," I say to the woman. "But it'll take about an hour."

45 She's grinning from ear to ear at my concession. "No problem at all! Thank you!" Customers regularly gush over my food; cakes and specialty pies have that effect on people. But this was different.

50 "So you really like speculaas," I say, after I've gotten the dough assembled and ready to slice. She starts babbling as if she's been waiting for me to ask. "Actually they're for my father. They were always his favorite, but I've never
55 seen them freshly made here in the States. My mother would bake them for him when they were courting in the Netherlands and every year on their wedding anniversary. But she's gone now. Where did you get your recipe?"

60 I fake a smug expression and decline to answer. But this makes me happy that I agreed to make them. I've experienced that same longing before, to recapture something from the past. It was touching that she wanted these
65 so badly for her father. Funny how something as innocent as a cookie from an earlier time is priceless later in life. When presented with the opportunity, we jump at the chance to buy back fond memories—to re-experience emotions.

70 These are the things that fill the pantry of our brains. Some of them are overturned, stale, discolored. Some of them are broken, having been long forgotten. Though sometimes hard to locate in dark, dusty corners way in the back,

11.3.1 Using Context

75 our life's clutter is what makes up our personal history. As time passes, we realize these small things take on immense personal value.

I knew the woman was hoping to illuminate a place deep in her father's heart. Sud-
80 denly, the soft chimes that would sound when I opened the door to my aunt's apartment was ringing in my ears.

I read an article about this. Snippets of time in our lives that seem ordinary in the
85 moment later prove to be profoundly meaningful when our memory is triggered. The smell of something baking in the oven can take us back to that time. I'll remember this the next time I don't feel like dragging myself into the bakery.
90 My life's work is much more than flour, sugar, and profit. I help make moments special and recreate the fondest of memories.

Reading Tip

Whenever you see *in context of the passage as a whole*, look at the context. Do not just look at the lines above and below. The ACT writers expect you to miss the bigger picture.

11.3.2 The Big Picture

Example 1:

1. The passage discusses the merits of healthy but expensive lunch options in schools. Several opinions from nutritionists, school administrators, and parents are included.
    A. Obesity will continue to be a problem for future generations.
    B. Current options are incredibly unhealthy for children.
    C. Nutritious food options will help students focus on academics.
    D. Making the right choices about nutrition is a crucial part of the real world.

Example 2:

2. The passage discusses how students can work faster when using calculators on math tests and assignments. There are several opinions in the passage, including those of math teachers, students, and parents.
    F. Calculators allow for more questions to be answered in a given time period.
    G. The use of a calculator is a skill within itself.
    H. Calculators are used in everyday life anyway.
    J. Calculators should be used in all classes.

Example 3:

3. The passage discusses the historic perspective provided by reading classic literature. Several opinions from writers, teachers, and politicians are presented for both sides of the argument.
    A. Classic literature challenges the reader.
    B. Classic literature allows students to see life through a different point of view.
    C. Classic literature builds the imagination.
    D. Classic literature shows how the world once was.

11.3.2 The Big Picture

1. Viewed in the context of the passage, Josiah's gasp (line 37) most likely reflects a feeling of:
   A. great surprise.
   B. intense pain.
   C. profound regret.
   D. witty sarcasm.

_____

_____

_____

_____

_____

_____

_____

_____

_____

_____

_____

_____

Reading Tip

Support and Scope: Always go back to the passage to support your answer, and the scope of your answer must fit the context of the passage. The key to ACT reading comprehension is to always investigate the answers.

This page is intentionally left blank.

11.4.1 Set One

Passage I

PROSE FICTION: This passage is adapted from *Everyday News* by Matthieu Langdon (©2015 by MasteryPrep). The narrator is a journalist who is assigned to cover the ninetieth birthday party of a war veteran.

My grandfather told me that everyone has a story. It's our stories that help define who we are and connect us to one another. My grandfather and his advice return to me as I stare at this ninety-year-old man. I wonder how
5 complex his story must be. He was a tail gunner in the South Pacific during World War II. Seventy years later, there can't be many of these guys left.

Joe Graham is seated at a table with balloons attached, while others scurry around to put the final touches
10 in place. I introduce myself and thank him for the opportunity to learn more about his life. And wish him "happy birthday," of course. He is kind, aware of my purpose, and welcoming.

Jane Graham's hair is pure white. It's perfectly
15 coiffed as if she's just come from the salon. It may not move for days. She can't be more than five feet tall, and she uses a walker as if she's gliding through water. She studies me for a moment and says, "I was a writer once. I hope you portray my husband as more than just a dried-up
20 old man who's made it to ninety."

"I look forward to getting to know you both," I reply. "What a terrific celebration! Your husband must be a remarkable man."

This softens her, and she smiles. "You just blend in
25 and enjoy yourself, honey. Your writing will be more authentic that way. Think of yourself as a guest instead of a newsperson."

I'm fairly new to my profession and eager to write a good piece. The local magazine I work for has given me
30 this assignment in an effort to shift the focus away from the usual "up and coming" citizens to the long-standing pillars of the community. At first, my coworkers chided me with jokes about the morning news show that devotes ten seconds a week to the washed-up weatherman and airs
35 pictures of old people on jelly jars. But I'm determined to portray this subject as a viable man—a war hero.

Jane is watching me with a smirk as I fumble to balance my notebook with the plate of food someone has given me. She swims over and says, "Glad to see you set-
40 tling in. Now let me tell you about my Joe."

She sits me down and gets right to it. "I met him when I was sixteen years old, through his sister Claire. He was already out of high school and working at a cash reg-

ister factory. It was impossible not to notice him because
45 he was loud and boisterous. And very handsome."

Joe has now joined us—someone has pushed his wheelchair over—and he's eager to join the conversation. "Most of you want to hear about the war. Do you want to hear about the war?" Together they look like a Norman
50 Rockwell painting. I grab my camera and take their picture.

"I'm telling her about our courtship, Joe." Then she leans in and whispers, "My mother thought he was a no-goodnik at first. He grew on her, though."

55 Joe chimes in with a smile. "She thought I was no-good until I spent half the night looking for their dog that had got out. When I brought that dumb thing home, her mother fell for me like rain."

I hear about their separation while Joe served over-
60 seas in the military, their marriage after the war ended, and Joe's leap of faith to move their young family to our then undeveloped small town. Several times during our conversation, Joe pauses to interject, "You know, when I got here, Northlake Boulevard was nothing but miles of
65 dirt." As the afternoon goes on, our interview ebbs and flows as I back away to share Joe with his real guests. Jane routinely nods off but then rejoins the celebration as if she had only taken a sip of punch. Family and friends tell me stories about this larger-than-life man who's been
70 around since forever. I leave the party like the rest: with a slice of cake on a plastic plate. I feel like I've been with my own family.

As I drive home, it occurs to me that I never heard much about Joe's service in World War II. A mere chapter
75 of his long story, it was overshadowed by family, celebration, and amusing anecdotes about this formerly boisterous man who touched many lives. My article will be much different than I originally anticipated. Joe won't be depicted as a frail war hero from the past or as an old man
80 on a jelly jar.

1. Within the context of the passage, Jane's smirk (line 37) most likely reflects her:

    A. sharp disapproval.
    B. slight amusement.
    C. mild fatigue.
    D. strong relief.

3 ▬▬▬▬▬▬▬▬▬▬▬▬▬▬▬▬▬▬▬▬▬▬▬▬ **3**

2. Viewed within the context of the passage, the narrator's portrayal of Jane's physical appearance (lines 14–17) conveys:

    F. her apparent frailty.
    G. the narrator's feelings of intimidation.
    H. her age, which is close to Joe's.
    J. her tailored appearance and adept mobility.

3. In the context of the passage, lines 78–80 most strongly suggest that the narrator:

    A. views Joe as more than a man who has lived to the age of ninety.
    B. has a strong dislike for jams and jellies.
    C. is not happy with the photograph she took of Joe and Jane.
    D. does not intend to submit Joe's picture to a morning news show.

4. Viewed within the context of the passage, Joe's statement in lines 62–65 most strongly suggests that:

    F. Joe was a city developer.
    G. Joe sometimes repeated himself in conversation.
    H. the town grew very quickly.
    J. Joe knows a lot about the history of the town.

5. In the context of the passage, the main purpose of lines 28–36 is to:

    A. illustrate the novice journalist's desire to write a well-rounded article.
    B. characterize her coworkers as mean-spirited and bored with history.
    C. introduce her growing relationship with Jane over a series of interviews.
    D. illustrate the claim made in the first paragraph that her grandfather inspired her to become a storyteller.

END OF SET ONE
STOP! DO NOT GO ON TO THE NEXT PAGE
UNTIL TOLD TO DO SO.

Entrance Ticket   Learning Targets   Using Context   The Big Picture   ACT Practice   Sum It Up

11.4.2 Set Two

Passage I

PROSE FICTION: This passage is adapted from *More Than Human: Looking Back at No Superman* by Sander Winans (©2015 by MasteryPrep).

My parents never dreamed I would become a doctor. My father was a self-made businessman, and my mother was a homemaker. Neither of them had gone to college, but we lived a comfortable life on the coast of Georgia.
5 When we were young, my brothers and I whiled away afternoons, weekends, and summers at the water's edge, fishing and crabbing. Many kids who lived in our area went on to obtain jobs in the fishing industry after high school, so it was assumed that I was likely to follow a
10 similar path. I had few thoughts about doctors, or medicine in general, until I was the one who was critically ill. At the age of ten, I was thrust into the world of hospitals and illness.

The last page of my memoir, *No Superman,* has a
15 photograph of a boy and a doctor sitting at a small table. Behind them is a big window with the sun shining through and a brightly colored wall decorated with colorful drawings. The boy is wide-eyed and laughing as the doctor smiles back, wearing a lab coat, stethoscope, and curly
20 blue wig. The picture is based on a story I tell in the book about the day I was told I had cancer. It was an extremely frightening time for me as a boy. I didn't quite grasp what was happening, though I could see the pain on my parents' faces. Beneath that, however, was a sense of calm-
25 ness and security. I was in a special place and with special people who, in the midst of a scary experience, made me laugh. Their mission was to make things bearable for kids like me. As I reflect on my own experience in the world of childhood cancer, this impression stands out.

30 When I think about my life before I got sick, there isn't much to relate it to, as I was fairly young. I do recall the carefree, sunburned days with my brother. We never wore shoes, though my mother hated it. When we weren't in school (I wasn't much of a student), we spent all day
35 outdoors, typical of most boys our age. At ten, I didn't think about what the future would bring, except for the next day's weather. Suddenly, however, the hospital became my second home. My treatment was an ordeal that lasted over two years, and it altered the course of my
40 future: from would-be fisherman to a well-respected pediatric oncologist. A formal education alone—if I were even destined to have one without my illness—would not have led me down this road.

It was, of course, a doctor who inspired my profes-
45 sional journey. Dr. Hanlon, a pediatric hematologist-oncologist at the children's hospital, was tall and foreboding from a distance. Up close, however, he was a teddy bear among men. His cadence when he spoke was soft and soothing, and he always made me feel like I was his favor-
50 ite "kid," as he called us. It was Dr. Hanlon who brought out my inner doctor. I learned from him how smart doctors must be: he used big words, pointed out numbers on a lab sheet, and talked in what seemed like another language. The nurses listened to him carefully and sometimes took
55 notes. But what I mainly felt from the brilliant Dr. Hanlon was his compassion. He seemed to be living the experience with me; he was sympathetic when I was ill and celebratory when I was well. He treated me like a boy and not like a patient. He was free with fist bumps and pats on
60 my head. And he always, always tried to make me laugh. Above all, the most valuable lesson I learned from him was indeed the importance of humor. I had always been a silly kid, I suppose, but it was Dr. Hanlon who taught me to harness that childhood spirit and use it to comfort and
65 to heal. From his early interactions with me while he wore that blue wig, he altered the face of medicine for me with his earnestness and easy sense of humor.

Today when I enter a hospital room to see my patients—newly diagnosed children in particular—I make
70 sure I have a red clown nose in my pocket. With a mindless prop, I can sometimes bring light to a frightened child and sweep the demons away. Though my profession is often deeply painful, the joy of making an ill child laugh is the greatest reward.

6. Viewed in the context of the passage, the statement in lines 41–43 is most likely intended to suggest that:

   F. educators should encourage students to consider careers in medicine, even if they do not show interest.
   G. if he had not gotten sick as a child, the narrator would have become a fisherman as an adult.
   H. the narrator has a negative view of formal education for the lack of guidance given to students.
   J. the narrator would not have chosen medicine as a career had he not experienced cancer as a child.

3　　　　　　　　　　　　　　　　　　　　　　　　**3**

7. Viewed in the context of the passage, the statement in lines 55–59 most likely suggests:

   A. Dr. Hanlon had a high level of education and taught those around him.
   B. Dr. Hanlon's expertise in his field made him appear intelligent to onlookers.
   C. Dr. Hanlon was respected by the parents and relatives of his patients.
   D. Dr. Hanlon had a serious disposition that made him seem stern.

8. In terms of the passage as a whole, the second paragraph (lines 14–29) mainly serves to:

   F. contrast the narrator's early childhood with the time of his treatment for cancer.
   G. argue for the hospital's need to provide emotional support to sick children.
   H. explain how the narrator's childhood experiences inspired him to become a doctor.
   J. introduce the narrator's mentor, who is discussed later in the passage.

9. If the first paragraph (lines 1–13) was deleted, the passage would lose all of the following EXCEPT:

   A. details about the narrator's medical diagnosis.
   B. background information about the narrator's family.
   C. a suggestion of the dominant economic industry in a specific locale.
   D. an indication of the narrator's profession at the time of writing.

10. The last paragraph (lines 68–74) differs from the rest of the passage in that it is composed of the:

    F. narrator revealing his hobby of performing as a clown.
    G. narrator emphasizing the role Dr. Hanlon played in his career.
    H. narrator discussing his current approach with patients.
    J. narrator indicating the difficult emotional aspect of childhood cancer.

END OF SET TWO
STOP! DO NOT GO ON TO THE NEXT PAGE
UNTIL TOLD TO DO SO.

Entrance Ticket　Learning Targets　Using Context　The Big Picture　ACT Practice　Sum It Up

11.4.3 Set Three

Passage I

PROSE FICTION: This passage is adapted from *Learning to Fly* by Haley Martinez-Ramos (©2015 by MasteryPrep).

For over two decades, I've worked on designing helicopters as an aeronautical engineer. Both of my parents encouraged me to find something I would love to do, but my mother in particular was always guiding me to con-
5 sider career choices. She was a teacher, so I think it was natural for her to weigh my observed interests against my practical skills. If she noticed I was in a drawing phase (I wasn't very good), she'd discuss with me art as a career field versus as a hobby. I'm very similar to my mother,
10 so I think she had hoped I'd pursue a career like hers; but ultimately she was the first one to encourage me to consider a profession in engineering. By the time I was in middle school, my aptitude for the mechanics of how things worked was clear. My abilities in math, on the
15 other hand, were a different story. I had teachers along the way who doubted my career aspirations because of the rigorous math courses required to get a degree such as mine—few suggested I major in business—but I made my way through.

20 When I was about twelve years old, my parents took us on a summer vacation to Washington, D.C. One of the Smithsonians—The Air and Space Museum—had an entire wing devoted to the exploration of flight. Dozens of airplanes from the early days of the Wright Brothers to the
25 modern commercial jetliner hung from the rafters under spooky, dim lights. I became fixated on an early version of the helicopter that hung in its own sacred spot, illuminated in a way that made it look almost magical. This grand aircraft was unlike other modes of flight, mysteriously so.
30 I leaned on a railing and got lost in my daydream, imagining how such an aircraft was conceived, how the design of the blades could make it lift and propel, and what it would feel like to fly one. I remember the feeling that came over me that day: it was a strong fascination that I couldn't
35 articulate at the time.

When I look back at my life as a teen, I remember the things that captivated the attention of my peers. For most it was sports—a drive to hurl themselves onto a field and compete like animals fighting for prey. I dabbled in
40 soccer, tried basketball a few times, and liked to watch baseball (my parents regularly took me to games), but I never really took to any of it. I didn't feel very typical of most boys my age. In my case, it was cars and planes and any kind of movable machine that held my attention.
45 I was similarly captivated by sharks when I was younger and the solar system before that. But it was my passion for how things worked, the mechanics of flight especially, that eventually became a thriving career.

Karl Shafer, our next-door neighbor, was the man
50 who sealed the deal. Tall and spindly, he personified a nerdy scientist from a comic book. He was reserved and talked mostly in monotone. That is, unless he was talking about his work. He was an engineer at Sykora Aircraft and worked on helicopter rotor design for military use.
55 I'd gotten the impression that most people either didn't understand or didn't show interest in what he did, so he didn't bother engaging in much conversation about his occupation.

Otherwise secure from the public, Sykora held a bi-
60 annual "family day" during which employees could bring guests to see what was happening there. I'm fairly certain my mother arranged it, but one year Mr. Shafer invited me to attend. I watched the experts facilitate test flights, met the pilots, examined designs, and explored the helicopters
65 from the inside out. That day with Mr. Shafer ignited a spark in my belly that couldn't be extinguished. I begged Mr. Shafer to take me under his wing. From him I learned the pros and cons of daily life at a job like his—most days didn't include the adrenaline-filled test flights that were
70 conducted the day I visited. I learned from him the importance of safety in everything his company did and the far-reaching effects of what his industry accomplished. But what I mainly got from Mr. Shafer was his enthusiasm; it was contagious for a kid like me. He wasn't an
75 athlete, and he didn't care for football; his sports were aeronautics, calculations, and experimentation. When he wasn't at work, he would toil away for hours in his garage, building everything from simple rockets to drones, getting lost in the process.

80 Above all, Mr. Shafer taught me the value of patience as an engineer. He demonstrated that his work took time, sacrifice, and tedious experimentation. But the reward was great when that persistence came to life—the implementation of a Sykora X2 rotor on a U.S. Army
85 Blackhawk helicopter, for example. To this day, when I see a helicopter overhead, I think about the unseen hours of dogged determination and devotion that made it possible.

Entrance Ticket Learning Targets Using Context The Big Picture ACT Practice Sum It Up

3   **3**

11. In the context of the passage, (lines 23–29) are best described as presenting images of:

    A. gloom, fear, and fascination.
    B. awe, anticipation, and respect.
    C. surprise, frustration, and uneasiness.
    D. hope, intimidation, and wonder.

12. Viewed within the context of the passage, (lines 74–79) are best described as presenting images of:

    F. steadfastness, dedication, and individualism.
    G. introversion, weakness, and anxiety.
    H. extroversion, cooperation, and motivation.
    J. isolation, listlessness, and dispassion.

13. Based on the passage as a whole, the narrator was invited to attend "family day" at Sykora Aircraft (lines 61–63) so that he would be able to:

    A. convince his teachers that he should stay in higher-level math classes.
    B. provide companionship for Mr. Shafer's children.
    C. explore the possibility of aeronautical engineering as a career.
    D. pilot the helicopter he had seen in Washington, D.C.

14. The main function of the third paragraph (lines 36–48) in relation to the passage as a whole is to:

    F. describe how the narrator's interests set him apart from his childhood peers.
    G. restate the narrator's passion for the mechanics of automotives.
    H. compare the narrator's interest in mechanics with his mother's career.
    J. argue that the helicopter is more sophisticated than other kinds of aircraft.

15. If the fourth paragraph (lines 49–58) were deleted, the passage would lose which of the following?

    A. Details that give insight about the narrator's view of himself
    B. A description of the main interests of the narrator's peers
    C. A suggestion that the narrator was ridiculed by his peers
    D. An introduction to someone who was a role model to the narrator

END OF SET THREE
STOP! DO NOT GO ON TO THE NEXT PAGE
UNTIL TOLD TO DO SO.

Entrance Ticket   Learning Targets   Using Context   The Big Picture   ACT Practice   Sum It Up

Sum It Up

Relate to Passage as a Whole

Context
Words that surround a certain word or phrase; clarifies the meaning

Tips and Techniques

Support and Scope: Always go back to the passage to support your answer, and the scope of your answer must fit the context of the passage. The key to ACT reading comprehension is to always investigate the answers.

Summarize Key Ideas and Details Part 1

CAPTION:

12.1 Entrance Ticket

Read the passage and answer the questions.

On June 7, 1900, fifty-three-year-old Carry Nation strode into a saloon in Kiowa, Kansas, holding a rock. As startled customers looked up from their drinks, she shouted, "Men! I have
5 come to save you from a drunkard's fate!" and began smashing the barroom's interior, taking particular glee in shattering the liquor bottles behind the bar. At the time, the American movement for temperance (abstinence from
10 alcohol) was being spearheaded by the Woman's Christian Temperance Union (WCTU), of which Nation was a member. But even though its members were dismayed by the scourge of alcoholism, hardly any were willing to take the
15 extreme step of destroying saloons themselves. Nation, on the other hand, was not only willing but also convinced that her actions were divinely ordained. She later described a revelation in which God came to her and told her, "Take
20 something in your hands and throw at these places in Kiowa and smash them."

So launched the career of one of America's greatest firebrands. But the seeds of Nation's revolt had actually been sown much earli-
25 er. As a young woman in 1867, she married Dr. Charles Gloyd, a physician and a former soldier in the Union army. Gloyd was a severe alcoholic,

and less than a year after the birth of their child, he died as a result of complications brought on
30 by alcoholism. After becoming a single mother, Nation developed a passionate attitude against the vice that had consumed her husband. She joined the temperance campaign and started a local branch of the WCTU, but she was dissat-
35 isfied with its lack of success in enforcing state bans on liquor sales. For Nation a more radical approach was necessary, and she envisioned herself "a bulldog running along at the feet of Jesus, barking at what He doesn't like."

40 After the Kiowa incident, Nation continued her destructive path through other Kansas towns, her fame growing along with her arrest record. Her uncompromising fanaticism took another step forward when she abandoned her
45 rocks in favor of a hatchet, the better for hacking and smashing bar fixtures and stock. As extreme as her actions have been considered to be, there is no questioning the attention they commanded, both in fighting alcoholism and in
50 raising awareness of government hypocrisy refusing to enforce prohibition laws. Nation bluntly rejected half-measures in the cause of temperance and remained faithful to her radical vision throughout her life.

Entrance Ticket   Learning Targets   Understanding Passage Structure   Reading Quickly   ACT Practice   Sum It Up

12.1 Entrance Ticket

1. The statement that Nation's husband "died as a result of complications brought on by alcoholism" (lines 29–30) is best described as:

    A. the main idea of the passage.
    B. a supporting point to emphasize Nation's strong Christian faith.
    C. a supporting point to emphasize the idea that many Union soldiers were alcoholics.
    D. a supporting point to show a possible reason for Nation's fanaticism.

2. The statement "Nation bluntly rejected half-measures in the cause of temperance and remained faithful to her radical vision" (lines 51–53) is best described as:

    F. the main idea of the passage.
    G. a supporting point to emphasize the dangers of alcoholism.
    H. a supporting point to emphasize Nation's religious fervor.
    J. a supporting point meant to show a reason for Nation's fanaticism.

3. The passage notes all of the following as reasons for Nation's fanatical approach to temperance EXCEPT that:

    A. her husband had died as a result of his alcoholism.
    B. she believed herself to be doing God's work.
    C. she was dissatisfied with the steps taken by the WCTU.
    D. she had a history of mental illness in her family.

12.2 Learning Targets

1. Read quickly and efficiently

2. Analyze the flow of a paragraph or passage

3. Understand main ideas and how to identify what supports them

Self-Assessment

Circle the number that corresponds to your confidence level in your knowledge of this subject before beginning the lesson. A score of 1 means you are completely lost, and a score of 4 means you have mastered the skills. After you finish the lesson, return to the bottom of this page and circle your new confidence level to show your improvement.

Before Lesson

1   2   3   4

After Lesson

1   2   3   4

12.3.1 Understanding Passage Structure

At the start of the 20th century, regional transportation in the United States was constrained by two factors: the location of railways and the accessibility of dirt roads for horse-driven coaches. The first automobiles had actually been invented roughly a decade earlier, but the general public still viewed them as frivolous toys for the extremely wealthy. Cars were expensive and unreliable, and there were hardly any roads on which to drive them.

Then, in 1908, Henry Ford introduced the Model T, a dependable, affordable car that revolutionized the fledgling auto industry. Competitors followed suit, and in a short time "automobiling" changed from a wealthy person's pastime to a legitimate mode of transportation for everyday Americans. By 1927, the year Ford stopped manufacturing the Model T, the company had sold almost 15 million models.

Even so, these millions of new vehicles still relied on smooth, safe roads to carry them, and that meant large investments in infrastructure for cities and towns. Streetcar and subway companies didn't mind shelling out millions for their own tracks, since they reaped huge profits from them. But because automobiles were individually owned and operated, their makers had to convince governments that building roads was a public concern.

This campaign proved largely successful throughout the 1920s and 1930s, as elected officials in many places agreed to use taxpayer money for the construction of new roads. The federal government generally split the cost with the states, but this arrangement was also subject to lengthy bureaucratic delays.

A network of high-speed interstate roads circulated as a topic in Congress for several years and was even granted funding and a detailed plan in the Federal Aid Highway Act of 1944. However, the war effort consumed every available dollar, and the execution of the plan withered from a lack of funding. In 1953 newly elected president Dwight D. Eisenhower decided to prioritize an interstate system. As an army general, Eisenhower had been impressed with Germany's national highway system while stationed there during World War II. He felt that the United States needed a similar network, especially given the perceived threat of nuclear attack by the Soviets.

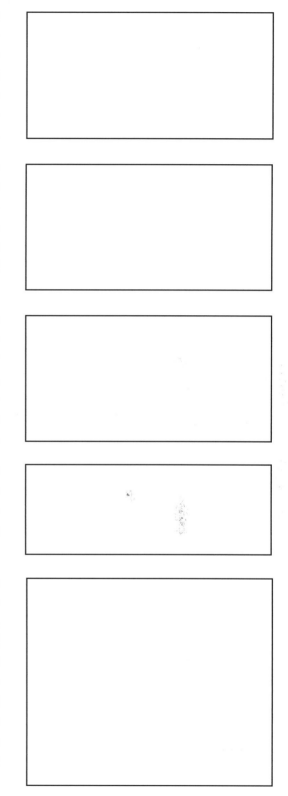

12.3.1 Understanding Passage Structure

The Federal Aid Highway Act of 1956 ushered in the largest public works project yet in American history, as it called for the construction of 41,000 miles of paved interstates. In order to support safe and efficient travel at high speeds, the new highways had design specifications of two twelve-foot-wide lanes going in each direction without any intersections, traffic signals, or rail crossings. Congress allocated $26 billion and directed the interstate road project to be finished "as nearly as practicable over a thirteen-year period." Though it would vastly exceed both budget and timeline, the Interstate Highway System also radically transformed both the U.S. economy and the American way of life.

The project was an economic success long before it was fully completed, as countless industries thrived on the building contracts. Raw materials and manufactured goods could be moved more easily on the new roads, cutting transportation costs for both producers and consumers. In addition, the promise of rapid interstate travel led to an even bigger boom in auto sales.

As highway connections spread, population centers shifted in response. The increased ease of travel attracted industries to new geographic areas and encouraged their expansion. A coastal port was no longer needed for a large city to develop, just as its labor force no longer needed to reside within its limits. From 1950 to 2000, the share of the U.S. population living in suburbs jumped from twenty-five to fifty-two percent.

The prosperity and sprawl engendered by the country's road networks gave rise to the American car culture. As car ownership became more and more normalized, people began to see cars as extensions of themselves. It also became increasingly common for families to have more than one car. In 1908, there was just one motorized vehicle on the road for every 18,000 Americans. By contrast, the 2012 census counted more than 250 million cars and trucks in the United States—almost one per person.

12.3.1 Understanding Passage Structure

Thanks to the Interstate Highway System, Americans today have relatively convenient access to friends, family, jobs, and leisure in other states. At the same time, however, highways have consistently undermined attempts at large-scale mass transit projects, which contributes to the fragmenting of both rural and urban communities. Increasingly those without personal transportation suffer a lack of access to both necessary and beneficial resources.

The legacy of America's interstate project may be mixed, but the sheer force of its cultural impact cannot be overstated. Drive-thrus, drive-ins, big box stores, and road trips are just a few of the deeply ingrained aspects of American culture fostered by the network of roads. Even though highways have shaped the national character in profound and unexpected ways, they remain quintessentially American in their vision to boldly access what was previously inaccessible.

12.3.1 Understanding Passage Structure

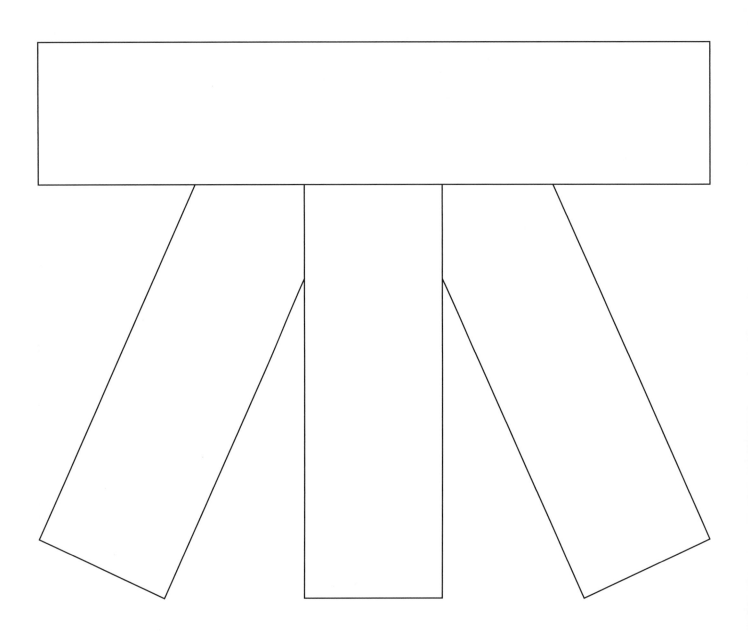

12.3.1 Understanding Passage Structure

Coral reefs are no strangers to hard knocks. Born and bred in tropical ocean shallows, these hardy marine organisms grow up in water with precious few nutrients, constantly battered by waves that would make even the toughest sea captain nauseated. Yet coral reefs flourish in these seemingly inhospitable neighborhoods, forming the backbone for some of Earth's most biologically diverse ecosystems. Sponges and sea urchins encrust their outsides, shrimp and lobsters scuttle between their crevices, and sharks and seabirds hunt among them. Reefs also afford nursery grounds for innumerable species of fish, which in turn feed turtles, eels, dolphins, and even sea snakes.

Although they cover less than one-tenth of one percent of the ocean's surface, coral reefs, amazingly, support over twenty-five percent of all marine species. They may look like rocks, but they're actually living colonies of tiny polyps embedded in calcium carbonate shells. The vast majority are found within thirty degrees of the Equator—where the sunlight necessary for their survival is most constant—and embody myriad colors and shapes, including table tops, antlers, and pillars. They can grow in isolated clusters or in networks spanning hundreds of miles, such as Australia's Great Barrier Reef. Whatever their location or appearance, reefs have one thing in common: they nurture life. Coral-associated bacteria are some of the only marine organisms able to process nitrogen from the water into compounds that can be used by algae. Waves breaking on rough coral edges then disperse algae throughout the surrounding water, creating the basis for a much larger food web. In turn, fish, sponges, and algae break down coral shells and redeposit them in the reef's nooks and crannies, where they bond and further strengthen the reef structure.

Reefs also protect coastlines from erosion by waves and currents. They absorb and dissipate up to ninety percent of wave energy before it reaches the shore, safeguarding beaches and helping to prevent flooding and damage during storms.

12.3.1 Understanding Passage Structure

Many nations with vulnerable coastlines have begun taking steps to preserve their reefs from the degradation of human activity. Overfishing, pollution, and tourism are all ongoing threats to coral ecosystems. In the United States, coastal storms account for seventy-one percent of annual disaster losses, and while not all of these events occur in areas that would naturally contain reefs, healthy reefs would certainly reduce the cost in regions that do. In Florida, for example, the absence of coral reefs would cause parts of the state to be submerged. In Belize, coastal protection afforded by reefs saves an estimated $231 million to $347 million in damages per year. By comparison, Belize's gross domestic product in 2007 was $1.3 billion.

For the past seventeen years, Andrew Bruckner, chief scientist at the Khaled bin Sultan Living Oceans Foundation, has been investigating a far less understood aspect of reef ecosystems: their potential role in life-saving medicines. Bruckner and his colleagues recently undertook a six-year expedition around the globe to map, characterize, and study coral reefs. He believes the prospect of finding a new drug among reef species may be 300 to 400 times more likely than isolating one from a terrestrial ecosystem, given that eighty percent of all life forms on earth are present only in the oceans.

Bruckner also points out that coral reefs contain a diverse assemblage of invertebrates—sponges, echinoderms, mollusks, and bryozoans—that are absent from terrestrial ecosystems. Because they can't move around to evade predators and other environmental stressors, these organisms use bioactive compounds to engage in a form of chemical warfare against predation and disease. The unique structures and properties of some of these compounds have already yielded revolutionary results: the antiviral drugs Ara-A and AZT and the anticancer agent Ara-C were developed from extracts of sponges found on a Caribbean reef.

12.3.1 Understanding Passage Structure

Even though reefs hold immense medical promise, Bruckner cautions that the initial focus must be on developing environmentally sustainable methods for collecting reef samples. Simply removing large chunks of coral damages the reef, and it doesn't even necessarily supply usable amounts of bioactive compounds. For this reason a new generation of specialized tools and processes for collection, identification, evaluation, and development is needed.

If scientists, resource managers, and industry leaders could operate in sync, the chances of developing a sustainable management plan would radically improve, says Bruckner.

Marine biotechnology is already a multibillion-dollar industry worldwide with a projected annual growth of fifteen to twenty percent during the next five years, according to the National Oceanic and Atmospheric Administration. Companies interested in cashing in would be smart to invest in environmentally sound plans for harvesting the reef's bounty, thereby ensuring its long-term availability.

12.3.1 Understanding Passage Structure

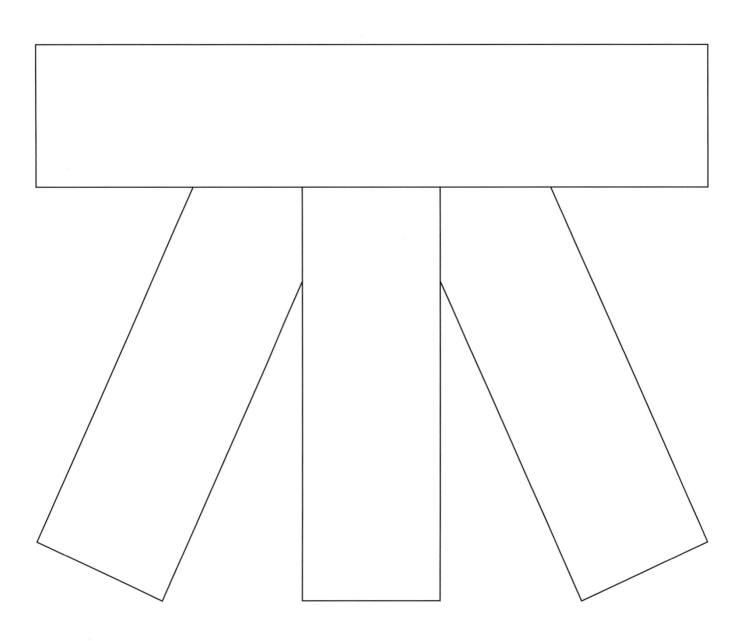

12.3.2 Reading Quickly

As the Great Depression deepened into the mid-1930s, President Roosevelt established the Works Progress Administration (WPA) in an effort to provide economic relief to citizens who were having trouble finding work. Several months later he created the Federal Art Project as a subdivision of the WPA. Its intention was twofold: to supplement artists' incomes and, more importantly, to fund patriotic art projects in an effort to rally dejected Americans. Prior to this project Roosevelt had made several other bids to provide relief for artists, but the larger-scale attempts had all fizzled. These included the Public Works of Art Project, which dissolved in 1934 after a single year.

To qualify for the new Federal Art Project, artists first had to apply for Home Relief to confirm they were impoverished and then submit samples of their work to demonstrate they were actively creating art. Once approved, an artist's weekly stipend was twenty-four dollars (equal to $420 in 2015). Submissions poured in, and just a few months after the program's inception, more than 1,100 artists were working for the Federal Art Project. One particularly robust section was the Mural Division; the roster included Stuart Davis, Jackson Pollock, and Arshile Gorky.

In November 1935 the Mural Division's director, Burgoyne Diller, assigned Gorky to draw some sketches for a mural to be installed at Brooklyn's Floyd Bennett Airfield. The piece, Diller told him, should portray "the first attempts to build flying machines." But Gorky, an expressionist, hated the idea of realistically depicting the evolution of aircraft design. He wanted instead to give his audience a *sense* of flying. When the location for the murals was changed to Newark Airport, in order to secure funding Diller had to reassure his new client that Gorky's murals would not be abstract. But they were, of course. Still, the airport accepted the design and unveiled the murals in June 1937. Gorky later wrote of one of the panels in the mural, *Early Aviation*: "I sought to bring into elemental terms the sensation of the passengers in the first balloon to the wonder of the sky around them and the earth beneath."

12.3.2 Reading Quickly

In philosophy circles, where meaning is continually examined and dissected, even the definition of knowledge can be a subject of argument. To understand how and why this is true, let us start with the Greeks. Plato is generally credited with defining *knowledge* as "justified true belief," or JTB. Along these lines, in order to know that a given proposition is true, one must not only believe the relevant true proposition but also have justification for doing so. An idea is *not* considered knowledge if it is true yet no one believes it. Similarly, it is not considered knowledge if everyone believes it and has good reason to do so but it is simply not factual. All three criteria must be satisfied in order for the Platonic definition of *knowledge* to apply.

However, in 1963 the American philosopher Edmund Gettier called this traditional theory into question by claiming that there are certain circumstances in which one does not have knowledge, even when all three conditions of JTB are met. For example, suppose that a clock on a college campus (which keeps accurate time and is well maintained) stopped working at 11:56 p.m. and has yet to be repaired. On the way to his noon class, exactly twelve hours later, Bill glances at the clock and forms the belief that the time is 11:56 a.m. His belief is true, of course, since the time is indeed 11:56. And his belief is justified, as he has no reason to doubt that the clock is working, and he cannot be blamed for basing beliefs about the time on what the clock says. Nonetheless, it seems evident that Bill does not *know* that the time is 11:56. After all, if he had walked past the clock a minute earlier or a minute later, he would have ended up with a false belief rather than a true one.

Most philosophers have accepted Gettier's argument, taking it to show that the three conditions of the JTB account—truth, belief, justification—are not, in general, sufficient for knowledge. But how must the analysis of knowledge be modified for it to withstand cases like Bill and the clock? This is what is commonly referred to as the "Gettier problem."

12.3.2 Reading Quickly

Technique 1 - No Lip Reading

After the campfire gathering, I go up to the main house for a glass of milk before bed. There are more little campers than usual inside tonight since the story was scary. They sit in clusters, munching cereal and nervously asking each other whether "Old Red Eyes" could still be alive. It reminds me of when I was nine years old and my camp counselor, Cabell, read a story about the boogeyman to me and the other boys in my cabin. I lay awake that night for what felt like hours, clutching my blanket and trying to convince myself that there was no way the monster could be real. The thing is, at that age you still don't know enough about how the world works to be sure about anything. You haven't yet sorted out the possible from the impossible. To make things even more disconcerting, you're constantly learning about awful things that really do happen, things you have never even thought about before.

The groups gradually break up and return to their cabins uphill. I stay at the house, washing dishes and chatting with some of the older camp counselors, most of whom are still a good ten years younger than me. As I'm about to depart, a battered green hardback on the coffee table catches my eye. It's an old copy of *The Fellowship of the Ring*, the first book in the *Lord of the Rings* trilogy.

The wet grass on the hillside soaks through my running shoes, but I barely notice as I trudge up toward the cabins. I'm thinking of Legolas and Aragorn, of Gandalf and the Ents, and of Frodo and Sam. I look up at the mountains silhouetted against the cloudy night and remember Rivendell, seat of the Elven kingdom. The characters and plot are pure fantasy, I think to myself, but this book is as good as any for teaching young readers about life on earth. There are scary parts—and disturbing ones—but nothing designed solely to terrify. Maybe I'm being overly optimistic, but as I crest the hill, I start to imagine the book in my hand as a powerful antidote to the confusion and fear that can infiltrate young lives. Here are characters striving for a moral purpose, enduring hardship and loss yet eventually reaching their goal. It is as inspirational a tale as you can find in any library.

12.3.2 Reading Quickly

Technique 2 - Finger Reading

The show begins with the improvisers—usually four to eight—taking the stage and asking the audience to shout out a suggestion. Once they have one, the group launches into an "opening" designed to mine the suggestion for ideas and material that will inform the scenes to come. The opening can take many different forms: it can be a word association game, a series of character monologues delivered to the audience, a single monologue by one of the actors, or something else entirely. However, its purpose is always the same: to lay a foundation for the show.

Afterward, the show shifts gears and becomes purely scenic. Two or more actors step out from the group and perform an improvised scene based on something that came up during the opening. In order for this improvisation not to fall flat, the performers generally follow certain "rules" in their play. Like all rules these can be broken, but in most cases they provide a basis for the scene to grow into something interesting. The dual concepts of agreement and heightening in an improv scene are frequently referred to by the term "yes, and." This means that if one actor initiates a scene by saying, "The sea looks rough today, Captain," then his partner has the responsibility to *agree* that he is the captain and they are on the ocean (the "yes" part) and *heighten* it by adding something else to the established reality (the "and" part). He might do this with the response, "Indeed it does, mate. The gods must be angry with us." In this way the actors enhance the scene and allow it to take shape.

The concept of time is always flexible in long-form improvisation. Not only do scenes *not* have to progress in chronological order, but characters can jump back and forth in time at a moment's notice. This grants the performers freedom to explore ideas and themes in countless ways. A character might be telling a story about something that happened to him in childhood and then suddenly shift from that reminiscence into the actual episode, playing his younger self. The rest of the cast will immediately support this new reality by playing ancillary characters, adding sound effects, or otherwise contributing color.

12.3.2 Reading Quickly

Technique 3 - Chunking

Although they live in many different regions and comprise dozens of species, deep-sea anglerfish as a group share many common traits. They inhabit freezing waters up to a mile below the surface of the ocean, where light is practically nonexistent. Since light is necessary for photosynthesis, on which nearly all known living creatures at least indirectly rely, prey is generally scarce for deep-sea anglerfish. As a result these strange and fascinating creatures have developed a mode of existence that is extremely low-energy, allowing them to survive for long periods between meals.

In the murky brine of the deep ocean, there is little use for the type of swimming motion employed by fish in shallower waters. Instead of darting and diving, anglerfish shuffle along through the dense water—a method toward which they devote just two percent of their energy intake. Because they don't need to swim quickly, anglers' bodies have evolved into a globular shape dominated by a huge head with small, weak fins on the top and sides. Like other fish, they sense changes in water pressure via organs in their skin called neuromasts. Unlike other fish, however, anglers' neuromasts are concentrated in the face. The location of these sensors is another energy-conserving adaptation because it allows the fish to wait for prey to pass in front of its mouth. When that happens the angler senses the water disturbance and strikes, opening its enormous crescent-shaped mouth and snapping down on its prey with long, sharp teeth.

Sometimes, though, prey doesn't arrive for a while. It is in those instances that anglerfish earn their name. Their most distinctive feature (though it is present only in females) is a piece of dorsal spine called the illicium that protrudes from the top of the head and hangs above the mouth like a fishing pole. At the end of the "pole" is an irregular growth of flesh called an esca, which can move in all directions. Anglerfish can wiggle the esca to make it resemble a prey animal, which lures the real prey close enough for it to be devoured. Some deep-sea anglers also emit light from their escae to attract prey. This bioluminescent glow—attractive in the abyss of the deep ocean—is a result of anglers' symbiosis with bacteria. Although the mechanism by which they harness the bacteria is unknown, it is thought that bacteria enter the esca from the seawater through small pores. Once inside, the bacteria multiply until they are packed so densely that their collective glow is very bright.

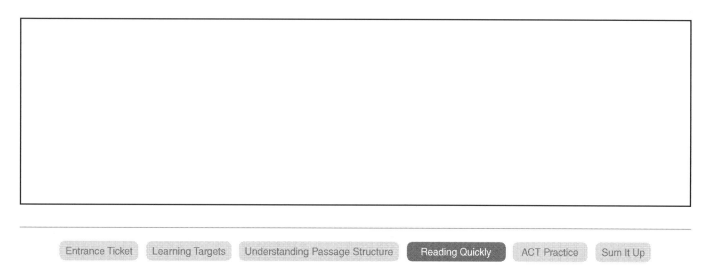

12.3.2 Reading Quickly

Technique 4 - Photograph Reading

The Turks and Caicos Islands, or TCI, make up a small archipelago about 200 miles northeast of Cuba's eastern tip. The land there is largely arid and sandy. Rainfall is scant, making fresh water a rare and precious commodity. But the opening of a cruise ship port on Grand Turk Island in 2006 has resulted in a tourism boom. Miles of once-wild coastline are now studded with mega-hotels and all-inclusive resorts. In 2014 more than a million people visited TCI, and that number is projected to keep growing.

In light of recent events, steps have been taken to protect the country's crown jewel of eco-tourism—its ocean waters and spectacular coral reef system. So far, these measures seem to be working. National marine park status has been conferred on and around nearly every island, even in areas outside park boundaries. Mooring buoys have been established at all dive sites and mooring areas to avoid possible damage from anchors. In addition, low-impact excursions are promoted by companies such as Big Blue Unlimited, which allows only biodegradable sunscreen on its tours (the chemical benzophenone-2, common in many commercial sunscreens, has been shown to be highly toxic to coral reefs).

Unfortunately, the sheer number of human visitors to this remote island has resulted in a sizeable carbon footprint. Almost ninety percent of the island's fresh food supply is still flown in daily. TCI also lacks cutting-edge recycling centers, so tourists' trash, plastic bottles, and batteries either pile up or have to be flown out for disposal. Still, the government is beginning to combat the islands' reliance on aircraft with agriculture initiatives. Subsidies are reviving a 143-acre working farm in Kew, which has produced fruits and vegetables for TCI inhabitants throughout the 20th century. The soil is much richer here than in other parts of the islands, ably supporting tomatoes, cucumbers, peppers, mangoes, bananas, melons, and herbs.

Reading Tip

Reading Level: A high reading level will send your ACT scores soaring. If you practice reading a little faster, your scores will continuously improve. The best way to practice is to read something from a novel, history book, magazine, or newspaper that you are interested in every day.

Entrance Ticket | Learning Targets | Understanding Passage Structure | Reading Quickly | ACT Practice | Sum It Up

This page is intentionally left blank.

3   3

12.4.1 Set One

Passage I

PROSE FICTION: This passage is adapted from *Mondays, Machines, and Memories* by Joachim Talmadge (©2015 by MasteryPrep).

Close to four o'clock, the first customer of the day pulls into the parking lot. A woman in her twenties with two small children walks in the front door. The kids immediately run over to the old Wurlitzer jukebox, mesmer-
5 ized by the rippling colors in its tubes.

The woman approaches me and gestures to the green Philco phonograph that I have perched on a stool in the store window. "Are you selling that old record player?" she asks.

10 "Sorry," I reply. "It's just for show. I couldn't part with it." I get a lot of young people asking if they can buy the phonograph, but they usually just want it to impress their friends at parties. I'd rather keep it in my window than sell it to someone who doesn't appreciate its history.

15 She nods and turns back to the children then sudden-
ly spins back around. "My grandmother's been looking for one like that for more than ten years," she says.

I frown and glance at the phonograph. It's a Philco TPA-1, the world's first all-transistor record player. It
20 came out in the fall of 1955 and was only manufactured for two years before new vacuum tubes made it obsolete. "Are you sure that's the right one?" I ask the woman.

"Uh-huh," she says. "It's a Philco TPA-1, right? Plays mono 45s?"

25 I have to admit, this changes things. This lady knows exactly what it is, and what's more, she wants it as a present for her grandmother. Chances are good that the old woman has a record collection already and just needs the player.

30 "Alright," I say. "But I can't let it go for less than two hundred."

The young woman smiles ecstatically. "Two hundred it is," she says. "Thank you so much."

I know I could've gotten more. After all, the TPA-1
35 is an extremely hard-to-find piece, and mine is in good working order on top of that. But I smile when I think of the old woman receiving a treasured gift from her granddaughter.

"Did your grandma have one of these same play-
40 ers?" I ask as I swipe her credit card. The phonograph is now wrapped in plastic on the counter between us.

"Yes. She lost it in a fire. It was her most prized pos-
session, one of the first things she ever bought for herself when she moved to New York."

45 I know exactly what it's like to move to a new place and struggle just to stay afloat, much less afford something nonessential like a record player. I still have the cheap little TV that I bought in Chicago when I was twenty. It wasn't even a nice model when it was new, but I've kept it
50 all these years because it reminds me of being young and out on my own. Reclaiming her old TPA-1 will probably mean a lot more to this woman's grandmother than just being able to play her records.

It reminded me of when Shelly and I got an apart-
55 ment together. We were unloading boxes from her car, and while I was inside I heard Shelly give a sharp yowl from the street. I ran outside, terrified that she had hurt herself. She was sitting on the curb, holding back tears, and clutching a broken glass jewelry box. The box had
60 been a gift from her aunt when Shelly was thirteen.

The force of her reaction to the box breaking sur-
prised even Shelly. Sure, she had loved it, but she'd never put her finger on exactly why. Now she understood: it was a memento from a specific time in her life—a promise
65 of her life to come. She had always admired her aunt's style and elegance, and receiving the jewelry box was like receiving a benediction. Shelly was still a girl, but she would grow into a glamorous, capable woman just like her aunt.

70 These types of keepsakes are more than personal effects. They represent our very identities or, more accu-
rately, the times in which we begin to form our identities. We all want to stay in touch with that heady feeling of possibility when our future seemed wide open, before we
75 started stacking commitments on top of commitments. As time passes, more and more of our dreams knock up against the hard ceiling of reality. If we are lucky and we work hard, we'll accomplish a handful of major life goals. But in the process we're forced to make sacrifices.
80 Even when we're at peace with that, the sacrifices remain meaningful.

Entrance Ticket   Learning Targets   Understanding Passage Structure   Reading Quickly   ACT Practice   Sum It Up

3 _____ **3**

1. According to the passage, Shelly was upset about the jewelry box breaking because:

   A. it was expensive and beautiful.
   B. it was a memento of an era in her life.
   C. she is mad at herself for being careless.
   D. her aunt will be disappointed in her.

2. According to the passage, which of the following is NOT a reason the narrator is happy to sell the phonograph to the young woman?

   F. She knows exactly what it is.
   G. She plans to give it to her grandmother as a gift.
   H. The narrator believes the young woman's grandmother will cherish it.
   J. The narrator is tired of having it sit unused in his record store.

3. According to the narrator, the record player's primary significance to the grandmother is that it may:

   A. evoke a time when her life was full of possibility.
   B. be capable of playing her old records.
   C. remind her of the fire in which she lost the original.
   D. improve her relationship with her granddaughter.

4. The passage most strongly emphasizes that sacrifices:

   F. can happen unexpectedly.
   G. are difficult for many people to accept and grow from.
   H. are an inevitable result of driving toward one's goals.
   J. have little meaning to the young.

5. The passage notes all of the following as reasons why people value certain objects EXCEPT that:

   A. they represent a time of identity forging.
   B. they can embody meaningful sacrifices.
   C. they are promises that people will achieve their goals.
   D. they can be resold for many times their original value.

END OF SET ONE
STOP! DO NOT GO ON TO THE NEXT PAGE
UNTIL TOLD TO DO SO.

Entrance Ticket   Learning Targets   Understanding Passage Structure   Reading Quickly   ACT Practice   Sum It Up

12.4.2 Set Two

Passage III

HUMANITIES: This passage is adapted from the article "Second City, First in Laughs" by Thomas Whittington (©2015 by MasteryPrep).

About a decade after the end of World War II, a serious social movement gained momentum in Chicago. It would eventually wield enormous influence over multibillion-dollar industries and millions of people, yet it started
5 with a group of actors playing games in a Hyde Park bar. The Compass Players, as they came to be known, were fed up with the staid conventions of Broadway at the time and wanted to embrace a new source of theatrical creativity: improvisation. With roots in *commedia dell'arte*—a
10 Renaissance-era genre in which actors improvised scenarios—the Compass collective quickly took on a contemporary identity of its own. Paul Sills, one of the founders, pioneered the use of theater games as the basis for topical skits sparked by audience suggestions. The company
15 folded in 1958, but Sills relocated to Chicago's north side and opened The Second City Theatre in December 1959.

From the start, Second City leaned toward parody and satire of social norms, political figures, and the current events. Using only a few costumes and props, the cast
20 presented blackouts, parodies, musical numbers, and improvisations. Over the ensuing decades the company expanded to a handful of other cities and became known as a breeding ground for some of the biggest names in American and Canadian comedy. Although these performers are
25 better known for their roles in television and movies, the work they did at Second City has remained central to their approach to acting. The principles of improvisation Sills and his cohorts established with the Compass have grown into a comedy movement that has helped define popular
30 entertainment ever since.

The driving forces behind Second City's style were more than just spontaneity and irreverence for the status quo. An ensemble mentality was key, with everyone willing to jump in and offer support to a faltering scene at
35 a moment's notice. Still, many times the improvisation simply wouldn't land with the audience, so the actors also had to be willing to endure failure on a nightly basis. The shared attitude was that everything was a bit of an experiment, with the benefit that when something worked,
40 it exuded a magic that exhilarated everyone in the room.

The early revues, performed in a converted cabaret space in Chicago's Old Town neighborhood, had names like "A View From Under the Bridge" and "Showdown at Credibility Gap." Audiences packed in to witness the
45 strange new theatrical format. The collective energy was intoxicating, and Second City rapidly became one of the hottest tickets in town. In 1973 the company expanded to Toronto, where it also became an immediate hit. Inadver-

tently the theater had come to define a new comic temper-
50 ament that resonated strongly with the youth movements in culture and politics. Two years later *Saturday Night Live* would debut and borrow heavily from both the style and cast of Second City.

On *Saturday Night Live* and its Canadian counter-
55 part, *Second City Television*, actors like John Belushi, Gilda Radner, and Martin Short performed characters inspired by—and sometimes lifted from—their nights at Second City. As before, improvisation figured prominently in the development of these personalities. To locate the
60 humor, the actors would focus on a handful of specific traits or mannerisms of their characters and then practice putting them in situations where those traits would be highlighted to comic effect. Often the characters were inspired by people the actors really knew, such as Belushi's
65 "cheezborger"-obsessed diner owner, whom he modeled after Sam Sianis, the owner of the Billy Goat Tavern in Chicago.

As the decades passed, many Second City alumni embarked on movie careers, and new generations of talent
70 refreshed the ranks. The 1990s saw Mike Myers, Chris Farley, and Bonnie Hunt become film stars at the same time that Steve Carell, Tina Fey, and Stephen Colbert took to the stage in Chicago.

The troupe continued to experiment with new show
75 concepts: 1995's "Piñata Full of Bees," directed by Mick Napier, was the first to have recurring characters and a cohesive theme. In 2009 Second City celebrated its fiftieth anniversary with a bash that included performances and reminiscences by dozens of alumni, many of them now
80 Hollywood A-listers. A common refrain in their speeches was how liberating and special their time at Second City had been and how influential it was on their careers.

Today, improvisation has deep credibility in showbiz circles as both a tool for writing and, increasingly,
85 as an art form in itself. While some of Second City's stars—such as Bill Murray—have achieved worldwide fame, most—such as T.J. Jagodowski—remain relatively obscure despite their immense talent and devotion to the craft. Although they do not reach the huge audiences of
90 their Hollywood counterparts, they continue to perform at improv theaters throughout the country, dazzling audiences with their wit, absurdity, and fearlessness.

Entrance Ticket   Learning Targets   Understanding Passage Structure   Reading Quickly   ACT Practice   Sum It Up

3 ████████████████████████████████ **3**

6. According to the passage, with which of the following groups did the comedic style of The Second City resonate most strongly?

   F. Broadway audiences
   G. Hollywood A-listers
   H. Youth in cultural and political movements
   J. Traditional comedic writers

7. According to the passage, Stephen Colbert and Bonnie Hunt are linked because:

   A. they both began their comedy careers at Second City.
   B. they are married to each other.
   C. they have a sincere admiration for each other's work.
   D. they were both cast members on *Saturday Night Live.*

8. According to the passage, the Second City style was originally defined by:

   F. strict adherence to the traditions of *commedia dell'arte*, including its Renaissance-era costumes and props.
   G. satirizing social norms, as well as the conventions of Broadway at the time.
   H. the prevailing trends in comedy at the time, which in turn defined American and Canadian entertainment.
   J. Broadway performers who were looking to supplement their work on New York stages.

9. The passage states that the development of the original characters in Second City sketches occurred in part as a result of inspiration from:

   A. the show's cohesive theme.
   B. people the actors knew.
   C. props and costumes.
   D. audience suggestions.

10. The passage indicates that, as a group, Second City performers have remained relatively obscure because only a select few:

    F. join the cast of *Saturday Night Live.*
    G. become film and television stars, thereby increasing their influence on popular comedy.
    H. are willing to make the leap to Hollywood from Chicago or Toronto.
    J. continue performing after they leave Second City.

END OF SET TWO
STOP! DO NOT GO ON TO THE NEXT PAGE
UNTIL TOLD TO DO SO.

Entrance Ticket   Learning Targets   Understanding Passage Structure   Reading Quickly   ACT Practice   Sum It Up

12.4.3 Set Three

Passage II

SOCIAL SCIENCE: This passage is adapted from *Progress Comes to Chinese Education* by Susumi Lee-Blair and Jin-Su Chang (©2015 by MasteryPrep).

In the midst of dramatically increasing population density, a rapidly evolving and changing economy, and a growing need for skilled laborers in a variety of industries, BN Vocational School is hard at work to make a
5 better future for China, one student at a time. Students don't pay tuition; the school operates as a non-profit; and its nine campuses are located in cities that have a need for workers in specific industries.

Over the last four decades, China's population has
10 undergone a sweeping shift from rural farming villages to rapidly expanding cities. Mandatory benefits and state-regulated wages have provided better prospects for migrant workers who don't mind doing the jobs urban residents consider "dirty" or too dangerous. However,
15 it is not as easy for the migrants' children. Unless they can acquire job-relevant training, many of these relocated families will find themselves unemployed as the economy transitions to a more specialized workforce. For this reason, free and low-cost vocational education is in high
20 demand; unfortunately, most state-run trade schools are suffering from budget shortfalls, inadequate training, and teacher shortages, unable to manage the many students seeking enrollment.

"After the Vocational Education Law passed in
25 1996, everything changed," explains Xiu Ying Liang, an education professor at Peking University. "Prior to the law, industries trained their own employees through the institution. Then, the government decided it was better to bring vocational schools under the wing of subsidized
30 education. Unfortunately, state-run vocational schools have less specialized courses, and so their graduates are not prepared for the skills and responsibilities required of them in their field."

Public perception of vocational schools, and how
35 this affects policy and legislation, has also done a disservice to the institution. Historically, the Chinese people have esteemed higher education and have a low regard for someone who works with his hands. State-run vocational schools are plagued by budget shortfalls, forced to
40 operate on a fraction of what the law dictates should be allocated to them. A domino-effect of problems follows: inadequate equipment, facilities in desperate need of updating, low wages for teachers, especially (and ironically) those who have practical experience in their fields.
45 Unable to keep up with the rapidly changing economy, curriculum tends to be general and thus insufficiently prepares students for the job market waiting for them. This knowledge gap hurts not only China's laborers but also the country's economic bottom line. Currently one-third
50 of Chinese products cannot meet quality-control standards because workers lack training in how to properly operate the machinery, resulting in a staggering loss of potential revenue each year.

BN Vocational School was established in 2005 to
55 address such a serious situation. Today, nine campuses are scattered across the country, offering tailor-made courses that place graduates directly into employment in their area. "In Dalian, mechanical operations has the largest class," says Qiang Liu, spokesperson for the BNVS
60 campus network, referring to the highly industrialized city in the north. "Whereas in Sanya," situated on a tropical island in the South China Sea, "most students enroll in air-conditioning operation and maintenance." The full curriculum available at various BNVS campuses includes
65 hotel management, tourism, web production, and graphic design—a first in China's history. They even offer a dozen or so "long-term development courses," such as financial literacy, philanthropy, and English.

Despite the successful rate of placing BNVS gradu-
70 ates into jobs, hurdles remain for this new model of industry-tailored education. For one, the cultural bias toward a university education is hard to overcome. "Many parents simply don't see the value of a vocational education," says Liu. "They think of the prestige that comes with a
75 degree. What they don't consider is that vast numbers of university graduates do not have the skills necessary for the emerging job market. Not to mention, the wages they can expect to earn are not competitive with graduates from vocational schools. They're spending more time and
80 money to earn the same income."

With the future economy expecting rapid growth and change, China has a vested interest in modernizing state-run trade schools so that its labor force is more fully educated and prepared. "China has hit its popula-
85 tion peak," explains economist Jie Zhang. "From now on, more people will be retiring from the workforce than will enter in. The focus of factories and industries is going to be narrowed onto those employees who can do more than a general work—specialization will be priority."

90 One obstacle has not been as daunting as might be expected. As a tuition-free school, BNVS must find alternate sources of revenue. However, domestic and international charities, corporations, and governments have seen the value and promise in such an enterprise and have
95 steadily given to the school since its inception. Financial donations are submitted from the world over. Philanthropic foundations and the national government award grants to keep the school campuses up-to-date. Dell and Motorola have donated equipment, and local businesses
100 near the campus offer their professionals as volunteer teachers, saving BNVS from a major expense.

3   **3**

The founder of BNVS, Yao Li, knows that better education leads not only to greater productivity but also to higher wages for Chinese workers. She considers that the
105 school fulfills a responsibility both to her government and to her fellow citizen. Her mission, she says, is to continue to "bring hope to the future of all of China's youth, regardless of their economic status."

11. According to the passage, one-third of domestically produced products in China do not meet quality-control standards because:

    A. the speed of production is too fast to ensure consistency.
    B. inferior materials are being used as a cost-cutting measure.
    C. workers are not adequately trained to operate machinery.
    D. the standards of quality control are impossibly high.

12. The passage indicates that significant funding is necessary to support China's vocational schools because:

    F. the majority of prospective students cannot afford to pay for tuition.
    G. the curriculums require that state-of-the-art machinery be installed in classrooms.
    H. corporations refuse to pay to educate potential employees.
    J. much of the money allocated to schools disappears within government bureaucracy.

13. The passage indicates that, as a group, the BN Vocational School students will positively impact China's economy because most of them:

    A. will become government officials and have an influence on labor policy.
    B. will contribute to economic growth in the cities where they work.
    C. will eventually go on to get a traditional university education.
    D. will bring skills back to their rural villages following graduation.

14. The passage indicates that BN Vocational School adapted the curriculums of its various campuses in order to:

    F. match graduates' skills with the demands of local industry.
    G. give students more options in what they are able to study.
    H. not compete with other regional trade schools.
    J. meet government regulations.

15. The passage makes clear that a main goal of the BN Vocational School's founder is to:

    A. take advantage of the tuition potential of more than 200 million migrant workers.
    B. give migrant workers a better chance to find stable, well-paying jobs.
    C. train government employees in how to design curriculum for China's state-run schools.
    D. encourage China's manufacturing economy at the expense of its service-oriented economy.

END OF SET THREE
STOP! DO NOT GO ON TO THE NEXT PAGE
UNTIL TOLD TO DO SO.

Entrance Ticket   Learning Targets   Understanding Passage Structure   Reading Quickly   ACT Practice   Sum It Up

Sum It Up

Summarize Key Ideas and Details Part 1

No Lip Reading
Read faster than you can say the words, and stop trying to sound them out.

Finger Reading
Run your finger along the words as you read to help you focus.

Chunking
Read the passage as chunks of words, not as individual words that need to be sounded out.

Photograph Reading
"Take pictures" of the word chunks with your mind as you read through the passage.

Tips and Techniques

Keep Your Pencil Moving: Use your pencil to jot down key ideas as you read. Just remember to keep your speed up.

Reading Level: Work on your reading level every day by reading a little from a novel, history book, magazine, or newspaper that you find interesting.

Summarize Key Ideas and Details Part 2

CAPTION:

13.1 Entrance Ticket

Read the passage and answer the questions below.

In his later years Vincent Wingfield would look upon a single event as the greatest reason for which he had become an esteemed and heralded horseman. Though his father—himself a
5 great rider and breaker of horses—had started him on the path early on, he had passed away as Vincent was coming of age. Thus, he was not able to nurture or appreciate his son's prowess for riding beyond his early childhood endeavors.
10 Vincent would later credit his swift ascent in the cavalry to Jonas, the caretaker of his family's grounds and stables.

Jonas spared no pains to gain the goodwill of Vincent. Jonas had set inquiries on foot and
15 had selected for him a horse which, for speed and bottom, had no superior in the state. One of Mrs. Wingfield's acquaintances, however, upon hearing that she had purchased the animal, angrily told her in front of Jonas that it was noto-
20 rious for its vicious temper. The groundskeeper defended himself by saying that he had certainly heard that the horse was spirited and needed a good rider—and that he only selected it know-ing that Vincent was a first-class rider—and
25 would not care to have a weak-willed horse that any child could manage. The praise was not undeserved. The gentlemen of Virginia were celebrated as good riders; Major Wingfield, himself a cavalry man, had been anxious that Vincent
30 should maintain the credit of his English blood and had placed him on a pony as soon as he was able to sit on one. He almost lived on horse-back, either riding about the estate or paying visits to the houses of other planters.

35 He exercised his father's horses for an hour or more every day in a paddock near the house—the major being wheeled down in an easy chair and superintending his riding. As the horses Jonas purchased were always full
40 of spirit, Vincent's powers were often taxed to the utmost, and he took many falls; however, the soil was light, and he had learned the knack of falling easily. By the age of fourteen, he was able to ride nearly any mount, absolutely fear-
45 lessly and without a saddle.

13.1 Entrance Ticket

1. The horse mentioned in the passage was described by an acquaintance of Mrs. Wingfield as:

   A. abandoned by its previous owners.

   B. notorious for its vicious temper.

   C. a beast both intelligent and handsome.

   D. a docile and gentle creature.

2. The author seems to attribute Vincent's eventual rise in the ranks of the cavalry primarily to:

   F. having been born into a long line of accomplished cavalrymen.

   G. possessing an innate ability to sense a horse's every move before it is made.

   H. an employee of his family who had the confidence to task him with a difficult horse.

   J. long hours of exercising the family horses on the estate with his father.

3. According to Jonas, as he is presented in the passage, purchasing a weak-willed horse for Vincent to train would have most likely resulted in:

   A. Jonas losing his position as caretaker because the purchase would have upset Mrs. Wingfield.

   B. an increase in admiration shown to him by the cavalrymen of Virginia and their wives.

   C. Vincent's abilities going unnoticed because the horse would not have provided a challenge.

   D. therapeutic exercise to relieve Vincent of the stress caused by not meeting his father's expectations.

Entrance Ticket | Learning Targets | Question Detangling | Scanning for Answers | ACT Practice | Sum It Up

13.2 Learning Targets

1. Decode questions quickly to understand what is being asked of them

2. Efficiently scan passages to sort out important and nonimportant information

Self-Assessment

Circle the number that corresponds to your confidence level in your knowledge of this subject before beginning the lesson. A score of 1 means you are completely lost, and a score of 4 means you have mastered the skills. After you finish the lesson, return to the bottom of this page and circle your new confidence level to show your improvement.

Before Lesson

1   2   3   4

After Lesson

1   2   3   4

13.3.1 Question Detangling

1. The passage indicates that horseshoe bats have developed a system of echolocation using sound waves because:

   _____

2. The passage states that the development of a fully resonant tone in singing occurs as a result of:

   _____

3. The passage makes clear that one reason Henry Ford established his original Model T factory in Detroit, Michigan, was to:

   _____

4. According to the passage, one reason the Galapagos Islands off the coast of Ecuador were attractive for NOAA's study on the effect of ecotourism on biodiversity is that the islands:

   _____

   _____

5. The author seems to attribute Spencer's ability to foresee impending natural disasters primarily to Spencer's:

   _____

6. The author indicates that Picasso's *Guernica* is connected to the Spanish Civil War in that the painting:

   _____

7. The passage indicates that the underwater submersion time of baleen whales is primarily determined by the:

   _____

8. The passage most strongly emphasizes that the chrysalis is crucial for the lepidopteran's transition from:

   _____

Reading Tip

Use Your Words: If you run into an unusual or confusing question, try focusing on the key words and reword the question in a way that you would ask a friend. If that does not clear it up, mark and move.

13.3.2 Scanning for Answers

Copernicus's theory of *heliocentricity*, or the idea that the earth and our planets revolve around the sun, was published in a book that—rumor has it—was placed in his hands as he lay dying in 1642. His monumental book is a rational and modern work in an age of astrology and superstition. His theory is a triumph of reason and imagination and is perhaps as original a work as any human being may be expected to produce. Copernicus was extremely reluctant to publish his book because of the misunderstandings and malicious attacks it would undoubtedly arouse, and he passed away unaware that his life's work appeared before the world not as a truth but as a mere hypothesis.

In the mid-1600s, the diffusion of the Copernican system was due in large part to the writings of Bishop Wilkins. The first, *The Discovery of a World in the Moon, or, a Discourse Tending to Prove That 'Tis Probable There May Be Another Habitable World in That Planet* appeared in 1638. The second book appeared two years later, titled *A Discourse Concerning a New Planet—Tending to Prove, That 'Tis Proba-ble Our Earth Is One of the Planets*. In the latter, Wilkins stated certain propositions as indubitable: that the scriptural passages intimating diurnal motion of the sun or of the heavens are fairly capable of another interpretation, that there is no sufficient reason to prove the earth incapable of those motions that Copernicus ascribes to it, and that it is more probable that the earth moves than the heavens move.

The appearance of Newton's *Principia* in 1687—with his statement of the universal application of the law of gravitation—soon ended hesitancy for most people about the Copernican system. Twelve years later John Keill, Scotch mathematician and astronomer, opened the first course of lectures delivered at Oxford on the new Newtonian philosophy. Not only were his lectures thronged, but his books advocating the Copernican system in full went through several editions in relatively few years.

13.3.2 Scanning for Answers

1. According to the passage, what is the Copernican theory?

   A. A theory that has come to be considered one of mere astrology and superstition

   B. A theory stating that it is very likely that the moon is habitable by humans

   C. A theory stating that the earth and its planets revolve around the sun

   D. The now world-renowned "statement of the universal application of the law of gravitation"

2. The passage makes clear that people were generally less hesitant to accept Copernicus's hypothesis after:

   F. Newton came out with *Principia*.

   G. the many editions of John Keill's books were published.

   H. Keill delivered his first well-attended lecture at Oxford.

   J. Bishop Wilkins published his writing, *The Discovery of a World in the Moone.*

3. In the passage, the significance of the year 1640 is that it is:

   A. the year when Copernicus finished the book that would be placed in his hands as he lay dying.

   B. the year in which Newton first began to study the Copernican theory of heliocentricity.

   C. the year during which Bishop Wilkins published one of his works supporting Copernicus's hypothesis.

   D. the first time that Copernicus's name would be uttered in a place of academia, Oxford University.

13.3.2 Scanning for Answers

The dusty window to the past has been favorable to Henry Ford, who is often credited with the invention of the first automobile. Many regard the Michigan-born engineer as the vi-
5 sionary who ushered in the age of motorized ground transportation with the unveiling of the Model T. What many do not realize, however, is that Ford's was not the first self-propelled automobile to be invented—or to be made available
10 to eager consumers.

The Model T made its debut via the Ford Motor Company in 1908 with a purchase price of $825. Over 10,000 vehicles were sold in its first year of production. By 1912 Ford had
15 dropped the price to $575, and sales had skyrocketed even further. Central to Ford's success was his ability to perfect the concept of the assembly line, which increased the efficiency of manufacturing the vehicle and thus lowered its

20 cost. The Model T quickly became recognized as the "Ford in your Future," and many Americans aspired to display the masterpiece in their garages.

But what was actually so historic about
25 Ford's masterpiece? The Model T was not the first automobile to be invented—Ford himself had previously invented the Quadricycle in 1896. Rather, the Model T was the first *affordable* automobile available to the average American.
30 Ford's invention was long-preceded by that of Karl Benz, who patented the first self-propelled motorwagon in 1886 in Mannheim, Germany. Benz's revolutionary vehicle was limited to the relatively few well-to-do consumers who could
35 afford to purchase it, but it sparked the legacy of innovation within the automobile industry that continues to this day.

Reading Tip

Scanning: When a question gives you a specific topic, do not rush when you scan the passage for the answer. Start at the beginning of the passage and carefully but quickly scan the passage, looking for the topic.

13.3.2 Scanning for Answers

1. According to the passage, what was a motorwagon?
   - A. Another name for the Ford Model T
   - B. The slang term for automobile that was common in the American vernacular by 1912
   - C. Henry Ford's earlier automobile invention, which predated the Ford Model T
   - D. An invention by Karl Benz that was a predecessor to Ford's Model T

2. The passage makes it clear that the Ford Model T was revolutionary because it:
   - F. was the first self-propelled automobile.
   - G. embodied the perfection of the assembly line.
   - H. debuted in 1908, when nothing of the sort had ever been seen in the United States.
   - J. was the highest selling automobile in history.

3. In the passage, the significance of 1896 is that it is:
   - A. the year in which Ford unveiled his first Model T.
   - B. a year in which multiple inventors came out with a "self-propelled 'motorwagon.'"
   - C. the year in which Ford made a predecessor to the Model T.
   - D. when Henry Ford first outsold Karl Benz.

3   3

13.4.1 Set One

Passage I

LITERARY NARRATIVE: This passage is adapted from *Rodney Stone* by Sir Arthur Conan Doyle (©1896 by D. Appleton & Co.).

Our family has for many generations belonged to the Royal Navy, and it has been a custom among us for the eldest son to take the name of his father's favorite commander. Thus we can trace our lineage back to old
5 Vernon Stone, who commanded a high-sterned, peak-nosed, fifty-gun ship against the Dutch. Through Hawke Stone and Benbow Stone, we came down to my father, Anson Stone, who in his turn christened me Rodney at the parish church of St. Thomas at Portsmouth in the year
10 of 1786.

My dear mother was the best that ever a man had. She was young when she married, and still so to me when I can first recall her busy fingers and her gentle voice. I see her as a lovely woman with kind, dove's eyes, somewhat
15 short of stature but carrying herself very bravely. I see her again in her middle years, sweet and loving, planning, contriving, achieving—with the few shillings a day of a lieutenant's pay on which to support the cottage at Friar's Oak—and keeping a fair face to the world.

20 As to my father, I can describe him best when I come to the time when he returned to us from the Mediterranean. During all my childhood he was only a name and a face in a miniature picture that hung around my mother's neck. At first they told me he was fighting the
25 French, and then after some years one heard less about the French and more about General Bonaparte. I remember the awe with which one day I saw a print of the great Corsican's portrait in a bookseller's window. This, then, was the archenemy with whom my father spent his life in
30 terrible and ceaseless contest. To my childish imagination it was a personal affair, and I forever saw my father and this clean-shaven, thin-lipped man swaying and reeling in a deadly, year-long grapple.

Only once in those long years did my father return
35 home. It was just after we had moved from Portsmouth to Friar's Oak when he came for a week before he set sail with Admiral Jervis to help him turn his name into Lord St. Vincent. I remember that he both frightened and fascinated me with his tales of battles, and I can recall, as
40 if it were yesterday, the horror with which I gazed upon a spot of blood upon his shirt ruffle, which had come, as I have no doubt, from a mischance in shaving. At the time, however, I never questioned that it had spurted from some stricken Frenchman or Spaniard, and I shrank from him in
45 terror when he laid his calloused hand upon my head. My mother wept bitterly when he was gone, but for my own part I was not sorry to see his blue back and white trousers going down the garden walk, for I felt, with the selfishness of a child, that we were closer together, she and I, when
50 we were alone.

It was during these times that my mother sparked my interest in music. She played the piano beautifully and would give me lessons every night. Soon my hands would begin to itch at mid-day if they had not yet run up and
55 down the black and white keys of the instrument in our music room.

However, this childhood fancy gave way to adolescence, and adolescence succumbed to adulthood. The time had come for me to continue the family tradition
60 that was the duty of all male members of the Stone family set forth by Vernon Stone himself. I was born into a Navy family, and I felt obliged to wear the same stripes as my father and his.

I can recall a heavy-hearted younger version of
65 myself wearing the uniform and engaging in battles in foreign lands in which I did not care to be. It all seemed an inevitable course and one that a heavy heart could not change.

Thus I did not know happiness until two decades
70 later, when an injury and subsequent infection rendered me useless to the Navy. In my hospital bed I began to hear in my head *Fur Elise* and Mozart's *Fifth Concerto*. The tunes I had played as a child called me back to my greatest passion and signaled a new chapter in my life.

75 Now as I call to my young son, Nelson, in the garden, I do so from the piano bench, where I met my first and greatest loves: ivory, ebony, and their gloriously infinite possibilities.

3   **3**

1. What does the narrator state was his mother's role in his interest in music?

   A. She warned him that it was not a proper hobby for a man in the Stone family.

   B. She sparked his interest in music by playing the piano and helped him learn to do so himself.

   C. She appreciated that he took an interest in music but urged him to hide it from his militaristic father.

   D. She wanted him to make music his profession and wept when he chose the Navy over his true passion.

2. The author indicates that his mother's feelings differed from his own about his father's departures in that:

   F. he was inconsolable at his father's parting, but she remained stoic.

   G. she would cry sorrowfully, but he was glad to see his father go.

   H. she was happy to be alone with her son, but he was angry.

   J. he wept for many days, but his mother became unusually cheerful.

3. Based on the passage, what reaction, if any, did the narrator have to his father returning home?

   A. He ignored his father because he wanted to spend time alone with his mother.

   B. He felt sorry for his father for having been injured in the war and attempted to console him.

   C. He was upset because he knew that his father would be leaving again and did not want to get attached to him.

   D. He was frightened by his father's stories of war and would shrink in terror from his father's touch.

4. According to the passage, one way in which the narrator was able to conceptualize the militaristic endeavors of his father was by:

   F. imagining that a spot of blood on his shirt was that of a foe he had battled.

   G. envisioning his father bellowing commands to General Nelson himself.

   H. playing Navy battle tunes on the piano during evening social hours.

   J. drawing portraits of the famous foes his father had fought at war, such as General Bonaparte.

5. What does the passage state is the means by which the narrator returned to his passion for playing music?

   A. He retired from the Navy and wanted to return to his childhood home.

   B. He decided that he did not want to carry the naval tradition into the next generation.

   C. He sustained an injury that forced him out of his naval duties.

   D. He jumped at the opportunity to pursue music as a full-time career.

END OF SET ONE
STOP! DO NOT GO ON TO THE NEXT PAGE
UNTIL TOLD TO DO SO.

Entrance Ticket   Learning Targets   Question Detangling   Scanning for Answers   ACT Practice   Sum It Up

13.4.2 Set Two

Passage II

SOCIAL SCIENCE: This passage is adapted from *Watts* by William Loftus Hare (©1910 by T.C. & E.C. Jack, Ltd.).

In July of 1904 the life of George Frederick Watts, famous for his series of private and public portraits, came to an end. Watts's first aspiration toward monumental painting began in the year 1843, when in a competition
5 for the decoration of the Houses of Parliament, he gained a prize of three hundred British pounds for his cartoon, *Caractacus Led Captive Through the Streets of Rome*. Young Watts won the prize in a field of competitors that was rich with talent. This group included well-known
10 historical painter Haydon, who, because of some financial difficulties and from the neglect, real or imagined, of the leading politicians, struggled emotionally from then on.

The winnings took Watts to Italy, where he stayed for four years as a guest of Lord Holland. Glimpses of the
15 Italy he gazed upon and loved are preserved in a landscape of the hillside town of Fiesole with blue sky and clouds, another of a castellated villa and mountains near Florence, and a third of the Carrara Mountains near Pisa. He also produced some beautiful works of portraiture during this
20 time, capturing the likenesses of both Lady Holland and Lady Dorothy Neville.

Italy, and particularly Florence, was perpetually fascinating and inspirational to Watts. There he was highly influenced by the painters Orcagna and Titian—influences
25 that were clearly represented in the next monumental painting he attempted. It came about that Lord Holland persuaded his guest to enter a fresh competition for the decoration of the Parliament Houses, and Watts won the prize with his *Alfred Inciting the Saxons to Resist*
30 *the Landing of the Danes*. The color and movement of the great Italian masters, noticeably absent from the *Caractacus* cartoon, were quite evident in this new effort, where the English King Alfred stands like a Raphaelesque archangel prominently in the painting.

35 In 1848 Watts attained the position of official historical painter to the state, a post that the unfortunate Haydon desired greatly. In 1853 he contributed an appendix to the *Diary of Haydon*—in itself an exciting document, showing how disheartening the life of an
40 official painter then might be—a note telling of the state of historical and monumental painting in the 1840s and of his own attitude toward it:

Patriots and statesmen will rue the day that shall
arrive when they realize that a great opportunity
45 *to spread great art throughout England was sadly*
missed. Haydon, for example, would have no doubt
worked as a historian in recording English battles in
many mighty and instructive works of art. England
50 *is a great and mighty country, and its government*
should undertake to decorate all of its public
buildings, like town halls, state-run schools, and
even train stations. We should consider the walls
as notebooks, like those of a school boy writing
his various assignments. We should paint what
55 *we can on them now, and when fine originals can*
replace them, we will replace them as such. The
process would carry an expense similar to that of
simply whitewashing them. For example, if an artist
were to paint the whole line of English kings on a
60 *public wall—with some information accompanying*
each figure, like the dates of their reign and any
noteworthy events in which they had a part—it
would be instructive to the public and provide lovely
decoration of the space.

65 During this time, Watts's personal life was pervaded by the influence of Lord and Lady Holland, who, having returned from Florence to London, had him as a constant visitor to Holland House. In 1850 he went to live at The Dower House, an old building in the fields of Kensington.
70 There as a guest of the Prinsep family, he set up as a portrait painter. His host and family connections were some of the first to sit for him, and he soon gained fame in this type of work.

In 1856 Watts traveled to the East, in the company of
75 Sir Charles Newton, for the purpose of opening the buried Temple of Mausolus at Halicarnassus. This gave Watts further insight into the old Greek world and stimulated his efforts in depicting incidents in classical lore. In a view of a mountainous coast called *Asia Minor*, and another, *The*
80 *Isle of Cos*, he produced two charming pictorial records of this important expedition. The next six years of his life were spent as a portrait painter—not as a professional who would paint anyone's portrait, but as a friend who loved to dedicate himself to his friends.

3 **3**

6. The author indicates that Watts's portraits of Lady Holland and Lady Dorothy Neville are similar in that:

   F. they are his first two commissioned works.
   G. they show how much the artist matured in his journey to the east.
   H. they are paintings created during Watts's stay in Italy.
   J. they are both parts of larger works that were created for public buildings.

7. What does the passage state is Watts's view of painting personal portraits after returning from his trip to the East?

   A. He considered it his greatest contribution to the world of art, far above that of his civic paintings.
   B. He did it purely for financial stability, since this was a slow period in his career.
   C. He loathed the subjects of his paintings, and this can be seen in the portraits themselves.
   D. He did not do it for economic reasons, but rather as an act of devotion to friends.

8. Based on the passage, what reaction, if any, did Watts's peer Haydon have to losing several painting competitions?

   F. He vowed to exact revenge against Watts for making a mockery of civic art.
   G. He altered his style to reflect that of Watts, changing from a more classic technique to painting cartoons.
   H. He became depressed in part due to financial difficulties and a perceived lack of recognition by political leaders.
   J. He championed Watts as the next great public servant and endorsed him for the position of official historical painter to the state.

9. According to the passage, the influence of Italy's great masters, Orcagna and Titian, can be seen in Watts's work, *Alfred inciting the Saxons to resist the landing of the Danes* in its:

   A. textured brushstrokes and attention to light.
   B. color and movement.
   C. portrayal of the king as an archangel.
   D. size and scale.

10. What does the passage state is Watts's view of the role of art in public and government buildings?

    F. Children ought to be given the freedom to paint whatever they please on government buildings.
    G. Fine art has no place in public buildings, such as town halls, national schools, and railway stations.
    H. Since most public art is of poor quality, it should be whitewashed wherever it is found.
    J. A public building ought to have art on its walls so as to teach history and inspire future generations.

END OF SET TWO
STOP! DO NOT GO ON TO THE NEXT PAGE
UNTIL TOLD TO DO SO.

Entrance Ticket   Learning Targets   Question Detangling   Scanning for Answers   ACT Practice   Sum It Up

13.4.3 Set Three

Passage IV

NATURAL SCIENCE: This passage is adapted from *Essays on Early Ornithology and Kindred Subjects* by James R. McClymont (©1920 by Bertrand Quaritch, Ltd.). Vasco da Gama (1460s–1524) was a Portuguese explorer and navigator who was the first European to travel from Europe to Asia by sea.

There exists an anonymous narrative of the first voyage of Vasco da Gama to India under the title *Roteiro da Viagem de Vasco da Gama em MCCCCXCVII*. Although it is called a *roteiro* (or Portuguese navigational map), it
5   is in fact a purely personal and popular account of the voyage and does not contain either sailing directions or a systematic description of all the ports that were visited, as one might expect. There is no reason to believe that it was written by Vasco da Gama himself. An officer in such
10 high authority would not be likely to write his narrative anonymously. The faulty and inconsistent orthography, or writing system, of the roteiro also renders improbable the hypothesis that the well-educated Vasco da Gama was the author.

15 The journal of the first voyage of Columbus contains many allusions to the birds that were seen in the course of it by the great discoverer. In this respect, the roteiro of the first voyage of Vasco da Gama resembles that of Columbus. The journal of Columbus is the earliest record
20 of an important voyage of discovery that recognizes natural history as an aid to navigators.

The author of the roteiro notes that birds resembling large herons were seen in the month of August 1497 at which time, I would imagine, the vessels of da Gama were
25 not far from the Gulf of Guinea, or were, perhaps, in the process of making their way across that gulf.

On October 27, as the vessels approached the southwest coast of Africa, whales and seals were encountered, and also *quoquas*, or shells that may have
30 been those of nautili.

On November 8, the vessels under the command of Vasco da Gama cast anchor in a wide bay that extended from east to west and was sheltered from all winds except those that blew from the northwest. It was subsequently
35 estimated that this anchorage was sixty leagues distant from the Angra de Sam Bràs, and as the Angra de Sam Bràs was estimated to be sixty leagues distant from the Cape of Good Hope, it follows that the sheltered anchorage must have been in close proximity to the Cape.

40 The Portuguese came into contact with the inhabitants of the country adjacent to the anchorage. These people had tan complexions and carried wooden spears tipped with horn—an *assegais* of a kind (an iron-
45 tipped spear used by Bantu peoples of South Africa)— and bows and arrows. They also used foxes' tails attached to short wooden handles. We are not informed for what purposes the foxes' tails were used. Were they used to brush flies away, or were they some insignia of authority?
50 The food of the natives was the flesh of whales, seals, and antelopes; the roots of certain plants; and crayfish and other shellfish. The author of the roteiro affirms that the birds of the country resembled the birds in Portugal and that amongst them were cormorants, larks, turtle doves, and gulls.

55 In December, the squadron reached the Angra de São Bràs, which is in close proximity to Mossel Bay. Here penguins, or *sotilicarios*, and seals were in great abundance. The sotilicarios, says the chronicler, could not fly because there were no quill feathers in their wings; in
60 size they were as large as drakes, and their cry resembled the braying of a mule. Manuel de Mesquita Perestrello, who visited the south coast of Africa in 1575, also describes the Cape penguin. From a manuscript of his roteiro, one learns that the flippers of the sotilicario were covered
65 with minute feathers and that these flightless birds dived after fish upon which they fed and on which they fed their young, which were hatched in nests constructed of fish bones. Most of the account is accurate until he mistakenly asserts that the penguins' nests were constructed of fish
70 bones; for this is not in accordance with the observations of contemporary naturalists, who tell us that the nests of the Cape penguin are constructed of stones, shells, and debris. It is, therefore, probable that the fish bones that Perestrello saw were the remains of seals and other larger
75 animals.

Seals, says the roteiro, were in great number at the Angra de São Bràs. On one occasion the number was counted and was found to be 3,000. Some were as large as bears, and their roaring was as deafening as the roaring of
80 lions. Others, which were very small, bleated like sheep. These differences in size and in voice may be explained by differences in the age and in the sex of the seals, for seals of different species do not usually resort to the same locality.

3 **3**

11. Based on the passage, what reasons, if any, are there to suggest that the *roteiro* attributed to Vasco da Gama may have been written by someone else?

   A. It is in almost illegible handwriting, which would have been uncharacteristic of da Gama.
   B. It imparts navigational and scientific information that is not typically found within a roteiro.
   C. It contains a faulty and variable writing system and was written anonymously.
   D. Historical research shows that da Gama was on board a different voyage at the time this roteiro was written.

12. What does the author state is an error made in the accounts found within the roteiro of Manuel de Mesquita Perestrello?

   F. It states that many of the birds observed off the coast of Africa resembled birds found in Portugal.
   G. It indicated that the Cape penguins used fish bones to construct their nests.
   H. It states that the explorers encountered native peoples who used fox tails attached to short wooden handles.
   J. It states that whales could be seen near the southwest coast of Africa.

13. The author indicates that the *sotilicario*, or Cape penguin, is flightless because:

   A. it is the size of a drake, thus too large to achieve flight.
   B. it has a cry like the braying of a donkey.
   C. its wings do not contain the necessary feathers.
   D. it does not have a need to travel long distances.

14. According to the passage, the roteiro of Vasco da Gama and the journal of Christopher Columbus's first voyage are similar in that:

   F. they both exclusively contain nautical directions and charts.
   G. they were both lost for many years and rediscovered in the 1900s.
   H. they were both likely authored by someone else.
   J. they both mention birds that were seen along their course.

15. What does the passage state is the process by which Cape penguins hunted for food?

   A. Skidding across the water and catching fish near the surface with their wings
   B. Waiting for seals to finish their meals and retrieving the scraps from the sand
   C. Diving down beneath the surface of the water to catch fish
   D. Stalking the smaller seal cubs of the Angra de São Bràs and attacking them as a group

END OF SET THREE
STOP! DO NOT GO ON TO THE NEXT PAGE
UNTIL TOLD TO DO SO.

Entrance Ticket   Learning Targets   Question Detangling   Scanning for Answers   ACT Practice   Sum It Up

Sum It Up

Tips and Techniques

Use Your Words: If you run into an unusual or confusing question, try focusing on the key words, and reword the question in a way that you would ask a friend. If that does not clear it up, mark and move.

Scanning: When a question gives you a specific topic, do not rush when you scan for the answer. Start at the beginning of the passage and carefully but quickly scan through the passage, looking for the topic.

Paraphrase

CAPTION:

14.1 Entrance Ticket

Paraphrase the paragraph, rewriting it in your own words and cutting where appropriate.

The folklore of dragons has a long and intricate history, with dragons appearing in the mythology of a variety of cultures and representing different symbols in each. For instance, Chinese dragons, often depicted as amalgams of different animals, traditionally symbolize power. Japanese dragons, by contrast, are often depicted as wingless, serpent-like water deities that sometimes grant wishes to the humans who approach them. Dragons also appear in old mythological stories. In *Beowulf*, the hero's realm is terrorized by a poisonous, fire-breathing dragon. In *The Epic of Gilgamesh*, the hero faces off against a monstrous beast that breathes fire and is covered in scales. In these and other epic stories, heroes must defeat these ancient beasts, often in pursuit of a quest.

_____

_____

_____

_____

_____

_____

_____

_____

_____

_____

_____

Entrance Ticket   Learning Targets   Paraphrase Identification   How to Paraphrase   ACT Practice   Sum It Up

14.2 Learning Targets

1. Locate details in passages and determine appropriate one- or two-word paraphrases of that information

2. Locate details in passages and determine appropriate one- or two-line paraphrases of that information

Self-Assessment

Circle the number that corresponds to your confidence level in your knowledge of this subject before beginning the lesson. A score of 1 means you are completely lost, and a score of 4 means you have mastered the skills. After you finish the lesson, return to the bottom of this page and circle your new confidence level to show your improvement.

Before Lesson

1   2   3   4

After Lesson

1   2   3   4

Entrance Ticket | Learning Targets | Paraphrase Identification | How to Paraphrase | ACT Practice | Sum It Up

14.3.1 Paraphrase Identification

1. I want to go watch the baseball game and eat snacks.

   _____

2. A girl had a lamb with white fur who followed her around.

   _____

3. Riding in a sleigh with bells on it is fun and makes everyone happy in the wintertime.

   _____

4. The light from the rockets showed that our flag was still waving.

   _____

14.3.1 Paraphrase Identification

Loquacious

_____ **1.** The day after today, I plan to venture down to the local market in order to procure some hors d'oeuvres for the gathering that will be taking place.

_____ **2.** Our mother has requested that on Saturday, numerous guests, who are related to us, will dine together at our house for the last meal of the day.

_____ **3.** Steven is participating in a performance with a few other members of his class and will be singing by himself for one particularly important moment of a song.

_____ **4.** We will be accepting a ride with a few other girls to the soccer game the day before Sunday and journeying with them to the event.

_____ **5.** Our canine companion rather despises the person who administers his vaccine shots and provides yearly check-ups on his health.

Paraphrasia

A. Steven has a solo in his class's concert performance.

B. Tomorrow I'm going to the grocery store to get some appetizers for the party.

C. Our dog hates the vet.

D. We're carpooling with some other girls to Saturday's soccer game.

E. Our mother has invited some family over for dinner this weekend.

Reading Tip

Fact Check: Always go back to the passage for any question that requires you to paraphrase. The ACT writers expect you to make memory mistakes, so do not fall into that trap. Check the passage every time.

14.3.2 How to Paraphrase

Jerzy Grotowski and Bertolt Brecht are just two of modern theatre's many theorists. Grotowski, a native of Poland, esta blished a theatre in his home country in 1959 that eventu-
5 ally toured around the globe, allowing his work to garner international attention. In 1982 he came to the United States to teach and direct but later moved to Italy, where he died in 1999.

While his early works had always involved
10 the audience in some way, Grotowski came to approach the notion of audience involvement in an entirely new manner: his "poor theatre" recognized the actor-audience relationship as the heart and soul of theatre, and he strove
15 to emphasize that in his work. However, Gro-towski found that by placing audience members onstage in an active role, he was actually in-hibiting their ability to participate: they became too involved in the action to the point of being
20 preoccupied and self-conscious.

As a result Grotowski gave up traditional performance altogether. His notion of "poor the-atre" came to include the use of attendees as part of the drama in keeping with his idea that
25 acting should involve those watching as well. The play became an interactive experience with audience members as part of the cast. Gro-towski's peak was the moment he did not make his acting a function of himself alone. He staged
30 workshops where the actors and audience par-ticipated together in the piece. Workshops in-cluded such concepts as the abstraction of everyday activities (cooking, walking, etc.) and group music-making where participants would
35 find rhythms and melodies using percussion and their own voices.

Grotowski came to include less structure in his theatrical technique, and he came to value the actor's ability to infuse his performance with
40 his own psyche, which, as described by Carl Jung, lay within the collective unconscious. He felt that this goal could be accomplished without the use of an actor's words. He used myths as a basis for some of his plays because he felt that
45 they evoked universal responses.

Eugen Berthold Friedrich Brecht was a native of Bavaria and a committed Marxist who was influenced by Charlie Chaplin's work. Brecht established a writing collective that pro-
50 duced many influential works. He left Germa-ny just after Adolph Hitler assumed power and moved around northern Europe before coming to the United States in 1941.

Blacklisted in Hollywood even though he
55 was not a card-carrying Communist, Brecht's political philosophy nevertheless informed his theater. He was particularly interested in theatre with an instructional purpose representative of his values. His work includes over forty plays
60 and copious amounts of theory in which he out-lines his specific techniques for performance and production. His "epic theatre" was devel-oped with the goal of eschewing the concept of theatre as an artistic pleasantry and implement-
65 ing it as a raw teaching tool. Brecht's desire was for his art to instruct, and he believed that the best way to do so was to abandon escapism and force the audience to evaluate the play not for its aesthetic but for its moral and sociocultur-
70 al value. The play was a sort of artificial reality that was changeable, much as the spectator's own reality.

14.3.2 How to Paraphrase

Brecht used the alienation effect to implement the social change he sought: by breaking the illusion that theatre so often presented, he thought that the audience would be forced to take a step back from the action; therefore, the play would have the biggest possible effect on them. There is merit to this, certainly—Brecht prevented his audience from becoming too caught up in the play itself, and subsequently they were better able to analyze the meaning of the piece. He utilized unique techniques—actors speaking directly to spectators, signs to explain ideas to the audience, brilliant lighting onstage, and songs that broke into the play's action.

Grotowski used his "poor theatre" to encourage self-revelation, while Brecht's "epic theatre" was meant to instigate social change. In their respective spheres, Grotowski minimized theatrical effects and included the audience in workshop-style performances; Brecht interrupted his narratives so as to alienate the audience. Grotowski took his philosophy a step further than Brecht: by engaging the audience rather than alienating them, he built upon Brecht's epic theatre tenets to affect the audience in a more personal way. Unlike Brecht, who used projectors, music, and other pomp to distance his spectators, Grotowski stripped the theatre to its bare minimum, and in doing so he explored the power of the live actor.

In terms of self-revelation, Grotowski's strategy of performance was more successful than Brecht's pursuit of social change. Even Grotowski's first few performances—the forced-participatory plays that he deemed as failures of the "poor theatre"—were inherently self-revelatory. The responses were not unlike spiritual awakenings. Grotowski's actors and audience members learned something about themselves because of the way his workshop format stimulated the creative brain. For Brecht, however, there was no guarantee of success. A play is not enough to galvanize society to change.

14.3.2 How to Paraphrase

1. _____

   _____

   _____

2. _____

   _____

   _____

3. _____

   _____

   _____

4. _____

   _____

   _____

This page is intentionally left blank.

14.4.1 Set One

Passage I

LITERARY NARRATIVE: This passage is adapted from *Swiss Family Robinson* by Johann David Wyss (©1812 by Johann Rudolph Wyss). The narrator is a man whose family was shipwrecked on an island in the East Indies. *Falconhurst* is the name given by the family to the treehouse they built for shelter.

The first thing to be done on the following day was to return to the Calabash Wood to fetch the sled with the dishes, bowls, and baskets we had made. Fritz alone accompanied me. I desired my other boys to remain with
5 their mother, intending to explore beyond the chain of rocky hills and thinking a large party may be undesirable for the trip.

An excellent supper was ready for us, and with thankful hearts we enjoyed it together. Then ascending
10 to our tree-castle and drawing up the ladder after us, we betook ourselves to the repose well-earned and greatly needed after this fatiguing day.

The idea of candle making seemed to have taken the fancy of all the boys. The next morning they woke,
15 one after the other, with the word "candle" on their lips. When they were thoroughly awakened, they continued to talk candles; all during breakfast, candles were the subject of conversation, and after breakfast they would hear of nothing else but setting to work at once and making
20 candles.

"So be it," said I. "Let us become chandlers."

I spoke confidently, but to tell the truth I had in my own mind certain misgivings as to the result of our experiment. In the first place, I knew that we lacked a very
25 important ingredient—animal fat—which is necessary to make candles burn for any length of time with brightness. Besides this, I rather doubted how far my memory would recall the various operations necessary in the manufacture.

Of all this, however, I said nothing. And the boys,
30 under my direction, were soon at work. We first picked off the berries and threw them into a large, shallow iron vessel placed on the fire. The green, sweet-scented wax was rapidly melted, rising to the surface of the juice yielded by the berries. This we skimmed off and placed in
35 a separate pot by the fire, repeating the operation several times until we had collected sufficient liquid wax for our purpose. I then took the wicks my wife had prepared and dipped them one after the other into the wax, handing them as I did so to Fritz, who hung them up on a bush to
40 dry. The coating they thus obtained was not very thick, but by repeating the operation several times, they assumed very fair proportions and became fairly sturdy candles. Our wax being at an end, we hung these in a cool, shady

place to harden. That same night we sat up like civilized
45 beings three whole hours after sunset, and *Falconhurst* was for the first time brilliantly illuminated.

We were all delighted with the success of our experiment.

We were soon obliged to acknowledge that the
50 light they gave was imperfect, and their appearance was unsightly. My wife, too, begged me to find some substitute for the threads of our cotton neckties, which I had previously used as wicks.

To give the proper shape and smoothness to the
55 candles, I determined to use the bamboo molds I had prepared. My first idea was to pour the wax into the mold, and when the candles were cooled, to slip them out. But I was soon convinced that this plan would not succeed. I, therefore, determined to divide the molds lengthways, and
60 then having greased them well, we might pour the melted wax into the two halves bound tightly together and be able to take out the candles when cool without injuring them.

The wicks were my next difficulty, and my wife positively refused to allow us boys to devote our ties and
65 handkerchiefs to the purpose. I took a piece of burnable wood from a tree, which I thought would serve our purpose; this I cut into long slips and fixed in the centers of the molds. My wife, too, prepared some wicks from the fibers of a karata tree, which she declared would entirely
70 surpass mine in quality. We put them to the test.

On a large fire we placed a pot in which we prepared our wax mixture—half beeswax and half wax from the candleberries. The molds, carefully prepared—half with karata fiber and half with wooden splint wicks—stood on
75 their ends in a tub of cold water, ready to receive the wax. They were filled, the wax cooled, the candles taken out and subjected to the criticism of all hands.

When night drew on, they were formally tested. The decision was unanimous: neither gave such a good
80 light as those with the cotton wicks, but even my wife declared that the light from mine was far preferable to that emitted by hers, for the former, though rather flaring, burned brilliantly, while the latter gave out such a feeble and flickering flame that it was almost useless.

Entrance Ticket   Learning Targets   Paraphrase Identification   How to Paraphrase   ACT Practice   Sum It Up

3 ▬▬▬▬▬▬▬▬▬▬▬▬▬▬▬▬▬▬▬▬▬▬▬▬▬▬ **3**

1. According to the passage, the family's final recipe for candle-making consisted of:

   A. candleberries, wooden splint wicks, and bamboo molds.
   B. fire, animal fat, and bamboo molds.
   C. candleberries, animal fat, and bamboo molds.
   D. handkerchiefs, fire, and wooden splint wicks.

2. The second paragraph (lines 8–12) describes the family as ending the day by:

   F. agreeing that they would make candles that evening.
   G. dining and going to bed in their tree-castle.
   H. returning to Calabash Wood to get items they had left there.
   J. falling asleep on the ground among the trees.

3. The third paragraph (lines 13–20) describes the Robinson sons waking to:

   A. discuss their previous candle-making experiences.
   B. complain that they had to eat breakfast without light.
   C. express the desire to make candles.
   D. have unrealistic desires regarding candle-making.

4. The narrator's wife refuses to allow him to use fibers from ties and handkerchiefs as wicks in which of the following ways?

   F. Shyly
   G. Angrily
   H. Pleadingly
   J. Comically

5. The light from the candles with karata fiber wicks is portrayed in the passage as being:

   A. ineffective.
   B. brilliant.
   C. useful.
   D. flaring.

END OF SET ONE
STOP! DO NOT GO ON TO THE NEXT PAGE
UNTIL TOLD TO DO SO.

Entrance Ticket   Learning Targets   Paraphrase Identification   How to Paraphrase   ACT Practice   Sum It Up

14.4.2 Set Two

Passage I

LITERARY NARRATIVE: This passage is adapted from *Dombey and Son* by Charles Dickens (©1848 by Bradbury & Evans).

When at last a son was born to Mr. Dombey, it wakened something at the bottom of his cold and heavy heart that he had never known before. He named the boy Paul and began at once to long for the time when he
5   should become old enough to be a real member of the firm in which all his own interest centered—Dombey and Son. So selfishly was the father's soul wrapped up in this that he scarcely ever noticed his poor, lonely little daughter, Florence, whose warm heart was starving for affection.

10   Little Paul's nurse was very fond of him and Florence, but she had children of her own also. One day, instead of walking up and down with Florence and the baby near the Dombey house, she took the children to another part of the city to visit her own home and children.

15   This resulted in a very unhappy adventure for Florence. On their way home, a mad bull broke away from its keepers and charged through the crowded street. There was great screaming and confusion, and people ran in every direction, Florence among them. She ran for a
20   long way, and when she stopped, her nurse and Paul were nowhere to be seen. Terrified to find herself lost in the great city, she began to cry.

The poor child could think of nothing else but to find her father's office at Dombey and Son, and for two hours
25   she walked, asking directions of everyone she met. She might not have found it at all, but at a wharf where she wandered, there happened to be a young clerk of Dombey and Son's.

This lad's name was Walter Gay. He lived with his
30   uncle, honest and kind-hearted old Solomon Gills—a maker of ship's instruments—who kept a little shop with the wooden figure of a midshipman outside. Very few customers ever came into the shop, and hardly anyone else, for Old Sol had only one intimate friend.

35   This friend was a retired seaman named Captain Cuttle who always dressed in blue as if he were a bird. He had a hook instead of a hand attached to his right wrist, a shirt collar so large that it looked like a small sail, and wherever he went he carried a thick stick that was covered
40   all over (like his nose) with knobs.

Captain Cuttle used to talk on land just as if he were at sea. He would say "Steady!" and "Belay, there!" and called Old Sol "Shipmate," as though the little shop was a ship.

45   But, in spite of his funny ways and talk, Captain Cuttle had a soft, kind heart. He thought old Solomon Gills the greatest man alive and was deeply fond of "Wal'r," as he called the nephew. And, indeed, Walter was as good a boy as he was handsome.

50   Walter soothed Florence's tears and took her, ragged clothes and all, straight home to Solomon Gills's shop, where his uncle gave her a warm supper. Walter ran to the Dombey house with the news that she was found and to retrieve a dress for her to wear.

55   So Florence's adventure turned out well in one way, since through it she met Walter Gay. But Mr. Dombey was angry that anyone should have seen his daughter in such a plight, and he harbored this anger against Walter. Florence, however, never forgot her rescuer after that day.
60   As for Walter, he fell quite in love with her.

It would be a long time until Florence and Walter could consider marriage, however. At home, there were more pressing matters to take up the young girl's attention. Florence loved her little brother very dearly, but Paul, in
65   the constant companionship of his father, grew up without boys or play. His face was old and wistful, and he had an old-fashioned way of brooding in his little armchair beside his father, looking into the fire. He asked strange, wise questions, and the only time he seemed childlike at
70   all was when he was with Florence. He was never well and strong like her. He grew tired easily and used to say that his bones ached.

Mr. Dombey at length grew anxious about Paul's health and sent him and Florence to Brighton, a town on
75   the sea coast, to the house of Mrs. Pipchin, a stooped old lady with a mottled face, a hooked nose, and a hard, gray eye.

Mrs. Pipchin took little children to board; her idea of managing them was to give them everything they didn't
80   like. She lived in a gloomy house, so windy that it sounded to anyone in it like a great shell, held to one's ear, like it or not. The children stayed most of the time in a bare room they called "the dungeon" with a big, ragged fireplace in it. They had only bread and butter and rice to eat, while
85   Mrs. Pipchin had tea and mutton chops and buttered toast and other nice things.

6. In the passage, when Walter found Florence, he calmed her by:

   F. taking her to Solomon Gills's shop.
   G. taking her to a shop to purchase a new dress for her.
   H. preparing her a warm supper.
   J. bringing her brother Paul to his uncle's shop to comfort her.

7. Lines 1–6 most nearly mean that Mr. Dombey:

   A. had been awakened to a deep paternal love when his son was born.
   B. was mainly focused on having his son follow in his footsteps.
   C. prevented his children from suffering ill health.
   D. devoted himself to being a companion for his two children.

8. Based on the passage, Captain Cuttle and Old Sol can reasonably be said to share the following characteristics EXCEPT:

   F. expertise with regard to seagoing vessels.
   G. a relationship with Walter Gay.
   H. a good-natured heart.
   J. experience in making devices for ships.

9. The passage indicates that Captain Cuttle's way of speaking could most likely be described as:

   A. anxious.
   B. reserved.
   C. volatile.
   D. entertaining.

10. In the passage, Mrs. Pipchin managed the children in her boarding house by:

   F. feeding them a poor diet in contrast to her own.
   G. taking them to the sea coast to get fresh air.
   H. making them clean "the dungeon."
   J. putting them in the care of a nurse.

END OF SET TWO
STOP! DO NOT GO ON TO THE NEXT PAGE
UNTIL TOLD TO DO SO.

Entrance Ticket   Learning Targets   Paraphrase Identification   How to Paraphrase   ACT Practice   Sum It Up

3 ▬▬▬▬▬▬▬▬▬▬▬▬▬▬▬▬▬▬▬▬▬▬ **3**

14.4.3 Set Three

Passage IV

NATURAL SCIENCE: This passage is adapted from *Island Fauna* by Pam Braud (©2015 by MasteryPrep).

The Tasmanian tiger, or thylacine, is an extinct mammal that was native to Tasmania. Contrary to its name, the thylacine did not resemble a tiger but rather resembled a large dog with dark stripes. The scientific
5 name of the Tasmanian tiger is *Thylacinus cynocephalus*, meaning "pouched dog with a wolf's head." The adult animal had a length of about six feet.

Originally, the tiger ranged throughout Australia and New Guinea; however, it is believed that its extinction in
10 those two locales was due to predation and competition with the dingo. When Europeans settled in Tasmania in 1803, Tasmanian tigers were prevalent, especially in eucalyptus forests, wetland areas, and native grasslands.

The Tasmanian tiger, though related to the
15 Tasmanian devil, was not as aggressive as either animal's name implied. It preferred to stay isolated from human contact, leaving its home to hunt in open areas at night or early in the morning. The thylacine was carnivorous, eating wallabies, birds, and small animals.

20 Though not particularly fast or graceful, it pursued its prey ceaselessly until the prey was too fatigued to run any farther. It rarely emitted sounds but was known to occasionally bark when agitated or yip when hunting. Unfortunately, no sound recordings of the thylacine's
25 bark exist.

The thylacine's breeding season was most likely during the winter and spring. As with other marsupials, the new babies, usually three in a litter, were tiny and had no hair at birth. The mother had a pouch into which
30 the new babies migrated to feed. When they were large enough to leave the pouch, they lived in a den, a cave, or another well-hidden location. Scientists believe that a thylacine's life expectancy was about five to seven years.

After Europeans arrived in Tasmania, the thylacine
35 was forced to begin a fight for survival. Because the animal preyed on sheep and poultry, the government established a bounty scheme that lasted from 1888 until 1909, which rewarded individuals for killing the animals. By the time the scheme was terminated, the thylacine was
40 rarely seen. A sought-after animal for captivity, the last thylacine was apprehended and sold to a zoo in 1933. It lived only until 1936, the same year the animal was placed on a list of protected wildlife. Unfortunately, in 1986, the thylacine was officially declared an extinct species. The
45 main causes of extinction were assumed to be hunting, the destruction of its habitat, and a disease similar in nature to distemper.

It is notable that in 1863, over a century before the animal became extinct, John Gould, a famous naturalist,
50 foretold the Tasmanian tiger's demise. He stated that when Tasmania "becomes more densely populated and its primitive forests are intersected with roads from the eastern to the western coast, the numbers of this singular animal will speedily diminish, extermination will have its
55 full sway, and it will then, like the wolves in England and Scotland, be recorded as an animal of the past ... "

Since the death of the last known thylacine in 1936, sightings have still been reported. Possibly mistaken, many people hold out hope that the animals they spot
60 are living thylacines even though no one has presented any real evidence of their existence. In an analysis of 320 reported thylacine sightings between 1934 and 1980, Steven Smith determined that about 150 could be considered "good sightings." None of the animals seen,
65 though, were conclusively proven to be Tasmanian tigers. These supposed sightings do not stand alone as trustworthy evidence; although we know that the tiger does not exist on mainland Australia, an equal number of sightings of good quality are reported there. Nevertheless, naturalists
70 have led expeditions into the northern part of Tasmania seeking the thylacine, and some reported finding only possible footprints. Searches of the Tasmanian Wildlife Park and other locales produced no evidence. Some authorities remain hesitant, however, to dogmatically
75 assert that the animal is extinct.

Even though the loss of the Tasmanian tiger is lamentable, the statistics of extinction on the Australian mainland provide some perspective. The thylacine is the only mammal to have disappeared since the time of
80 European settlement, whereas almost half of Australia's native mammals have become extinct over the past two centuries.

Recently, the idea of cloning the thylacine has gained attention. Even if cloning were feasible, some ask,
85 "What about the many other Tasmanian species that are nearly extinct? Is it not more important to discontinue the destruction of the *their* habitats?" The loss of the Tasmanian tiger illustrates the crucial need to maintain Tasmania's natural wealth.

Entrance Ticket   Learning Targets   Paraphrase Identification   How to Paraphrase   ACT Practice   Sum It Up

3 　　　　　　　　　　　　　　　　　　　　　　　　　　 **3**

11. According to the passage, the main focus of naturalists' expeditions into northern Tasmania was:

   A. determining why the Tasmanian tiger is most likely extinct.
   B. conducting scientific research to better understand the thylacine's diet.
   C. finding suitable specimens of the Tasmanian tiger to clone.
   D. searching for possible surviving Tasmanian tigers.

12. According to the passage, the main focus of legislation in the late 1800s to the early 1900s was:

   F. saving the tiger from extinction in Australia and New Guinea.
   G. placing thylacines in zoos around the world in order to preserve them.
   H. hunting thylacines that preyed on farm animals.
   J. declaring the thylacine among Australia's endangered species.

13. Which of the following does NOT reasonably describe the transition the author presents in lines 34–35?

   A. Silent to audible
   B. Predator to prey
   C. Free to threatened
   D. Unlimited to limited

14. Which of the following does NOT reasonably describe the transition the author presents in lines 57–58?

   F. Final to unsettled
   G. Inaccurate to accurate
   H. Conclusive to inconclusive
   J. Impossible to possible

15. The author characterizes the effect of the Tasmanian tiger's extinction most nearly as:

   A. upsetting but blameless.
   B. lamentable and unavoidable.
   C. regretful and insightful.
   D. interesting but insignificant.

END OF SET THREE
STOP! DO NOT GO ON TO THE NEXT PAGE
UNTIL TOLD TO DO SO.

Entrance Ticket　　Learning Targets　　Paraphrase Identification　　How to Paraphrase　　ACT Practice　　Sum It Up

Sum It Up

Paraphrase

Paraphrase
To express the meaning of a passage in different words, often for conciseness and clarity

Tips and Techniques

Fact Check: Always go back to the passage for any question that requires you to paraphrase. The ACT writers expect you to make memory mistakes, but do not fall into that trap. Check the passage every time.

Point of View

CAPTION:

15.1 Entrance Ticket

In one paragraph (5-7 sentences), explain what is happening in the cartoon below.

_____

_____

_____

_____

_____

_____

_____

_____

_____

_____

_____

_____

15.2 Learning Targets

1. Identify the narrator in ACT Reading passages

2. Infer a narrator's opinion and/or attitude

3. Identify which characters hold certain opinions in the Reading passages

Self-Assessment

Circle the number that corresponds to your confidence level in your knowledge of this subject before beginning the lesson. A score of 1 means you are completely lost, and a score of 4 means you have mastered the skills. After you finish the lesson, return to the bottom of this page and circle your new confidence level to show your improvement.

Before Lesson

1   2   3   4

After Lesson

1   2   3   4

15.3.1 Point of View as Perspective

15.3.1 Point of View as Perspective

_____

_____

_____

_____

_____

_____

_____

_____

_____

_____

_____

_____

_____

_____

_____

_____

_____

Reading Tip

In point of view ACT questions, you must choose the answer choice that best completes the following statement: _The point of view from which the passage is told is best described as that of..._ When faced with this kind of question, you must:

1. Identify the narrator.
2. Find details describing the narrator.
3. Choose the answer supported by those details.

15.3.1 Point of View as Perspective

If we enter some profession, we find ourselves constantly faced by the need to persuade people above us, below us, and all around us. So all-inclusive is this power that if we will think the matter out clearly, we will see that the answer to the problem of every human being, diverse as these problems are, may be summed up in two brief colloquial injunctions, namely: first have the goods, then be able to sell them. Salesmanship is only the commercial name for persuasion.

Perspective:_____

Laura's mother, Avis, always keeps her houses as "neat as a pin." Though Laura tries her best to avoid adopting her mother's personality quirks, that phrase was likely passed down by Avis herself. Avis calls a small gift a "happy," and Laura, too, finds herself picking up little tokens for friends and passing them along with, "Just a little happy. Thinking of you.

Perspective:_____

15.3.2 Point of View as Opinion

"Maybe these new glasses will help you see things
from my perspective!"

15.3.2 Point of View as Opinion

Not one of the Old Italian Masters has taken such a firm hold upon the popular imagination as Raphael. Other artists wax and wane in public favor as they are praised by one generation of critics or disparaged by the next, but Raphael's name continues to stand in public estimation as that of the favorite painter in all of the world. The passing centuries do not dim his fame, though he is subjected to severe criticism; and he continues, as he began, as the first love of the people.

The subjects of his pictures are nearly all of a cheerful nature. He exercised his skill for the most part on scenes that were agreeable to contemplate. Pain and ugliness were strangers to his art; he was preeminently the artist of joy. This is to be attributed not only to his pleasure-loving nature but also to the great influence upon him of the rediscovery of Greek art in his day, an art which dealt distinctively with objects of delight.

Moreover, Raphael is compassionate toward mind as well as heart; he requires of us neither too strenuous feeling nor too much thinking. As his subjects do not overtax the sympathies with harrowing emotions, neither does his art overtax the understanding with complicated effects. His pictures are apparently so simple that they demand no great intellectual effort and no technical education to enjoy them. He does all the work for us, and his art is too perfect to astonish. It was not his way to show what difficult things he could do, but he made it appear that great art is the easiest thing in the world. This ease was, however, the result of a splendid mastery of his art. Thus he arranges the fifty-two figures in The School of Athens or the three figures of Madonna of the Chair, so simply and unobtrusively that we might imagine such feats were an everyday affair. Yet in both cases he solves most difficult problems of com¬position with a success scarcely paralleled in the history of art."

Opinions: _____

_____

_____

_____

_____

_____

_____

_____

15.3.2 Point of View as Opinion

"There is one name," according to Elbert Hubbard, "that stands out in history like a beacon after twenty-five hundred years have passed, just because the man had the sublime genius of discovering ability. That man is Pericles. Pericles made Athens, and today Athens is being sifted and searched for relics and remnants of the things made by people who were led by the men of ability who were discovered by Pericles."

The remark of Andrew Carnegie—that he won his success because he had the knack of picking the right men—has become a classic in current speech. Augustus Caesar built up and extended the power of the Roman Empire because he knew how to select the right people. The careers of Charlemagne, Napoleon, Washington, Lincoln, and all the empire builders hold their places in history because these men knew how to recognize, how to select and how to develop the abilities of their colleagues—how to unearth men of genius.

The glory that was Greece shined forth because Pericles kindled its flame and ushered in a Golden Age. He could have done the same in any time and among any people. Had Carnegie lived in any other day and sought his industrial giants, he would no doubt have found them. If a supreme judge of latent talent can always find greatness, it follows that humanity is rich in undiscovered genius—that, in the human race, there are untapped possibilities for a millennium of Golden Ages. Psychologists tell us that only a very small percentage of the real ability and energy of the average man is ever developed or used. There has been only one Pericles in all of history. Great geniuses in the discovery, development, and management of men are rarely acknowledged. Most men never meet them.

Opinions: _____

_____

_____

Reading Tip

When questions ask whether a statement or description is *best described as the opinion of...* you must:

1. Assess the answer choices. Can you remember the opinions or ideas of any of these people?
2. Make sure you can find details in the passage to support the answer choice you think is correct.
3. If you cannot remember or find who held that opinion, eliminate answer options that are not supported by the passage.

3 ▬▬▬▬▬▬▬▬▬▬▬▬▬▬▬▬ **3**

15.4.1 Set One

Passage III

HUMANITIES: This passage is adapted from the essay "On Lying Awake at Night" by Stewart Edward White, which appeared in Christopher Morley's *Modern Essays* (©1921 by Harcourt, Brace).

Every so often you are due to lie awake at night. Why this is so I have never been able to discover. It apparently comes from no predisposing uneasiness of indigestion, no rashness in the matter of too much tea, no excitation of
5　unusual incident or stimulating conversation. In fact you turn in with the expectation of rather a good night's rest. Almost at once, however, the little noises of the forest grow larger, blending in the hollow bigness of the first drowse; your thoughts drift idly back and forth between
10　reality and dream, when—snap!—you are broad awake!

Perhaps the reservoir of your vital forces is full to the overflow, or perhaps, more subtly, the great Mother insists that you enter the temple of her larger mysteries.

For, unlike mere insomnia, lying awake at night in
15　the woods is pleasant. The eager, nervous straining for sleep gives way to a delicious indifference. You do not care. Your mind is cradled in an exquisite poppy-suspension of judgment and thought. Impressions slip vaguely into your consciousness and as vaguely out again. Some-
20　times they stand stark and naked for your inspection; sometimes they lose themselves in the mist of half-sleep. Always they lay soft velvet fingers on the drowsy imagination, so that in their caressing you feel the vaster spaces from which they have come. Peaceful brooding your fac-
25　ulties receive. Hearing, sight, smell—all are preternaturally keen to whatever sensations of sound and sight and woods are abroad through the night; yet at the same time, active appreciation dozes, so these things lie on it sweet and cloying like fallen rose leaves.

30　In such circumstance you will hear what the voyageurs call the voices of the rapids. Many people never hear them at all. Their speech is soft and low and distinct beneath the steady roar and dashing, beneath even the lesser tinklings and gurglings whose quality superimposes
35　them over the louder sounds. They are like the tear-forms swimming across the field of vision, which disappear so quickly when you concentrate your sight to look at them and reappear so magically when again your gaze turns vacant. In the stillness of your hazy half-consciousness,
40　they speak; when you bend your attention to listen, they are gone, and only the tumults and the tinklings remain.

Nothing is more fantastically unreal to tell about—nothing more concretely real to experience—than this undernote of the quick water. And when you do lie awake at
45　night, it is always making its unobtrusive appeal.

Gradually its hypnotic spell works. The distant chimes ring louder and nearer as you cross the borderland of sleep. And then outside the tent, some little woods noise snaps the thread. An owl hoots, a whippoorwill
50　cries, a twig cracks beneath the cautious prowl of some night creature—at once the yellow sunlit French meadows puff away—you are staring at the blurred image of the moon spraying through the texture of your tent.

No beverage is more gratefully received than the
55　cup of spring water you drink at such a time—no moment more refreshing than that in which you look about you at the darkened forest. You have cast from you with the warm blanket the drowsiness of dreams. A coolness, physical and spiritual, bathes you from head to foot. All
60　your senses are keyed to the last vibrations. You hear the littler night prowlers; you glimpse the greater. A faint, searching woods perfume of dampness greets your nostrils. And somehow, mysteriously, in a manner not to be understood, the forces of the world seem in suspense, as
65　though a touch might crystallize infinite possibilities into infinite power and motion. But the touch lacks. The forces hover on the edge of action, unheeding the little noises. In all humbleness and awe, you are a dweller of the Silent Places.

70　At such a time, you will meet with adventures. One night we put fourteen inquisitive porcupines out of camp. Near McGregor's Bay, I discovered in the large grass park of my campsite nine deer, cropping the herbage like so many beautiful ghosts. A friend tells me of a fawn that
75　every night used to sleep outside his tent within a foot of his head, probably by way of protection against wolves. Its mother had in all likelihood been killed. The instant my friend moved toward the tent opening, the little creature would disappear, and it was always gone by earliest
80　daylight. Nocturnal bears in search of pork are not uncommon. But even though your interest meets nothing but the bats and the woods shadows and the stars, the few moments of the sleeping world force a spiritual experience to be gained in no other way. You cannot know the night by
85　sitting up; she will sit up with you. Only by coming into her presence from the borders of sleep can you meet her face to face in her intimate mood.

The night wind from the river, or from the open spaces of the wilds, chills you after a time. You begin to
90　think of your blankets. In a few moments, you roll yourself in their soft wool. Instantly it is morning.

And, strange to say, you have not to pay by going through the day unrefreshed. You may feel like turning in at eight instead of nine, and you may fall asleep
95　with unusual promptitude, but your journey will begin clear-headedly, proceed springily, and end with much in reserve. No languor, no dull headache, no exhaustion follows your experience. For this once, your two hours of sleep have been as effective as nine.

Entrance Ticket　Learning Targets　Point of View as Perspective　Point of View as Opinion　ACT Practice　Sum It Up

3 3

1. The passage is best described as being told from the perspective of an outdoorsman who is:

   A. describing the ways in which camping in the solitude of the forest has cured him of insomnia.
   B. presenting a detailed list of encounters with forest inhabitants on one particular camping trip.
   C. advocating engagement with the forest in ways that will bring restfulness and spiritual fulfillment.
   D. reflecting on the fear and loneliness he felt during his first night camping in the forest.

2. Which of the following statements about nature would be most aligned with the narrator's opinions?

   F. Communing with nature can be exhausting and lonely but full of adventure.
   G. The most rewarding aspect of outdoor camping is a long and peaceful sleep.
   H. The cacophony of noises in the forest at night make it impossible to rest.
   J. Nighttime envelops the woods, transcending time and refreshing the mind.

3. The author's perspective on the atmosphere of the forest at night is most nearly that of:

   A. admiration and reverence.
   B. disinterest and ambivalence.
   C. excitement and confusion.
   D. abhorrence and discomfort.

4. The author presents the qualities of the woods at night as exceptional because at night he:

   F. is able to experience the most peaceful qualities of the forest.
   G. is not in a rush like he is during the day.
   H. is able to get a long and restful sleep on the forest floor.
   J. has delightful dreams about the woods and nature.

5. The passage suggests that while lying in his tent and hearing nighttime animal noises in the forest (lines 46-51), the narrator feels:

   A. exhausted and would rather be at home in his own bed instead of his tent.
   B. terrified by the nearness of the animals, afraid of a bear attack.
   C. accepting of the interruption but unable to sleep through them.
   D. refreshed after his long sleep and ready to get back to his everyday life.

END OF SET ONE
STOP! DO NOT GO ON TO THE NEXT PAGE
UNTIL TOLD TO DO SO.

Entrance Ticket   Learning Targets   Point of View as Perspective   Point of View as Opinion   ACT Practice   Sum It Up

3 ⬛⬛⬛⬛⬛⬛⬛⬛⬛⬛ 3

15.4.2 Set Two

Passage I

LITERARY NARRATIVE: This passage is adapted from the novella *The Metamorphosis* by Franz Kafka (©1915 by Kurt Wolff Verlag).

One morning, when Gregor Samsa woke from troubled dreams, he found himself transformed into a cockroach. He lay on his armor-like back, and if he lifted his head a little, he could see his brown belly, slightly
5 domed and divided by arches into stiff sections. The bedding was hardly able to cover it and seemed ready to slide off any moment. His many legs, pitifully thin compared with the size of the rest of him, waved about helplessly as he looked.

10 "What's happened to me?" he thought. It wasn't a dream. His room, a proper human room although a little too small, lay peacefully between its four familiar walls. A collection of textile samples lay spread out on the table—Samsa was a traveling salesman—and above
15 it there hung a picture that he had recently cut out of an illustrated magazine and housed in a nice, gilded frame. It showed a lady fitted out with a fur hat and fur boa who sat upright, raising a heavy fur muff that covered the whole of her lower arm towards the viewer.

20 Gregor then turned to look out the window at the dull weather. Drops of rain could be heard hitting the pane, which made him feel quite sad. "How about if I sleep a little bit longer and forget all this nonsense," he thought, but that was something he was unable to do because he
25 was used to sleeping on his right, and in his present state he couldn't get into that position. However hard he threw himself onto his right, he always rolled back to where he was. He must have tried a hundred times, shutting his eyes so that he wouldn't have to look at the floundering legs,
30 and he only stopped when he began to feel a mild, dull pain there that he had never felt before.

"Oh, dear," he thought, "what a strenuous career it is that I've chosen! Traveling day in and day out. Doing business like this takes much more effort than doing your
35 own business at home, and on top of that there's the curse of traveling, worries about making train connections, bad and irregular food, contact with different people all the time so that you can never get to know anyone or become friendly with them." He felt a slight itch up on
40 his belly, pushed himself slowly up on his back toward the headboard so that he could lift his head better, found where the itch was and saw that it was covered with lots of little white spots that he didn't know what to make of, and when he tried to feel the place with one of his legs, he
45 drew it quickly back because as soon as he touched it he was overcome by a cold shudder.

He slid back into his former position. "Getting up early all the time," he thought, "it makes you stupid. Other traveling salesmen live a life of luxury. For instance,
50 whenever I go back to the guest house during the morning to copy out the contract, these gentlemen are always sitting there eating their breakfasts. I ought to just try that with my boss; I'd get kicked out on the spot. If I didn't have my parents to think about, I'd have given my notice
55 a long time ago. I'd have gone up to the boss and told him just what I think, tell him everything I would, let him know just what I feel. He'd fall right off his desk! Well, there's still some hope; once I've got the money together to pay off my parents' debt to him—another five or six
60 years I suppose—that's definitely what I'll do. First of all, though, I've got to get up; my train leaves at five."

And he looked at the alarm clock, ticking on the chest of drawers. "Good heavens!" he thought. It was half past six, and the hands were quietly moving forward. Had
65 the alarm clock not rung? He could see from the bed that it had been set for four o'clock, as it should have been; it certainly must have rung. Yes, but was it possible to quietly sleep through that furniture-rattling noise? True, he had not slept peacefully, but probably all the more
70 deeply because of that. What should he do now?

The next train went at seven; if he were to catch it, he would have to rush like mad, but the collection of samples was still not packed, and he did not at all feel particularly fresh and lively. And even if he did catch the train, he
75 would not avoid his boss's anger, as the office assistant would have been there to see the five o'clock train go, and he would have put in his report about Gregor's not being there a long time ago. The office assistant was the boss's man—spineless and with no understanding.

80 What if he reported sick? But that would be extremely strained and suspicious, as in fifteen years of service Gregor had never once yet been ill. His boss would certainly come round with the doctor from the medical insurance company, accuse his parents of having a lazy
85 son, and accept the doctor's recommendation not to make any claim, as the doctor believed that no one was ever ill but that many were workshy. And what's more, would he have been entirely wrong in this case? Gregor did, in fact, apart from excessive sleepiness after sleeping for so
90 long, feel completely well and even felt much hungrier than usual.

Entrance Ticket · Learning Targets · Point of View as Perspective · Point of View as Opinion · ACT Practice · Sum It Up

3   **3**

6. The passage is best described as being primarily focused on Gregor Samsa, a man who has:

   F. undergone a transformation but is distracted by other problems.

   G. become fed up with his menial job and is considering quitting.

   H. missed the early train to the city and is rushing to catch the next one.

   J. called in sick to work but is feeling guilty for his laziness.

7. Which of the following statements best describes Gregor Samsa's primary state of mind when he wakes up on the morning recounted in the passage?

   A. He feels that his parents have always been more worried about him than they should be.

   B. He is unsure how to balance being a vermin with his career as a salesman.

   C. He wants his new illness to remain hidden from his boss, as well as the office assistant.

   D. He takes his transformation rather well, focusing more on how he will get to work.

8. Gregor Samsa's perspective of and approach toward his job as a salesman is most nearly that of:

   F. a diligent and tireless go-getter.

   G. a burnt-out but obligated workhorse.

   H. a carefree and lazy dreamer.

   J. an uncomplaining but dishonest employee.

9. One of the main points in the sixth paragraph (lines 62–70) is that, concerning his being late to work, Gregor Samsa is most nearly experiencing the emotion of:

   A. panic.

   B. anger.

   C. apathy.

   D. triumph.

10. The passage suggests that concerning his current predicament, Gregor Samsa feels:

   F. nervous that his parents will be upset when they learn he has undergone a transformation.

   G. concerned about being late for work but unconcerned that he has turned into a vermin.

   H. upset that his boss has sent for his doctor but grateful that he is not ill.

   J. confident that he has enough time to get to the station and make the early train to work.

END OF SET TWO
STOP! DO NOT GO ON TO THE NEXT PAGE
UNTIL TOLD TO DO SO.

Entrance Ticket   Learning Targets   Point of View as Perspective   Point of View as Opinion   ACT Practice   Sum It Up

15.4.3 Set Three

Passage IV

NATURAL SCIENCE: This passage was adapted from the "Veta la Palma" by Seymour Pacheco (©2015 by MasteryPrep). *Aquaculture* is the farming of water-based organisms, such as fish and crustaceans.

The Veta la Palma Estate is one example of how commercial aquaculture has been integrated into the surrounding environment in an effort to improve sustainability while maintaining a sought-after product
5 for food distributors and chefs.

"For the past 50 years, we've been fishing the seas like we clear-cut forests," lamented Dan Barber, a food activist and James Beard Award-winning chef. "It's hard to overstate the destruction." With wild fish stocks
10 declining precipitously around the globe, aquaculture has emerged as perhaps the only viable way to satisfy the world's appetite for fish fingers and maki rolls. But most fish farms—even ones heralded as "sustainable"—create as many problems as they solve, from fecal contamination
15 to the threat that escaped cultivated fish pose to the gene pool of their wild cousins. Veta la Palma is meant to stand as proof that fish can be raised in a manner that actually enhances its surrounding ecosystem.

Located on an island in the Guadalquivir River
20 in southwestern Spain, the estate holds the unusual distinction of being a commercial fish farm that doubles as an important habitat for wintering and breeding bird populations, including some rare and endangered species.

The marsh certainly looks different today than it did
25 thirty-three years ago, when it was an Argentine-owned beef cattle farm. "They did it by draining the land," said Barber. "Ecologically, it was a disaster. It killed like ninety percent of the birds." The Spanish company Pesquerías Isla Mayor, S.A. (PIMSA) purchased the land in 1982,
30 intent on building economic value, while improving the ecology of the area.

The result was a pioneering integration of aquaculture with the recovery of disturbed salt marshes. Using a pump system and the original drainage channels to bring in
35 water from the estuary, PIMSA reflooded the wetlands to create a 27,000-acre fish farm comprised of forty-five interconnected ponds, which are joined to the local river system. The brackish water teems with microalgae and tiny translucent shrimp, which provide natural food for
40 the fish that Veta la Palma raises. This is another rarity for an industry in which feed sourcing has become an essential concern. "Take tuna," said Barber. "It takes fifteen pounds of wild fish to get you one pound of farm

tuna—not very sustainable." But by hewing as closely as
45 possible to nature, Veta la Palma avoids this and many of the problems that plague other aquaculture projects. Low density—roughly four kilograms of fish to every cubic meter of water—helps keep the fish free of parasites. And the abundant plant life circling its ponds acts as a filter,
50 cleansing the water of nitrogen and phosphates.

Miguel Medialdea, a biologist on the estate, acknowledges that allowing the farm to function as a wild bird sanctuary does impact the bottom line. Looking out on the carpet of flamingos that covers one of the lagoons,
55 he shrugged. "They take about twenty percent of our annual yield," he said, pointing at a blush-colored bird as it scoops up a sea bass.

But the birds are also a sign of Veta la Palma's ecological health, something on which its clients place
60 a high value. The farm produces 1,500 tons of sea bass, bream, red mullet, and shrimp each year for gourmet food shops, high quality food distributors, and haute cuisine chefs in Germany, the United States, and Mediterranean countries.

65 Having experts like Dan Barber advocate its methods has also raised the farm's public profile, potentially leading to wider adoption of its model. His 2010 TED Talk on Veta la Palma, titled "How I Fell in Love with a Fish," currently has more than 1.7 million views.

70 But sustainability is only part of the draw for chefs like Barber; the other is superior flavor. Chef Dani García, of the Michelin-starred restaurant Calima in Marbella marvels that the estate's catch "actually tastes better than most wild sea bass."

75 Medialdea is proud to point out that Veta la Palma's mission goes beyond simply "provisioning" for its ecosystem. By reflooding the drained wetlands and creating more than 100 islands for nesting waterfowl, the farm has actually boosted the region's biodiversity.
80 "Because of our artificial intervention, the natural environment is improved," he said. "The point isn't to make use and conservation compatible. The point is to use in order to conserve."

The possibility now exists that Veta la Palma's model
85 will help shape public policy, at least in Europe. As a result of its efforts to integrate aquaculture and marsh area restoration, the estate has been included as a partner in the SEAFARE project (Sustainable and Environmentally Friendly Aquaculture in the Atlantic Region of Europe)—
90 led by an interregional European consortium—which is focused on the need for environmentally sustainable aquaculture.

Entrance Ticket   Learning Targets   Point of View as Perspective   Point of View as Opinion   ACT Practice   Sum It Up

3 ▬▬▬▬▬▬▬▬▬▬▬▬▬▬▬▬ **3**

11. The passage is best described as being told from the point of view of a someone who is:

   A. cataloguing instances of fish stock shortages in the Guadalquivir River.
   B. chronicling the key events in Veta la Palma's transformation from cattle farm to sustainable aquaculture.
   C. outlining the novel farming methods employed at Veta la Palma, along with their benefits to both the environment and the fish market.
   D. advising farmers on how to update their commercial aquaculture operations.

12. In the passage, the idea that traditional tuna farming is not sustainable is most clearly described as the opinion of:

   F. Dan Barber, which he gives as a reason for not supporting aquaculture.
   G. Dan Barber, which he voices in reference to the high ratio of feed required.
   H. Miguel Medialdea, which he states to the author in support of Veta la Palma.
   J. Dan Barber, which contradicted his earlier endorsement of tuna farming methods.

13. The author's attitude toward Dan Barber in the passage is best described as that of:

   A. a close friend but professional rival.
   B. a skeptical food critic and opponent.
   C. an enthusiastic but misguided admirer.
   D. an unbiased and optimistic reporter.

14. The point of view from which the passage is told is best described as that of:

   F. a young tourist traveling through an estuary in southern Spain.
   G. an environmental activist concerned about the need for sustainable aquaculture.
   H. a reporter describing the significance of an unusual method of fish farming.
   J. a reporter cataloguing the history of commercial aquaculture.

15. That Veta la Palma's farm-raised sea bass taste better than most wild sea bass is most clearly described in the passage as the opinion of:

   A. Dani Garcia.
   B. the founders of PIMSA.
   C. Dan Barber.
   D. traditional aquaculturalists.

END OF SET THREE
STOP! DO NOT GO ON TO THE NEXT PAGE
UNTIL TOLD TO DO SO.

Entrance Ticket   Learning Targets   Point of View as Perspective   Point of View as Opinion   ACT Practice   Sum It Up

Sum It Up

Point of View

Inference
A conclusion based on evidence and reasoning

Point of View
The position from which a story is told or observed

First Person
I do / I eat / I run

Second Person
you do / you eat / you run

Third Person
he does / she eats / it runs

Tips and Techniques

In point of view ACT questions, you must choose the answer choice that best completes the following statement: *The point of view from which the passage is told is best described as that of...* When faced with this kind of question, you must:

1. Identify the narrator.
2. Find details describing the narrator.
3. Choose the answer supported by those details.

When questions ask whether a statement or description is *best described as the opinion of...* you must:

1. Assess the answer options. Can you remember the opinions or ideas of any of these people?
2. Make sure you can find details in the passage to support the answer choice you think is correct.
3. If you cannot remember or find who had that opinion, eliminate answer options that are not supported by the passage.

Compare Two Texts

Passage A

Passage B

CAPTION:

16.1 Entrance Ticket

Read the passage below and answer the questions.

Passage A

High schools are institutions of learning with a primary goal of preparing young adults for the real world. The sizes of high schools usually allow the student population to be well acquainted with one another. The smallest high schools may have less than one hundred students while the very largest may be home to a few thousand high school students. Usually, high schools are structured so that students can become tightly knit in their communities. This way, everyone is in the same boat.

Students often share many classes with the same group of students over several years, and attendance policies in high schools are rigid. In high school students must attend class; the law requires that all minors attend school without truancy issues until they reach a certain age. This policy has been adopted in the hopes of ensuring as many students as possible complete their high school educations and are able to continue their educations or enter the workforce.

Passage B

University campuses can often look as large and rich as sprawling cities. In fact, over the years, many universities have grown to accommodate student populations in the tens of thousands. The hustle and bustle is constant. At all times of the day (and night), students come and go, rarely seeing the same people more than once in a day. This accounts for fewer people being acquainted with each other, and contributes to the city-like atmosphere of a university campus.

University life also introduces students to new responsibilities. There are no laws that require students to come to class; any attendance policy, if there is such a policy at all, is only between the professor and the student. Even if they do miss or skip classes, students may generally refer to the class syllabus or talk with their classmates and instructors to make up missed assignments or tests. This newfound responsibility, coupled with increased academic rigor in coursework, creates an opportunity for students to develop and face the challenges of professional life.

1. Provide one similarity between high schools and universities as found in the passages. What do high schools and universities have in common?

_____

_____

Entrance Ticket   Learning Targets   Comparing Two Texts   Different Perspectives   ACT Practice   Sum It Up

16.1 Entrance Ticket

2. Provide one difference between high schools and universities as found in the passages. What are some features of high school that are not present in universities? Features of universities that are not present in high school?

_____

_____

3. Which of the passages describes a change over time for one of the institutions? What change occurred?

_____

_____

4. Identify the use of figurative or metaphorical language from each passage. What was this language used to describe?

_____

_____

16.2 Learning Targets

1. Identify similarities between two different reading passages

2. Analyze the content of two reading passages together

Self-Assessment

Circle the number that corresponds to your confidence level in your knowledge of this subject before beginning the lesson. A score of 1 means you are completely lost, and a score of 4 means you have mastered the skills. After you finish the lesson, return to the bottom of this page and circle your new confidence level to show your improvement.

Before Lesson

1   2   3   4

After Lesson

1   2   3   4

16.3.1 Comparing Two Texts

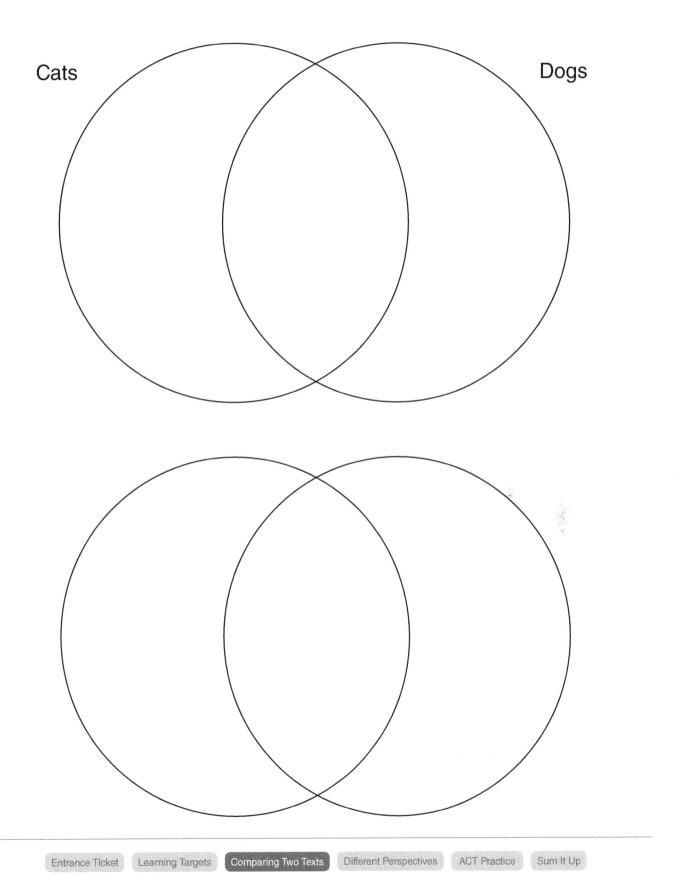

Cats   Dogs

16.3.1 Comparing Two Texts

Passage A

When it comes to flying, people have long lists of complaints: canceled flights, system crashes that keep people from checking in, long lines in security, and crowded airplanes. I, however, have found much to enjoy about flying. I travel a few times out of the year to visit family or go on vacation in Florida. These trips by car would take several days and lots of money spent on gas and hotels; by plane I can get there
5 in a day, and with frequent flyer miles I usually get a discount on tickets. I love the sensation of being in airports: it's like I'm in a completely new world, joined together with people of every culture and color. I feel like a seasoned traveler as I navigate the terminals, reading gate signs, noting where the best food options are located, eyeing the arrivals and departures screens as I bustle down the moving sidewalk. I have very little on me: flipflops so I can kick them off in security, a light jacket if the plane is cold, and a pen
10 and notebook so I can jot down the interesting people and scenes I witness while waiting to soar 30,000 feet above the earth.

Passage B

With the slam of car doors and the turn of a key, we are on our way. Over breakfast, the weatherman on TV said to expect another scorcher, but cool air comes through our rolled down windows as I pull the car out of the hotel parking lot. My friend in the passenger seat scans the radio for music, and all
15 of us laugh about who snored the loudest last night. In minutes we're on the interstate, and within an hour everyone but me has fallen asleep. As my hotel coffee went from steaming to lukewarm, the city had dropped away from the interstate. Now there are only random towns taking advantage of travelers looking for gas or a restroom. The road rumbles endlessly under the wheels, carrying me into the horizon, stretched green and flat across my windshield. It sounds lonely to drive for hours through the middle of
20 nowhere while a car full of friends catch up on lost sleep. But this is my favorite part of road trips: when it's just me and an empty road going wherever, forever. When the scenery opens up to large bands of sky and fields, suddenly possibilities seem endless, the future looms just as large and full of just as much promise.

Reading Tip

One at a Time: When you see two texts in a reading passage, read Passage A and then answer the questions designated to that passage. Do this *before* you move onto Passage B and its questions so that you don't confuse which detail came from which passage.

16.3.2 Different Perspectives

Passage A

Ongoing research confirms the belief that participating in school sports is quite beneficial for young people. Rates of depression and anxiety are lower for student athletes, compared to their peers who do not participate in sports. Various factors indicating health, socialization, and community values rank higher in this group as well as predictable long-term effects. In other words, a teenager who spends four years in
5   high school playing for a sports team is more likely to choose athletic extracurriculars in college, and he or she is more likely to continue an active lifestyle as he or she grows older, enters the workforce, and starts raising children. Additionally, despite the negative stereotype of the "dumb jock," statistics prove that young people who play competitive sports during middle school and high school tend to have a higher GPA and spend more hours studying than students who are not involved in any extracurricular activity.

Passage B

10   I play defense on my high school's soccer team. Game days are always exciting, and I admit it's hard to focus on whatever is going on in class that day. Practice days can be pretty grueling—especially drills—but it pays off when we score a victory. Most of my friends are also on the team. Since we spend several months playing and practicing, it's natural to spend our free time together, too. When we win a game, we usually celebrate by going out to eat or getting together at a teammate's house. Right now I have
15   a lingering ankle sprain that I have to keep on ice. I'm disappointed that I can't play in the tournament this weekend, but at least I can cheer on my friends and teammates from the sidelines.

If the writer of Passage A were to add more information to Passage B, he would likely give details that describe:
A. the narrator's study habits and school grades.
B. what a typical day of practice is like.
C. how many students suffer from anxiety who do not play sports.
D. the various positions one can play on a soccer team.

Reading Tip

Put Yourself in Their Shoes: If a question asks what one passage would say or do about another passage, pretend that you are the writer for the first passage. Ask yourself what details are most important to you, and look for answers that are similar to these details.

16.4.1 Set One

Passage II

SOCIAL SCIENCE: Passage A is adapted from the book *Split: The Intersection of Pleasure and Purpose in Modern Art* by Emmanuel Nguyen (©2017 MasteryPrep). Passage B is adapted from the article "The Unvalued *Parade*" by Johnathon Simien (©2017 by MasteryPrep).

Passage A by Emmanuel Nguyen

Surrealism was just entering the art world, and its introduction was the type of wonderful scandal that amused only the artists themselves. Patrons were scandalized by what an art critic at the time described as a "destructive
[5] thing." In the buildup to the second world war, surrealist artists throughout Europe had not yet achieved any goal except offending those whom they disdained.

For good reason, of course. Surrealism represented a rejection of form and logic, incorporating base objects
[10] and propaganda, flying in the face of proper society, and blasting social mores in the most dramatic and gasp-worthy fashion. The gatekeepers of the art world reacted in a predictable, pearl-clutching fashion. They penned scathing articles in their art magazines, writing in painstaking
[15] detail about the risk such artists posed to society, religion, and the world as a whole. They refused to show any surrealist works in their studios and responded derisively when more enlightened critics lobbied on behalf of the artists. Some offended critics even took artists to court based on
[20] their coarse subject matters and presentations.

Angry art socialites were hardly the only problem. Early surrealists, who called themselves Dadas, found it difficult to expand their audience beyond their own circle of likeminded artists. Their target audience was not the
[25] average person, and their art was not so much presentation as commentary against the "bourgeoisie" who they felt were responsible for the war. Unfortunately, these targets of their social commentary did not receive the criticism except to dismiss it as crude and unpalatable. Instead of
[30] comprehending the implications of the work and internalizing those criticisms, the intended targets merely sneered.

A work which is now held in great esteem, Duchamp's *The Fountain*, was rejected outright from the Society of Independent Artists exhibition. Indeed, so initial-
[35] ly ineffective was the attempted social commentary that deriding the surrealist artists became a popular pastime among the social elite.

Passage B by Johnathon Simien

In 1917, Jean Cocteau debuted a one-act ballet called *Parade* that included music by Erik Satie, choreog-
[40] raphy by Léonide Massine, and costume and set design by none other than Pablo Picasso. The creators came up with some innovative ideas. Instead of the ornate sets of typical ballets, *Parade* was set on the common streets of Paris and involved a lowly troupe of entertainers desperately trying
[45] to gain an audience. It was edgy! It was exciting!

Unfortunately, it was also strange. The ballet audience had little experience or appreciation for such things. At the premiere, this traditional audience "exploded in a sea of boos and hisses," reported one art historian, "they
[50] just did not understand what Cocteau was trying to say."

Parade didn't have the expected tropes or visuals common to the ballets of the time. Instead of ethereal waifs dancing around a garden, audiences were treated to cubist buildings and carnival barkers. The costumes,
[55] while visually striking, were comprised of cardboard which hindered the dancers' movements. Movement is an important part for dance, of course, but other parts of the ballet worked well. The score, for example, contained various "noise makers" such as typewriters, horns. . . and
[60] an assortment of milk bottles. The audience thought they were being tricked!

After May 18, 1917, Cocteau's Friday night debut, *Parade* was performed only six more times in the next 50 years. Though some critics understood and appreci-
[65] ated what the collaborators were attempting, the ballet simply could not find an audience. "Even fans of Picasso and other progressive artists were dismayed because they felt that he had sold out by working to produce a ballet," explained historian James Hayden, "they considered that
[70] art form to be the epitome of the classist, materialistic art that they fought against. They were disgusted."

But angry, progressive fans were hardly the biggest issue. The choreographer, Massine, while skilled and brilliant, directed his dancers to make complicated and gro-
[75] tesque facial expressions. His instructions included orders such as "flex your cheekbones" and "pretend you've swallowed an egg and it is coming out of your foot."

Another significant problem was that some people misinterpreted the frivolity and levity as dark and demente-
[80] ed, primarily due to a misunderstanding of the sets and costumes. People outside the burgeoning surrealist art movement simply did not grasp the message that Picasso had hoped to convey.

Cocteau promised a dynamic collaboration between
[85] some of the world's most innovative and daring artists. Sadly, aside from the six showings in 1917, this collaboration went completely unappreciated until 1973 when, at last, Robert Joffrey revived *Parade*, which finally received the recognition and applause that it had always deserved.

Entrance Ticket   Learning Targets   Comparing Two Texts   Different Perspectives   ACT Practice   Sum It Up

3   3

| Questions 1–2 ask about Passage A. |

1. Which statement best explains how Passage A characterizes the struggles of the surrealist art movement?

   A. Its development was slow and its artists hardly noticed by the others.
   B. The artists failed very quickly even though surrealism was initially successful.
   C. It failed to find an appreciative audience and its intended targets did not understand the artists.
   D. Other artists were finding much success, which only further embarrassed the surrealist artists.

2. Passage A indicates that the author considers that all surrealist artists believe they:

   F. are superior artistically to traditional artists.
   G. are engaging in important social commentary with their art.
   H. are not technically proficient enough to engage in traditional art forms.
   J. are not "real" artists.

| Question 3 asks about Passage B. |

3. According to Passage B, progressive artists believe that ballet has typically been an art form reserved for:

   A. the average person
   B. the privileged class
   C. the politically uninterested
   D. music lovers

| Questions 4–5 ask about both passages. |

4. Based on the passages, surrealist art and the *Parade* ballet are similar in that:

   F. both were misunderstood and struggled to find receptive audiences.
   G. both were desperate for affirmation from respected art critics.
   H. both were intended to promote art for the "common man."
   J. both were failures that never found respect.

5. Based on the passages, Dada art and the *Parade*'s approach to social commentary was similar in that:

   A. they both openly mocked the wealthy.
   B. they both called attention to the poor treatment of the lower classes of society.
   C. they had little to do with politics but were concerned with making art for art's sake.
   D. they both rejected the conventions of the day and sought to change common understanding of art.

END OF SET ONE
STOP! DO NOT GO ON TO THE NEXT PAGE
UNTIL TOLD TO DO SO.

Entrance Ticket   Learning Targets   Comparing Two Texts   Different Perspectives   ACT Practice   Sum It Up

16.4.2 Set Two

Passage III

HUMANITIES: Passage A is adapted from the essay "Un, Deux, Quoi?" by Lucille Prudeaux (©2017 by MasteryPrep). Passage B is adapted from the article "Progressive Regression" by Lawson Richard (©2017 by MasteryPrep).

Passage A by Lucille Prudeaux

I considered I was more than qualified to study abroad one summer in Québec City, having spent the last fourteen years studying French. No sooner had I disembarked the plane than I found myself having my first real
5 French conversation at the airport café. Timidly, I ordered a coffee, and my jaw slowly dropped as what sounded like gibberish tumbled from the barista's mouth. "I speak French," I thought to myself, "but whatever she's speaking is definitely not." This was not the language I had studied.

10 For the next few weeks, I navigated my new world in a daze. Wherever I went, people seemed to understand me, but I could never quite grasp what they were saying. I attended a concert in the middle of the city square one night when, late into the show, I tried to ask a group of
15 young people next to me what band was playing next. One of the teenagers cocked her head to the side and eyed me. "You aren't from around here are you?" she asked in English. At the time, I assumed something about my dress or looks kept me from blending in. Only later did I realize
20 that though I spoke French words to these native French speakers, to them I was still speaking a foreign language. We were speaking the same language, yet, somehow, we weren't.

With every conversation, I learned I was seeking
25 something elusive, two people who spoke a language as it existed in the pages of a grammar book. In our actual use, neither I nor the Quebecois could provide such a manifestation. We ourselves were just the conduits for communication. Moreover, the words we used could not exist with-
30 out the necessity that called them into use, as language evolves to fit the human need. In reality, words peeled off the pages of austere books are just a tool to assuage the human desire for connection, and, once applied, are required neither to adhere to grammar rules nor typical-use
35 conventions but rather often yield to the preferences of the user.

At the heart of my experience I uncovered a revelation: language is not immune to the environment it exists in; it changes over time as a result of its use. This new,
40 complex awareness was my snippet of wisdom, the missing piece to my language studies. The words I had learned after many years via nose stuck in a French book was incomplete without an understanding of the people—their culture, technology, and values—who used those words.

45 What mattered most was not how to form the past participle, but the power of the French language to embody its history and tell the story of its speakers. The words of a grammar book are only the raw material; what matters is the people who bring the words to life.

50 Language belongs to the category of art, not science. It is misguided to expect a language to follow a set of unchangeable rules as though the speaker owes the world the same predictability and literal accuracy that is owed the construction of a bridge or airplane. The speaker, in
55 fact, owes nothing. Instead, to employ language is to use words to paint a picture of the immediate and rudimentary message or need, highlighted with colorful flecks of every moment in history or culture each element of language inherently carries with it.

Passage B by Lawson Richard

60 The emphasis on prescriptive versus descriptive language regulation is a constant debate among linguists, and the renowned *Académie Française* often finds itself in the center. As history marks the pervasive creep of the English language into every corner of the world, the académie has
65 faithfully maintained its zealous devotion to prevent the Anglicization of the French language. By coining new French alternative words, the académie has sought to prevent the adoption of English loanwords such as *hamburger*, *weekend*, and *email*. Undoubtedly, the Académie
70 Française plays a vital role in preserving the French language. However, it has come under increased scrutiny for being overly conservative in its efforts to do so.

The académie is often criticized as an elitist club catering to aging linguistic reactionaries. Composed of 40
75 members who serve a lifelong membership, the council of "immortals" has received such distinguished members as Voltaire, Victor Hugo, and former French president Valérie Giscard d'Estaing. Each year, hundreds of new French words are created as the académie endeavors to counter-
80 act the virulent spread of Anglicisms. Native speakers, however, are quick to point out that many of these words rarely make it off an administrative page to successfully thrive in the wild. Even the académie's more liberal efforts to embrace language change have not wholly pleased
85 the layperson. When the académie proposed instituting certain spelling changes in order to standardize and simplify the language and thereby make it easier for learning, protests erupted against the perceived attack on the rich history and unique grandeur of the French language.

90 While it is impossible to confine language to a textbook or dictionary, one can conclude that authoritative prescriptions and guidelines are both necessary yet controversial. When mandates are placed on a deeply natu-

3   **3**

rally occurring human structure, such efforts at codifi-
95   cation produce two results—i.e., to preserve, instruct,
and support the capacity for communication but also to
limit the natural evolution and growth that comes with
daily use. Such institutions as the Académie Française
stand as a fascinating specimen of this dichotomy, a
100   martyr for the preservation of history who struggles to
balance and accommodate the often uncomfortable but
necessary demand for flexibility and change.

> ### Question 6 asks about Passage A.

6.   The main purpose of the first two paragraphs of Passage
A (lines 1–23) is to:

   F.   give credibility to the narrator's ability to speak
French by describing her efforts to communicate
with people in Québec.
   G.   demonstrate the narrator's pleasure with putting her
French study to practical use.
   H.   present examples of how a language learned in
school does not fully prepare one for conversations
with native speakers.
   J.   argue that language study should be categorized as
science, not as art.

> ### Question 7 asks about Passage B.

7.   Which of the following quotations from Passage B most
directly relates to French citizens' disagreement with
the changes suggested by the Académie Française?

   A.   "The académie has sought to prevent the adoption
of English loanwords" (lines 67–68).
   B.   "Many of these words rarely make it off an administrative page to successfully thrive in the wild"
(lines 81–83).
   C.   "The académie is often criticized as an elitist club"
(line 73).
   D.   "It is impossible to confine language to a textbook
or dictionary" (lines 90–91).

> ### Questions 8–10 ask about both passages.

8.   Both Passage A and Passage B highlight a modern
French speaker's use of:

   F.   spelling changes for easier language learning.
   G.   gestures and movement to communicate across language barriers.
   H.   metaphor to present a complicated emotional experience.
   J.   language and personal expression regardless of
grammatical purity.

9.   If a tourist had decided to communicate with the teenagers in Passage A using the new French words described
in Passage B, the teenagers would most likely have expressed:

   A.   confusion about vocabulary that did not fit well
with their natural way of speaking.
   B.   joy at learning new words in their own language.
   C.   disappointment that the speaker was not proficient
in the French language.
   D.   admiration that the speaker knew the ancient origins in their own language.

10.   Another author wrote the following about the role of
cultural immersion in learning a new language:

> By living where a language is spoken, the brain
> can more naturally acquire a new language out of
> necessity rather than through empty memorization.

Which passage most closely reflects the opinion presented in this quotation?

   F.   Passage A, because it describes a story about what
happens when you interact with someone who does
not speak the same language as you.
   G.   Passage A, because it emphasizes that language
proficiency also requires use in normal interactions
with other native speakers.
   H.   Passage B, because it states that the Académie
Française rejects all proposed changes to the French
language.
   J.   Passage B, because it states that the Académie
Française rarely accommodates English words into
official French dictionaries.

END OF SET TWO
STOP! DO NOT GO ON TO THE NEXT PAGE
UNTIL TOLD TO DO SO.

Entrance Ticket   Learning Targets   Comparing Two Texts   Different Perspectives   ACT Practice   Sum It Up

16.4.3 Set Three

Passage III

HUMANITIES: Passage A is adapted from the essay "Considering Ophelia" by Rebekah Olivier (©2017 by MasteryPrep), which is the preface to the first edition of Olivier's novel *Passing through Fire*. Passage B is adapted from *Passing through Fire* (©2017 by MasteryPrep). A *cauponae* is a place of eating in ancient Rome.

Passage A by Rebekah Olivier

My first taste of creative writing came in third grade. I was tasked with writing the script for an Odyssey of the Mind sketch that was to be loosely based on a Shakespearian play. At the time, I was not aware that I was so
5 indebted to Shakespeare for much of the success of our little production. The words were mine, but they had been carefully molded, squeezed, and shoveled into the beats and plotting of the greater work. Within that framework, nearly any collection of words and ideas could spread its
10 wings, look up into the sunlight, and soar to great heights.

It was to my great shock and dismay, then, that when I first set pen to paper to write my own creation, I could not simply rely on clever turns of phrase to carry my narrative, but instead had to sit down, think carefully, and
15 craft the bones of the story that I hoped to tell.

I would wrestle endlessly with stories in my mind, carefully molding the characters into the people I envisioned them to be and constructing the places I needed them to explore, and hope that somehow out of this rumi-
20 nation they would spontaneously arrange themselves into a cohesive plot. The exercise was frustrating and excruciating. I quickly discovered that this process was not how I could continue to write fiction.

Following this epiphany, I dove into books on writ-
25 ing in hopes that those more learned than myself could offer insight on how to combine interesting characters, ideas that frightened and excited me, and lush settings into a compelling story.

Then, I took long journeys through books that had
30 first stirred within me the desire to write and that I had loved as well as those that had perplexed and pushed me out of my comfort zone into new worlds and new heights, and I began to emulate them.

I had to bury myself deeply in the world of literature,
35 with pages as spades, to break open the hidden structure of stories and let their roots take hold in my subconscious.

And so from high school until many years after college, not a week passed that I wasn't buried in a book exploring some great ancient society, looking for a hidden
40 map that guided the reader from a beggar's street corner to a royal feast, desperately searching for words and phrases that tied a life, a love, a heartache, or some great passion together to create A Story.

Along the way, I stumbled and crashed, though blunt
45 force reading, into old and true stories. I borrowed hooks and frameworks from science fiction authors and planted them in my own historical fiction so that I could breathe life into a stagnant page.

On my path, I sat in on countless conversations,
50 scenes, and character development that married together to bring suspense and joy.

Thus, I discovered plotting. I fell upon the simplest and best way of writing. Through a deep and vast diet of literature I was taken by surprise when stories at last
55 began leaping from my fingers like frogs on a still pond. I learned to craft stories by reading all that I could get my hands on and then ruthlessly deconstructing them. I let the books themselves tell me their secrets and my hunger for knowledge teach me their truths.

Passage B by Rebekah Olivier

60 What can be known of Pompeii is easily accessible. On August 24, CE 79, a single day after the people celebrated the Roman god of fire, a week after smoke began spilling from the summit, and 17 years since the city had escaped mass destruction from an earthquake, Mount
65 Vesuvius erupted. The heat from the eruption reached people in an instant, the ash enshrining them eternally. It hit quickly. It destroyed totally. It was not merciful. It was catastrophic. It destroyed the old and the young, the rich and the poor, and the just and the unjust. It was, in fact, the
70 only force any had ever known to equalize so completely.

It spared no one, save a man and his apprentice who presently walked across the ash-speckled ground, the fire raging around them with heat that whipped round with the wind and sent smoke sailing into the pewter sky. A sky
75 now thick and heavy as a wet pot on a wheel.

The apprentice walked slowly, feeling that the destruction would go on forever. The sound of the man's incantations, keeping them safe as they walked their path, were beyond his understanding; He followed silently.

80 The man suddenly ceased his mumbled spell. The apprentice stopped in his tracks and looked up at him.

"Master, why have you stopped?"

"You know the answer to that, Cato."

"Did you say that we are leaving—forever?"

Entrance Ticket   Learning Targets   Comparing Two Texts   Different Perspectives   ACT Practice   Sum It Up

3 3

85   The man took a sheepskin parchment solemnly from his pouch and showed it to his apprentice.

    "How can that possibly be?" said the apprentice. "The whole city! We were to study in the cauponae tonight! How could this, written so long ago, possibly

90 know? These people have been here since ancient days! It can't simply end in an instant!"

    "It's the Zoroaster," said the man. "He saw this long ago. The signs only confirmed it today."

    They sat down on the singed grass. Beyond the

95 smoke and the soot, Pompeii was engulfed in flames, the columns of the prominent temple beginning to sink. The apprentice wanted to run back to his family, find some way he might stop what was foretold. But he didn't run. And away from the city, through the smoke,

100 he saw a door appear from nowhere. He turned around one last time, and then stood to open it.

Questions 11–12 ask about Passage A.

---

11. As it is used in the passage, the term *interesting characters* (line 26) serves mostly as a:

  A. description of the author's work, made by a literary critic.

  B. name for the type of people that were made famous by the author.

  C. label for the type of character that the author hoped to write.

  D. term used sarcastically by the critics of the author.

12. The author's claim "I would wrestle endlessly with stories in my mind," (line 16) most strongly suggests that when she first began to write, the author would:

  F. attempt to find the one character who would be interesting enough to tell a story about.

  G. usually turn down stories for not helping her dig into the hidden structure of narratives.

  H. make a conscious decision to only write about ideas that frightened her.

  J. feel as though she could not form the ideas in her head into a compelling, readable story.

Question 13 asks about Passage B.

---

13. Based on Passage B, the accuracy of the parchment's message is particularly surprising because:

  A. it was written long ago and yet predicted exactly what was happening to the apprentice.

  B. it conflicted with other writings the apprentice had read about the volcanic eruption.

  C. the apprentice could not find any other writings to support what the parchment said.

  D. the apprentice believed that the parchment was true, but his family did not believe it.

Questions 14–15 ask about both passages.

---

14. Based on the passages, it can be reasonably inferred that the author would agree that when it comes to combining genres in a piece of fiction, a writer should:

  F. never attempt to insert elements from one into the other.

  G. leave out supernatural elements that might confuse the reader.

  H. have the liberty to mix elements from different genres if that helps her tell the best story she can.

  J. only write facts that have documentation to back them up.

15. Which element in the literary industry does the author of Passage A mention, which is not referred to in Passage B?

  A. Science fiction

  B. Historical fiction

  C. Books on writing

  D. Books on research documentation

END OF SET THREE
STOP! DO NOT GO ON TO THE NEXT PAGE
UNTIL TOLD TO DO SO.

Entrance Ticket   Learning Targets   Comparing Two Texts   Different Perspectives   ACT Practice   Sum It Up

Sum It Up

Compare Two Texts

Comparison
To look at two items and explain how they are similar or different.

Tips and Techniques

One at a Time: When you see two texts in a reading passage, read Passage A and then answer the questions designated to that passage. Do this *before* you move onto Passage B and its questions so that you don't confuse which detail came from which passage.

Put Yourself in Their Shoes: If a question asks what one passage would say or do about another passage, pretend that you are the writer for the first passage. Ask yourself what details are most important to you, and look for answers that are similar to these details.

Reading Strategy

CAPTION:

17.1 Entrance Ticket

Read the passage and answer the questions.

The skunk cabbage, or *Symplocarpus foetidus* as it is properly known, is distributed from Nova Scotia to Florida. Found in swamps and wetlands, the skunk cabbage blooms from
5 February to April and develops small, foul-smelling flowers. These flowers are colored an unappealing purple-brown or yellow-green.

This despised relative of the stately calla lily proclaims spring in the very teeth of winter,
10 being the first bold adventurer above ground. When the lovely lily is still awaiting her bloom, wrapped in her fuzzy furs, the skunk cabbage's dark, incurved horn shelters within its hollow, tiny, malodorous florets. Why is the entire
15 plant so fetid that one flees the neighborhood, pervaded as it is with an odor that combines a suspicion of skunk, putrid meat, and garlic? After investigating the carrion flower and the purple trillium, among others, we learned that
20 certain flies delight in foul odors loathsome to higher organisms. Plants dependent upon these pollen carriers woo them from long distances with such a stench. These flowers' natural color palletes—flesh tones, as well as pinks and
25 reds—also lure flies, carrion beetles, and other scavengers of nature in their resemblance to decaying meat both in appearance and in odor. In such marshy ground as the skunk cabbage lives, many small flies and gnats live in embry-
30 os under the fallen leaves during the winter, awaiting adulthood before seeking such pollen as that of the malodorous skunk cabbage. But even before these embryos hatch, the hive bees, natives of Europe and with habits not per-
35 fectly adapted as yet to our flora, are seeking after pollen.

After winter blooms have faded, the vivid green crowns appear, and they, at least, please the eye. Lizards make their homes beneath
40 them, and many a yellowthroat, taking advantage of the plant's foul odor, gladly puts up with it herself and builds her nest in the hollow of the cabbage to protect her eggs and young from four-footed enemies. Cattle leave the plant
45 alone, although such tender, fresh, bright foliage like the hellebore's must be especially tempting after a dry winter diet. With many potential predators, the cabbage takes protective measures: cattle stay away because of the stinging, acrid
50 juices secreted by its leaves, and most other herbivores avoid such rancid aroma.

1. It is most accurate to say that the information about the skunk cabbage in this passage is organized in a way that is:
   A. strictly chronological.
   B. loosely chronological.
   C. not chronological at all.
   D. in reverse chronological order, starting from most recent and working backward.

2. According to the passage the "scavengers of nature" referred to in line 26 can accurately be described as all of the following EXCEPT:
   F. carrion beetles.
   G. flies that delight in foul odors.
   H. gnats.
   J. cattle.

Entrance Ticket · Learning Targets · Reading Strategy · ACT Practice · Sum It Up

17.1 Entrance Ticket

3. As it is used in line 16, the word *pervaded*
    most nearly means:
    A. polluted.
    B. penetrated.
    C. depleted.
    D. extended.

17.2 Learning Targets

1. Recognize when to use appropriate strategies to answer standard ACT questions

2. Develop a method to address difficult questions during the test

Self-Assessment

Circle the number that corresponds to your confidence level in your knowledge of this subject before beginning the lesson. A score of 1 means you are completely lost, and a score of 4 means you have mastered the skills. After you finish the lesson, return to the bottom of this page and circle your new confidence level to show your improvement.

Before Lesson

1   2   3   4

After Lesson

1   2   3   4

Entrance Ticket   Learning Targets   Reading Strategy   ACT Practice   Sum It Up

This page is intentionally left blank.

17.3.1 Scope and Support

It is asserted that the way in which modern composers write vocal music is the cause of its deterioration. In the compositions of the Old Italian masters, the voice is studied, and nothing is
5 introduced that is hurtful or disadvantageous. Awkward intervals are avoided, no fatigue is caused, and everything is eminently *singable*; however, the music is not always expressive of the sense of the words, which are clearly con-
10 sidered to be of minor importance.

Modern composers, on the other hand, tend to emphasize the importance of the words themselves over the beauty of the melodic line. What is possible or impossible for the voice is,
15 since the time of Beethoven, rarely considered. Many composers—even the most distinguished ones—have evidently little knowledge of the most beautiful of instruments for which they are nevertheless continually writing.

20 When one of the greatest living masters introduced the harp into his works, he wrote for it as though it were a piano—as though it were to be played upon with the thumb and four fingers. But it so happens that on that instrument,
25 the fourth finger is never used. Consequently it came to the point that harpists could not play that gentleman's compositions, and they had to first rewrite them. Here, of course, the composer was found out immediately, and he or any other
30 man would have the same fate if he attempted to write for an instrument the properties of which he did not fully understand. But with the human voice, the case is different. Every musician believes himself to be competent to write
35 for it, though he may possibly be wholly unacquainted with its many peculiarities. It is to be feared, therefore, that modern composers must be held largely responsible for the sad state of affairs concerning vocal art at the present time.

40 Well might they learn a lesson from Mozart, who, in spite of his genius, first carefully studied the human voice and then wrote for it.

Another reason for the decline of singing is that the tuning of pitch has gradually and
45 considerably risen during the last 150 years. As orchestras increasingly tune at higher frequencies, the vocal apparatus has been unable to bear the strain to which it is now subjected. With regard to tenors, however, the greater evil
50 is that they disregard the falsetto register, singing everything, however high, in chest voice. I am afraid it cannot be said even that they have been beguiled into this serious mistake by the imperceptible rise of tuning pitch just mentioned.
55 The truth is that they have committed this fatal blunder knowingly and willfully—because they saw that it was more exciting to the public and knew it would draw in larger audiences.

1. The passage strongly implies that the author views modern composers as:
   A. strongly dedicated to their craft.
   B. largely unqualified to write vocal music.
   C. more concerned with melody than with lyrics.
   D. less concerned with financial gain than previous generations were.

Scope in the question: _____

Support in the passage: _____

17.3.1 Scope and Support

2. Through his comparison of German composers and Italian composers, the author reveals his belief that modern vocal music is:

    F. overly fussy.

    G. the perfect balance of musicality and lyrical genius.

    H. unbalanced and lacking in true mastery.

    J. inaccessible to the average person.

Scope in the question: _____

Support in the passage: _____

3. In the context of the passage, the significance of Mozart is that he:

    A. was an unparalleled musical genius.

    B. was able to write music in one sitting.

    C. was a superior composer to Beethoven.

    D. studied the voice before he wrote for it.

Scope in the question: _____

Support in the passage: _____

4. According to the passage, the rise of tuning pitch in music occurred:

    F. during Beethoven's time.

    G. along with the rise in German composers.

    H. during the last 150 years.

    J. within the last decade.

Scope in the question: _____

Support in the passage: _____

Reading Tip

Scope and Support: There are two key features of every correct answer on the reading test: a correct answer must be supported directly by the passage, and it must fit the scope of the passage.

Entrance Ticket   Learning Targets   Reading Strategy   ACT Practice   Sum It Up

17.3.2 Process of Elimination

Thales of Miletus, 600 BCE, discovered the properties of amber: when rubbed, it had the power to attract and repel light substances, such as straw, dry leaves, etc. From the Greek
5 word for amber—*elektron*—came the name *electricity*, denoting this peculiar property. Theophrastus and Pliny made the same observations, the former about 321 BCE, and the latter about 70 CE It is also said that the ancients had
10 observed the effects of animal electricity, such as that of the fish called the *torpedo*. Pliny and Aristotle both spoke of its power to paralyze the feet of men and animals and to first stun the fish they preyed upon. It is also recorded that a
15 freedman of Tiberius was cured of the gout by shocks of the torpedo. It is further recorded that Wolimer, the King of the Goths, was able to emit sparks from his body.

Coming down to more modern times—
20 1600 CE—we find Dr. Gilbert, an Englishman, taking up the investigation of the electrical properties of various substances when submitted to friction and compiling them in order of importance. In these experiments we have the begin-
25 nings of what has since developed into a great science. He made the discovery that when the air was dry, he could quickly electrify the substances rubbed, but when it was damp, it took much longer and sometimes failed altogether.

30 The full number of investigators is so great that not all of them can be named. It often happens that those who do the most for a science are never known to fame. A number of people will make small contributions until the structure
35 has by degrees assumed large proportions; then finally someone comes along and puts a gilded dome on it, and the whole structure takes his name. This is eminently true of many of the more important developments in the science

40 and applications of electricity during the last twenty-five or thirty years.

One such example is the Leyden jar, which was invented in 1745. It takes its name from the city of Leyden, where its use was first
45 discovered. It is a glass jar, coated inside and out with tin foil. The inside coating is connected with a brass knob at the top, through which it can be charged with electricity. The inner and outer coatings must not be continuous but insu-
50 lated from each other. The author's name is not known, but one manuscript claims that three different persons invented it independently—a monk by the name of Kleist, a man by the name of Cuneus, and Professor Muschenbroeck of
55 Leyden. The Leyden jar was quite an important invention, as it was the forerunner of Benjamin Franklin's discoveries and was a necessary part of his outfit with which he established the identity of lightning and electricity. Every American
60 schoolboy has heard from Fourth of July orations how "Franklin caught the forked lightning from the clouds and tamed it and made it subservient to the will of man."

1. Based on the passage as a whole, the Leyden jar (lines 55–59) had which of the following effects on Benjamin Franklin?
   A. He used the Leyden jar as inspiration for his lightning experiments.
   B. He considered the Leyden jar a failed but important experiment.
   C. He was unimpressed by the Leyden jar and doubted its effectiveness.
   D. He sought out the work of Cuneus to learn more about the Leyden jar.

_____

_____

_____

17.3.2 Process of Elimination

2. Regarding electricity, which of the following is NOT mentioned in the passage as a major scientific discovery?
   F. The electric properties of amber
   G. Franklin's innovative work with lightning
   H. The effect of humidity on electricity
   J. The positive and negative forms of energy

   _____

   _____

   _____

   _____

3. It can be reasonably inferred from the passage that which of the following discoveries about electricity had the LEAST amount of scientific importance?
   A. The discovery that amber had the power to attract and repel substances
   B. The claim that Wolimer could emit sparks from his body
   C. The invention of the Leyden jar
   D. The discovery of the electrical properties of lightning

   _____

   _____

   _____

   _____

4. It can most reasonably be inferred from the passage that which of the following statements is true about scientific discoveries?
   F. They are often a collaborative effort by many people who will never receive credit.
   G. They are often the result of the genius of a single individual.
   H. They are often named for the incorrect scientist or city.
   J. They are often overlooked until a future scientist recognizes their importance.

   _____

   _____

   _____

   _____

Reading Tip

Process of Elimination: No other test benefits from the process of elimination as much as the reading test. You should use the process of elimination on every question you answer. Use your pencil to cross out any choice that exaggerates the passage, comes from the wrong part of the passage, or is not supported by the passage.

17.3.3 Keep Your Pencil Moving

To the Europeans who lived before the Age of Discovery, only a very small portion of the Earth's surface was known. Their geography was confined to the regions lying immedi-
5 ately around the Mediterranean and Europe, the north of Africa, and the west of Asia. Around these there was a margin, obscurely and imperfectly described in the reports of merchants, but by far the greater part of the world was utterly
10 unknown. Great realms of perceived darkness stretched all beyond and closely hemmed in the little circle of light. In these uncharted lands people loved to imagine that all things strange and mysterious existed. They believed that
15 whoever reached far enough into these territories would find countries where inexhaustible riches were to be gathered without toil from fertile shores or marvelous valleys. Wild tales were told of the dangers supposed to fill these
20 regions, yet to the more daring and adventurous, these only made the visions of boundless wealth and enchanting loveliness all the more fascinating.

Thus, as the art of navigation improved—
25 finally making long voyages possible—courageous adventurers were tempted to venture out into the great unknown expanse. Columbus carried his trembling sailors over great tracts of uncharted ocean and reached the two conti-
30 nents of America; Vasco da Gama sailed far to the south and rounded the Cape of Good Hope; Magellan, passing through the straits now called by his name, was the first to enter the Pacific Ocean. In the case of a hundred others,
35 courage and skill carried the hardy sailors over many seas and into many lands that had lain unknown for ages.

Australia was one of the last parts of the
40 world to be visited and explored by Europeans in the Age of Discovery. In the year 1600 during the times of Shakespeare, the region to the south of the East Indies was still as little known as ever. The crude maps of those days had only
45 a great blank where the islands of Australia should have been. Most people thought there was nothing but the ocean in that part of the world. Because the voyage was dangerous and very long, requiring several years for its com-
50 pletion, scarcely anyone cared to run the risk of exploring it.

1. The passage is best described as being told from a historian who is:
   A. presenting in chronological order the modern history of Australia.
   B. discussing the issues faced by expeditions led by Magellan and other explorers.
   C. describing European exploration by sea leading up to the discovery of Australia.
   D. advising other historians on the importance of studying the history of mapmaking.

2. Based on the passage, which of the following was most likely to draw the author to this subject?
   F. Australia's inexhaustible resources
   G. The sense of adventure in discovery
   H. Wild tales of dangerous weather
   J. A love of ships and sailing

17.3.3 Keep Your Pencil Moving

3. The main purpose of the last paragraph is to:
   A. acknowledge Shakespeare's role in the discovery of Australia.
   B. describe the process of mapmaking in the context of long voyages.
   C. explain Australia's geographic relationship to the East Indies.
   D. reveal why Australia was explored much later than most of the world.

4. The passage indicates that prior to the Age of Discovery, many European nations were:
   F. unaware of the geography outside their immediate proximity.
   G. constantly seeking new lands to conquer and new goods to trade.
   H. interested solely in exploration for the sake of science.
   J. concerned with mapmaking as an art form rather than as a practical tool.

Reading Tip

Keep Your Pencil Moving: The reading test requires you to read a large amount of text, from the passages to the questions and answers. One of the best ways to keep it all straight is to use your pencil as you work: underline or jot down the key points in each paragraph, box the key topic in each question, mark the answers to highlight the parts you think are important, and cross out incorrect answers.

17.3.4 Skimming

Have you ever tried to eat a peach elegantly and gracefully? Of course you have. Show me a person who has not tried to do so, especially when under the eye of human surveillance. There is no fruit, certainly, that has so fair and alluring an exterior. However, few content themselves with feasting their eyes upon it. How fresh and ripe it looks as it lies upon the plate, and the fragrance, so suggestive of its rich, delicious flavor—who can resist? Bitterly you shall repent your rashness. Any other fruit can be eaten with comparative ease and politeness, but a peach was evidently intended only to be looked at or enjoyed beneath your own tree, where no eye may watch and criticize your motions.

I see you, in imagination, standing in the middle of the room at a party, plate in hand, regarding your peach as if it were some great natural curiosity. A sudden jog of your elbow compels you to a succession of most dexterous balancing, as your heavy peach rolls from side to side, knocks your knife to the floor, and threatens to plunge after it when you stoop to regain it. You look distractedly around for a table, but all are occupied. Even the corner of the mantelpiece holds a plate, and you enviously see the owner thereof leaning carelessly against the chimney and looking placidly upon his less fortunate companions. You glance at the different groups to see if anyone else is in your most unenviable predicament.

Ah, yes! Across the room stands a gentleman worse off yet, for in addition to your perplexities, he is talking with a young, laughing girl, who is watching his movements with a merry twinkle in her bright eyes. He evidently wishes to astonish her by his dexterity and disappoint her clumsy expectations. He holds his plate firmly in his left hand and proceeds at once to cut his peach into halves. Deuce take the blunt silver knife! The tough skin resists its pressure. The knife and plate clash loudly together; the peach bounds and rolls at the very feet of the young lady, who is in an ecstasy of laughter. Ah! She herself has no small resemblance to a peach: fair, beautiful, and attractive, but I sadly fear, with a hard heart beneath.

Are you yet more miserable than before? Turn then to that serious-looking gentleman over there, who certainly seems well-positioned to perform the difficult maneuver. He has the advantage of a table to be sure, but that is not everything. He begins correctly by deliberately removing the woolly skin. Now he lays the slippery peach on his plate and makes a plunge at it with his knife. A sharp, prolonged screech across his plate salutes the ears of all the bystanders, and a fine slice of juicy pulp is flung unceremoniously into the face of the gentleman opposite, who certainly does not look very grateful for the unexpected gift.

1. The point of view from which the passage is being told is best described as that of:
   A. an observer relating a series of events.
   B. a narrator unfolding a hypothetical situation.
   C. a child watching the situation unfold.
   D. a man trying to eat a peach politely.

17.3.4 Skimming

2. The passage contains references to all the following EXCEPT:
   F. a man dropping his peach to ground.
   G. a laughing young woman with bright eyes.
   H. a gentleman with peach flung onto his face.
   J. a child reaching for her mother's plate.

3. The passage establishes all of the following about the narrator EXCEPT that he:
   A. considers it impossible to eat peaches politely.
   B. finds absurdity in dinner party situations.
   C. dislikes peaches because of their wooly skin.
   D. believes that peaches are enjoyable when eaten without social judgment.

4. It can reasonably be inferred from the passage that the narrator thinks that dinner parties can often be:
   F. awkward and embarrassing for the participants.
   G. a fun way to meet and socialize with people.
   H. best avoided by those without proper table manners.
   J. good practice for perfecting polite eating habits.

Reading Tip

Skimming: In order to use any of the other techniques effectively, you will need enough time. Considering you don't have much time on the reading test, it is important that you learn to skim the passage as fast as you can. Look for key topics and mark them, or just read the first sentence of each paragraph. Either way, finish reading in no more than three minutes.

Entrance Ticket   Learning Targets   Reading Strategy   ACT Practice   Sum It Up

17.3.5 Scanning

People often talk about a gnat stinging or a stinging fly. It may be difficult to define exactly what "to sting" means, but a good rule of thumb is that a sting is inflicted by the tail end
5 of the creature and a bite by the mouth. A fly or gnat no doubt inserts its proboscis—protruding mouth and nose—into one's flesh just as a wasp does its stinger, but the actions of such opposite parts of the body surely demand distinct
10 names. The "aculeate" or stinging *Hymenoptera* are divided into sections and families according to their structures. The two groups that stand out most clearly in regard to their habits are the solitary and social species.

15 The vast majority of the aculeate *Hymenoptera* are what are called "solitary," which means one male and one female alone are interested in the production of the nest. There are also three "social" groups: the ants, the true
20 wasps, and the bumble and hive bees. These are called social because they form communities and all work together toward the maintenance of the nest. In the social species, there are two forms of the females: the queens and
25 the workers. The latter have an imperfectly developed reproductive system, and in the bumble bees and wasps, their smaller size is the only differentiating characteristic that sets them apart from fully developed females or queens.
30 In the ants, however, the workers are wingless and of a very different form from that of the queen. The role of these workers seems to be doing the general work of the nest. They have been known to lay fertile eggs, but the resulting
35 offspring have always been male.

We know of no type of aculeate *Hymenoptera* that exhibits behavior between the polar opposite solitary and social types. We do not seem to see any attempts on the part
40 of solitary bees to become social or vice versa. The only condition known that could possibly be considered as intermediate is shown in certain species where a number of individuals make their nests close to each other in some particu-
45 lar bank, forming a colony. These colonies are sometimes very extensive, and the burrows of the individual bees are very close together. It has also been shown that the burrows sometimes unite, but there seems to be no positive
50 evidence that there is any work done in the colony that could be considered as done for the common good.

1. Which of the following facts has the largest impact on classifying stinging insects?
   A. Flies and gnats bite, but they do not sting.
   B. Stinging insects are either solitary or social, without an intermediate group.
   C. Stinging insects often live in individual nests but work together for the common good.
   D. Stinging insects all have queens and workers within each nest.

2. The passage states that the vast majority of aculeate *Hymenoptera:*
   F. are solitary.
   G. are social.
   H. are a combination of solitary and social.
   J. are neither solitary nor social.

17.3.5 Scanning

3. The passage notes that people refer to gnats and flies as stinging insects but that:

    A. only gnats truly sting.
    B. only flies truly sting.
    C. neither gnats nor flies truly sting.
    D. both gnats and flies inflict mild stings.

4. The passage indicates that some solitary stinging insects live near one another but:

    F. these communities tend to be short lived.
    G. there is no work toward a common good.
    H. a queen usually arises and turns them into social communities.
    J. the males tend to fight for dominance within the nest.

Reading Tip

Scanning: Around half of the questions on the reading test will not give you a line reference. You will have to scan to find the topic in the passage instead. If you develop the ability to scan quickly and accurately, you will be much better at answering these kinds of questions.

3   3

17.4.1 Set One

Passage II

SOCIAL SCIENCE: This passage is adapted from *Favorite First Ladies: Ladybird to Michelle* by Catherine Holmes and Frederick Gilkes (©2015 by MasteryPrep).

Nancy Reagan is one of the most fascinating first ladies in United States history. Her journey from Hollywood to the White House was neither typical of her predecessors nor altogether effortless. She was born of humble
5   roots in New York City, the daughter of an aspiring actress. While working side jobs, Reagan was able to pursue her own acting career. She even obtained a few minor Broadway roles before securing a contract with MGM Studios in Hollywood. She has mentioned many times
10 that her acting career was, in fact, very good training for her future in the political sphere.

In 1949 Reagan (then Davis) fell in love with Ronald Reagan, a fellow actor and the president of the Screen Actors Guild. Despite his wariness to remarry
15 after a painful divorce, they began dating and were married in 1952. Even though she completed an additional three films after marrying, Reagan relished most being a mother to the couple's two young children, as well as to her husband's two children from his previous marriage.

20 When her husband was elected governor of California, Reagan refused to live in the Governor's Mansion, deeming it outdated and unsafe. She and her family instead moved to a private Sacramento neighborhood. She received criticism for this but defended the necessity of
25 the move for her family's well-being. The snobbish public image she had acquired eventually abated in response to her involvement in youth advocacy programs like the Foster Grandparents Program and her subsequent book, *To Love a Child*. During her time as California's first lady,
30 Reagan ceaselessly visited and aided many veterans, elderly, and handicapped people of the state.

Reagan transitioned to her role as first lady of the United States when her husband was elected president in 1980. In her first year in the White House, she con-
35 tinued spending time with impoverished Americans and showcased the talents of young performers in the Executive Mansion on the PBS program *In Performance at the White House*. The first lady helped to upgrade the White House both aesthetically and structurally. She was again
40 criticized for unnecessary spending, even though the changes were privately funded by donation.

The first lady was finally able to turn her critics around when she launched her own innovative platform, the "Just Say No" campaign. Now she had a cause of her
45 own to promote and champion. She believed that young people's inexperience made them more vulnerable to the dangers of drug and alcohol abuse than older demograph-

ics but that their youth also made them receptive to intervention. She traveled throughout the country touring drug
50 and alcohol rehabilitation centers and reviewing hundreds of drug prevention programs in public schools. She invited the first ladies of over fifteen countries to the White House to devote international attention to the issue. Her "Just Say No" program eventually resulted in over 10,000
55 after-school clubs around the world as well as the Drug-Free America Act, signed into law in 1986.

Alongside her particular causes and platforms, Reagan also took it upon herself to be her husband's personal protector. An assassination attempt in 1981 made the
60 first lady fearful for her husband's life. Not only was she in the perpetual confidence of President Reagan himself, but she demanded knowledge of all his appointments and proceedings. When criticized for her micromanagement of the president, she said that she was "doing everything
65 [she] could think of to protect [her] husband and keep him alive." She became so much the coordinator of his daily events that the White House chief of staff resigned after much dispute with the formidable first lady.

When the Reagan Administration ended, the couple
70 retired to California and established the Nancy Reagan Foundation to promote "Just Say No" worldwide. The relaxation of their retirement was cut short when the former president was stricken by Alzheimer's disease in 1994, and their focus shifted to raising awareness and under-
75 standing of the mysterious illness. Since her husband's death in 2005, Nancy Reagan has tirelessly advocated for a cure through the National Alzheimer's Association.

Throughout her life, Nancy Reagan has been an actress, a mother, a wife, and a first lady. She is lauded for
80 her integrity and her unrivaled devotion to both sincerity and human compassion. "These ideals have endured," she asserted, "because they are right and are no less right today than yesterday." She has stood up against everything that has been thrown her way and has undoubtedly
85 come out no worse for wear.

Entrance Ticket   Learning Targets   Reading Strategy   ACT Practice   Sum It Up

3 ▓▓▓▓▓▓▓▓▓▓▓▓▓▓▓▓▓▓▓▓▓▓▓▓▓▓ **3**

1. As she is depicted in the passage, Nancy Reagan is best described as:

   A. politically outspoken and privately frivolous.
   B. morally controversial but publically charismatic.
   C. tirelessly philanthropic but deeply envious.
   D. personally dedicated and socially concerned.

2. The author presents Nancy Reagan's achievements as especially remarkable because:

   F. she had a unsuccessful career as a movie star.
   G. she made aesthetic and structural renovations to the White House.
   H. she invited young performers to demonstrate their talents from the Executive Mansion.
   J. with a steadfast dedication to her causes, she won over critics.

3. According to the passage, Nancy Reagan did all of the following during her first year as first lady of the United States EXCEPT:

   A. become president of the Foster Grandparents Program.
   B. spend time with impoverished and disabled Americans.
   C. make renovations to the White House.
   D. showcase young performers through PBS.

4. Based on the passage, Nancy Reagan's involvement in her husband's daily life can best be described as:

   F. aloof and disinterested.
   G. concerned and relentless.
   H. unapologetic and domineering.
   J. patient and sympathetic.

5. It can reasonably be inferred from the passage that at the time Nancy Reagan launched the "Just Say No" Program, the United States was:

   A. oversaturated with drug abuse prevention programs.
   B. resistant to implementing the program in public schools.
   C. supportive of the first lady's crusade against drug abuse.
   D. unconcerned with the harmful effects of drug and alcohol abuse.

END OF SET THREE
STOP! DO NOT GO ON TO THE NEXT PAGE
UNTIL TOLD TO DO SO.

Entrance Ticket   Learning Targets   Reading Strategy   ACT Practice   Sum It Up

17.4.2 Set Two

Passage IV

NATURAL SCIENCE: This passage is adapted from the article "Lightning Distinction Theory" by Larrie Anne Brandon (©2015 by MasteryPrep).

At last science may solve the mystery of the floating orbs of light that have plagued sailors and UFO hunters for years. Though these phenomena have been witnessed the world over, they are such rare and unpredictable oc-
5 currences that studying and replicating anything was nearly impossible until Carl Travis stepped up to the plate.

Travis is the American scientist whose studies would have him contend that the broad term *ball lightning* is far too generic to accurately classify each of the many
10 natural phenomena that cannot fit into the category of normal lightning—such as bead lightning, aurora, or St. Elmo's Fire—and that a new classification is necessary. His theory and call for further research caused the highly distinguished scientist to gain a reputation among his col-
15 leagues as a man on a fool's errand.

Travis and his team member, Erik Farmer, regained some of their credibility when they conducted preliminary experiments that provided skeptics with evidence of some kind of difference between these illuminations. Instead of
20 boasting or expecting special recognition, Travis was sat-isfied that he could finally begin research aimed toward giving each lightning phenomenon a separate and individ-ual distinction.

"At first I did not realize how overwhelming the
25 dissent amongst my colleagues would be," he admitted. "I thought there may have been a handful of people who would be fully supportive, but when the votes came in, it was only myself and my team." He goes on to say that with a few long months of persuasion (in the form of
30 house calls and low-key lunch meetings), the team was finally given the green light to commence a legitimate study.

It may seem strange to receive this amount of reluc-tance from other scientists. After all, isn't science about
35 welcoming new information regarding the world around us? It would seem that every scientist would be eager to replace old ideas with his or her own. This is the case in theory, but in reality scientists are nearly as hesitant to accept wholly radical ideas as is the rest of the world.

40 "Becoming a scientist throws you into this life of constant duality," asserts Chairman Thomas Woo of the National Science Committee. "You have to be willing to believe and question those beliefs in almost the same breath." He contends that cynics can get nowhere in sci-
45 entific studies, but being too unquestioning may lead to heartache.

It was in 1900 that Nikola Tesla allegedly created ball lightning in his Colorado Springs laboratory, but none of his records have enabled scientists to do the same. In
50 their papers, Travis and Farmer describe that the amal-gamation of previous research and experimentation had generated a gaseous, glowing discharge of plasma sus-pended by electricity over a solution of electrolytes. As they evaluated these accounts, they discovered the vary-
55 ing descriptions of results, from sharp and jagged purple hissing plasmoids to spheres of blue and green light that hovered near the scientists' heads.

Fascinated by the mystery of the case, Travis and Farmer tried again and again to recreate these specta-
60 cles to a degree that was suitable for significant analysis; however, their creations were initially either too small or flashed too briefly. Finally, by fine-tuning all the method-ology gathered thus far, Travis's team adjusted over and over again the acidity of the electrolyte solution to create
65 larger and longer-lasting data specimen. With increased funding, the team was able to use high-speed cameras to capture the images of their creations. Furthermore, they were able to use video and infrared cameras to monitor the spheres' changes in density and structure.

70 The ability to replicate such intense and visual nat-ural reactions between the atmosphere, electricity, and air molecules can provide further knowledge about the Earth and its anatomy. This new field of study could explain how these natural wonders spontaneously form in houses and
75 airplanes and are able to pass effortlessly through glass.

More and more scientists are jumping aboard to bring further research to Travis's theory. A newly re-viewed mathematical theory—which explains the birth, or initiation, of ball lightning—may be the next step in the
80 investigation of lightning phenomena. The otherworldly and seemingly immaterial illuminations that have led wild and imaginative theories may finally have a scientific ex-planation.

Certainly, Travis's findings shed light on the differ-
85 ences between these previously conflated lightning types. They are as yet unsure of distinct classifications of each type, but this research has successfully opened up ques-tions for further study. Unfortunately, if he had been less prestigious in his field, Travis's theories may sadly have
90 been thrown out to sea.

3   **3**

6. Which of the following conclusions about new theories in science can be reasonably inferred from the passage?

   F. The scientific community will eventually accept new theories, even if they are controversial.
   G. Scientists welcome the opportunity to throw out old ideas in favor of their own unusual theories.
   H. Scientists are more likely to accept unusual new theories proposed by well-respected colleagues.
   J. People in general do not encourage the introduction of new, nontraditional theories.

7. Which of the following best describes how Travis's colleagues perceived him after he first presented his lightning theory and expressed a desire for further study?

   A. They feared he had damaged his reputation as a legitimate scientist beyond repair.
   B. They respected him for his work on other subjects but felt his theory was a waste of his time.
   C. They were impressed that Travis had worked so hard to analyze his findings.
   D. Their skepticism about the theory caused them to question his other unrelated work.

8. The passage indicates that at the time Travis and Farmer presented new evidence supporting their lightning theory, Travis most nearly felt:

   F. eager to begin substantial research on his theory.
   G. resentful of his colleagues and their treatment of him.
   H. devastated that his theory was disproven.
   J. self-satisfied and anticipating praise of his work.

9. The author uses the fifth paragraph (lines 33–39) primarily to:

   A. reveal the difference between theoretical and practical scientific research.
   B. acknowledge and then undermine common perceptions about science.
   C. depict the role the scientist plays in society.
   D. retract his earlier statements on the uselessness of science.

10. According to the passage, it can reasonably be inferred that the study leading to Travis's new lightning theory began when:

    F. Travis's colleagues persuaded him that he was wasting time studying ball lightning.
    G. Nikola Tesla's instruction manuals were discovered in Tesla's Colorado Springs lab.
    H. the scientific community voted that Travis should further his research by conducting many experiments.
    J. studying ball lightning led Travis to realize the existence of many varying phenomena.

END OF SET TWO
STOP! DO NOT GO ON TO THE NEXT PAGE
UNTIL TOLD TO DO SO.

Entrance Ticket   Learning Targets   Reading Strategy   ACT Practice   Sum It Up

17.4.3 Set Three

Passage I

LITERARY NARRATIVE: This passage is adapted from *Kidnapped* by Robert Louis Stevenson (©1886 by Cassell and Company Ltd.). The narrator is a young man fleeing British soldiers with the help of Alan, a more experienced fugitive.

The soldiers kept stirring all day in the bottom of the valley, now changing guard, now hunting in patrolling parties among the rocks. These lay 'round in so great a number that to look for men among them was like look-
5   ing for a needle in a stack of hay. We could see the sol-
diers pike their bayonets among the heather, which sent a cold thrill into our veins, and they would sometimes hang about our rock so that we hardly dared to breathe.

The tediousness and pain of these hours upon the
10 rock only grew greater as the day went on: the rock get-
ting still hotter and the sun fiercer. There was dizziness and sickness to be kept at bay. Indeed it was only by luck that neither of us were sun-broiled, especially myself, unused to the intensity of its rays.

15 At last it was beyond our bearing, and there was now temptation to resist, as well as pain to endure. For the sun being now a little into the west, there came a patch of shade on the east side of our rock, which was the side sheltered from the soldiers.

20 Alan motioned to the shadowy side and dropped soundlessly onto the ground. I followed him at once and instantly fell all the length, so weak was I and so dizzy with that long exposure. He helped me sit and bid me hush. And here we lay for an hour or two, aching from
25 head to foot, as weak as water and lying quite clearly to the eye of any soldier who should have strolled that way. None came, however, all passing by on the other side so that our rock continued to be our shield even in this new position.

30 With the soldiers lying presently on the other side, Alan proposed that we should try a start. I was, by this time, afraid of but one thing in the world: to be set back upon the rock. Anything else was welcome to me; so we got ourselves at once in marching order and began to slip
35 from rock to rock, one after the other, now crawling flat on our bellies in the shade, now making a run for it, heart in mouth.

The soldiers, having searched this side of the valley intently enough, and being perhaps somewhat sluggish
40 with the sultriness of the afternoon, had now given up much of their vigilance and stood dozing at their posts or only kept a lookout along the banks of the river. In this way, staying along the valley and moving steadily toward the mountains, we drew away from their camp. But the

45 business was the most tiring I had ever taken part in. A man needed a hundred eyes in every part of him to keep concealed in that uneven land and within earshot of so many scattered sentries. When we had to pass through an open field, quickness was not all, but we needed a swift
50 judgment of the solidity of every stone on which we must set foot. The afternoon had now fallen so breathless that the rolling of a pebble sounded from afar like a pistol shot and would start the echo calling among the hills and cliffs.

By sundown we had made some distance, even at
55 our slow speed, though the sentry on the rock was still plainly in our view. Now we came onto something that put all fears out of season, and that was a deep berm that rushed down to join the glen river. At the sight of this, we threw ourselves to the ground and plunged head and
60 shoulders into the water. I cannot tell which was the more pleasant: the great shock as the cool stream went over us or the greed with which we drank of it.

We lay there (for the banks hid us) drinking again and again; and at last, being wonderfully renewed, we got
65 out the meal bag and made drammach in the iron pan. This, though it is but cold water mingled with oatmeal, does much good for a hungry man; where there are no means of making fire, or good reason for not making one, it is the chief standby of those who have taken to the Scot-
70 tish heath.

The moon rose at last and found us still on the road. It was only a thin sliver, but after a while it shone out brightly and showed me many dark tops of mountains and was reflected far underneath us onto a narrow strip of sea.
75 At this sight we both paused: I was struck with wonder to find myself walking (as it seemed to me) upon clouds, and Alan sought to make sure of his direction.

Seemingly he was pleased at our location, and he must certainly judged us out of earshot of all our enemies;
80 for throughout the rest of our night-march, he passed with the whistling of many tunes: warlike, merry, plaintive; reel tunes that gratefully made the foot go faster; tunes of my own south country that made me wish to be home from my adventures.

Entrance Ticket · Learning Targets · Reading Strategy · ACT Practice · Sum It Up

3 ████████████████████████████████████ **3**

---

11. The main theme of this passage concerns the:

    A. difficulty soldiers encounter when scouting the Scottish wilderness.

    B. narrator's homesickness for the songs of his country.

    C. fleeing of two men from soldiers who wish to capture them.

    D. daily meals shared by soldiers beside a battlefield.

12. Which of the following questions is NOT answered by the information in the passage?

    F. What is the narrator's relationship to his companion?

    G. What do the narrator and his companion eat for meals?

    H. Which of the two companions is the more experienced traveler?

    J. When did the narrator and his companion come upon the river?

13. The narrator draws which of the following conclusions about the soldiers that leads to the success of the men's escape?

    A. They were talking among themselves next to the river.

    B. They had become drowsy and less attentive in the afternoon heat.

    C. They had been ordered to leave the area that morning.

    D. They were distracted by what sounded like a pistol shot.

14. In terms of developing the narrative, the first paragraph primarily serves to:

    F. describe the discomfort and pain the narrator felt hiding on the rock.

    G. portray the narrator's suspicion of Alan's sense of direction.

    H. depict the narrator's desire to return home to England.

    J. provide details about the terrain and the danger of the soldiers.

15. It can be most reasonably inferred from the passage that when the narrator says, "where there are no means of making fire, or good reason for not making one" (lines 67–68), he is most nearly indicating that:

    A. he dared not attract the soldiers with the smoke of a fire.

    B. he preferred to eat his drammach cold, but Alan wished to cook his.

    C. neither he nor Alan knew how to build a cooking fire.

    D. the blade of their axe was too blunt to chop wood.

END OF SET ONE
STOP! DO NOT GO ON TO THE NEXT PAGE
UNTIL TOLD TO DO SO.

Sum It Up

Reading Strategy

Scope and Support: Every answer needs to be correct, supported by the passage, and have a scope that fits the question and the passage.

Process of Elimination: The process of elimination is the most important technique on the reading test. Make sure you eliminate incorrect answer choices for each question before you select the correct answer.

Keep Your Pencil Moving: Use your pencil to keep track of the key points in the passage, the major topics in the questions and answers, and the incorrect answers.

Scanning: Develop your scanning skills to aid you on all of the questions without line references.

Skimming: Whether you look for the "hashtag" in each paragraph or read the topic sentences, remember to spend no more than three minutes reading the passage.

Reading Pacing

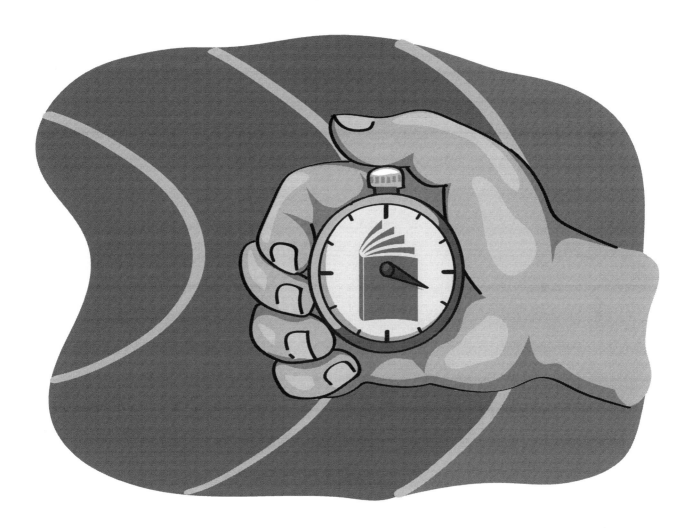

CAPTION:

18.1 Entrance Ticket

What are your goals for the ACT reading test? How do you plan to achieve them?
What could stand in your way?

_____

_____

_____

_____

_____

_____

_____

_____

_____

_____

_____

_____

_____

_____

_____

_____

18.2 Learning Targets

1. Set a personalized pacing goal for the reading test based on ACT scoring tables

2. Follow a personalized pacing plan for the reading test

Self-Assessment

Circle the number that corresponds to your confidence level in your knowledge of this subject before beginning the lesson. A score of 1 means you are completely lost, and a score of 4 means you have mastered the skills. After you finish the lesson, return to the bottom of this page and circle your new confidence level to show your improvement.

Before Lesson

1   2   3   4

After Lesson

1   2   3   4

18.3.1 Setting a Pacing Plan

Scale Score	Raw Score (Correct answers)	Scale Score	Raw Score (Correct answers)
36	40	18	21
35	39	17	19
34	39	16	18
33	38	15	16
32	37	14	14
31	37	13	13
30	36	12	12
29	35	11	10
28	34	10	8
27	33	9	7
26	32	8	6
25	31	7	5
24	30	6	4
23	29	5	4
22	27	4	3
21	26	3	2
20	24	2	1
19	22	1	0

18.3.1 Setting a Pacing Plan

Goal Scale Score: _____

Overall Goal Raw Score: _____

Target Raw Score (1–10): _____
Actual Raw Score (1–10): _____

Target Raw Score (11–20): _____
Actual Raw Score (11–20): _____

Target Raw Score (21–30): _____
Actual Raw Score (21–30): _____

Target Raw Score (31–40): _____
Actual Raw Score (31–40): _____

Reading Tip

Mark and Move: Since difficult questions are distributed throughout the test, you should be prepared to use the mark and move technique quite often. As soon as you get stuck on a question, eliminate what you can, mark your best guess, and move on. If you finish the passage before your eight minutes are up, go back and try the hard questions. Otherwise, move on to the next passage.

18.4.1 Mini-Test 1

Passage I

LITERARY NARRATIVE: The following passage is an excerpt from *Peter and Wendy* by J.M. Barrie (©1911 by Charles Scribner's Sons).

All children, except one, grow up. They soon know that they will grow up, and the way Wendy knew was this: one day when she was two years old, she was playing in a garden, and she plucked another flower and ran with it to
5 her mother. I suppose she must have looked rather delightful, for Mrs. Darling put her hand to her heart and cried, "Oh, why can't you remain like this forever!" This was all that passed between them on the subject, but henceforth Wendy knew that she must grow up. You always know
10 after you are two. Two is the beginning of the end.

The Darlings lived at number 14, and until Wendy came, her mother had been the chief one. Mrs. Darling was a lovely lady with a romantic mind and such a sweet mocking mouth. Her romantic mind was like the tiny
15 boxes, one within the other, that come from the puzzling East; however, no matter how many you discover there is always one more, and her sweet mocking mouth had one kiss on it that Wendy could never get, though there it was, perfectly conspicuous in the right-hand corner.

20 The way Mr. Darling won her was this: the many gentlemen who had been boys when she was a girl discovered simultaneously that they loved her, and they all ran to her house to propose to her except Mr. Darling, who took a cab and nipped in first, so he got her. He got
25 all of her except the innermost box and the kiss. He never knew about the box, and in time he gave up trying for the kiss. Wendy thought Napoleon could have gotten it, but I can picture him trying and then going off in a passion, slamming the door.

30 Mr. Darling used to boast to Wendy that her mother not only loved him but respected him. He was one of those deep ones who knows about stocks and shares. Of course no one really knows, but he quite seemed to know, and he often said stocks were up and shares were down in a way
35 that would have made any woman respect him.

Mrs. Darling was married in white, and at first she kept the books perfectly, almost gleefully, as if it were a game. Not so much as a Brussels sprout was missing, but by and by whole cauliflowers dropped out, and instead
40 of them there were pictures of babies without faces. She drew them when she should have been totting up. They were Mrs. Darling's guesses.

Mrs. Darling loved to have everything just so, and Mr. Darling had a passion for being exactly like his neigh-
45 bors; so, of course, they had a nurse. As they were poor, owing to the amount of milk the children drank, this nurse was a prim Newfoundland dog called Nana, who had belonged to no one in particular until the Darlings engaged her. She had always thought children were im-
50 portant, and the Darlings had become acquainted with her in Kensington Gardens, where she spent most of her spare time peeping into baby carriages. She was much hated by careless nursemaids whom she followed to their homes and complained of to their mistresses. She proved to be
55 quite a treasure of a nurse. How thorough she was at bathtime, and she was up at any moment of the night if one of her charges made the slightest cry. Of course her kennel was in the nursery. She had a genius for knowing when a cough was a thing to have no patience with and when
60 it needed a stocking around your throat. She believed in old-fashioned remedies like rhubarb leaf to her last day, and she made sounds of contempt over all this new-fangled talk about germs and so on. It was a lesson in propriety to see her escorting the children to school, walking
65 sedately by their sides when they were well behaved and butting them back into line if they strayed.

No nursery could possibly have been conducted more correctly, and Mr. Darling knew it, yet he sometimes wondered uneasily whether the neighbors talked.

---

1. What does the author mean when he writes that Mrs. Darling's mind was like tiny boxes?

A. Mrs. Darling is a complex and secretive person.
B. Mrs. Darling is a deep and respectful person.
C. Mrs. Darling is a simple-minded person.
D. Mrs. Darling has a very good memory.

2. Mr. Darling can best be described as:

F. a bold, pretentious man.
G. a family man of great character.
H. a strict authoritarian parent.
J. a gentle and caring man.

---

3 ████████████████████████████████████ **3**

3. Why did Mrs. Darling begin shirking her book-keeping duties?

   A. She started growing vegetables instead.
   B. Someone was stealing cauliflower from their garden.
   C. She wanted children and couldn't focus.
   D. Mr. Darling decided to do the books instead.

4. Nana did all of the following EXCEPT:

   F. bring the children to school.
   G. give the children baths.
   H. sleep at the foot of the children's bed.
   J. cure the children when they were sick.

5. The narrator explains that women respected Mr. Darling because:

   A. he was rich and smart.
   B. he understood stocks and shares.
   C. he was a romantic.
   D. he demanded respect wherever he went.

6. It can be reasonably inferred from the passage that Wendy:

   F. is the center of attention in the house.
   G. is a neglected child.
   H. is adventurous and innocent.
   J. has been full of contempt since the age of two.

7. It is implied in lines 43–44 that:

   A. Mr. Darling valued his reputation a great deal.
   B. Mr. Darling felt it was important for the sake of his children's health to have a nurse.
   C. the neighbors did not have nurses for their children.
   D. Mr. Darling's neighbors envied him.

8. The narrator claims the Darlings are poor because:

   F. Mrs. Darling does not work.
   G. Mr. Darling lost his job.
   H. Mr. Darling's job is based on an unreliable market.
   J. the children drink too much milk.

9. Why is Mr. Darling worried about what the neighbors think?

   A. Because they are poor
   B. Because Mrs. Darling wears extravagant clothing
   C. Because their nurse is a dog
   D. Because their children drink too much milk

10. What does the author imply about Nana's care for the children?

   F. Nana is a more prominent character in the novel than the Darlings.
   G. Nana is going to be the main protagonist of the novel.
   H. Nana played a larger role in the children's lives than their parents did.
   J. The neighbors want to replace their nurses with a dog like Nana.

END OF MINI-TEST ONE
STOP! DO NOT GO ON TO THE NEXT PAGE
UNTIL TOLD TO DO SO.

18.4.2 Mini-Test 2

Attempts: _____   Correct: _____

Passage II

SOCIAL SCIENCE: This passage is adapted from *Our Vanishing Wild Life* by William T. Hornaday (©1913 by Charles Scribner's Sons).

The preservation of animal and plant life and of the general beauty of nature is one of the foremost duties of men and women today. It is an imperative duty because it must be performed at once, for otherwise it will be too
5 late. Every possible means of preservation—sentimental, educational, and legislative—must be employed.

The present warning issues with no uncertain sound because this great battle for preservation and conservation cannot be won by gentle tones nor by appeals to the aes-
10 thetic instincts of those who have no sense of beauty or enjoyment of nature. It is necessary to sound a loud alarm, to present the facts in very strong language backed up by irrefutable statistics and by photographs that tell no lies, to establish the law, and to enforce it with a bludgeon if
15 needed.

This book is such an alarm. Its forceful pages remind me of the sounding of the great bells in the watchtowers of the cities during the Middle Ages. These bells called the citizens to arms to protect their homes, their liberties,
20 and their happiness. It is undeniable that the welfare and happiness of our own and of all future generations of Americans are at stake in this battle for the preservation of nature against the selfishness, the ignorance, and the cruelty of her destroyers.

25 We no longer destroy great works of art. They are treasured and regarded as priceless, but we have yet to attain the state of civilization in which the destruction of a glorious work of nature—whether it be a cliff, a forest, or a species of mammal or bird—is regarded with equal
30 abhorrence. The whole earth is a poorer place to live in when a colony of exquisite egrets or birds of paradise is destroyed so their plumes may decorate the hat of some lady of fashion and ultimately find their way into the rubbish heap. The people of all the New England states are
35 poorer when ignorant residents destroy the robins and other songbirds of the North for a mess of pottage.

Travels through Europe, as well as over a large part of the North American continent, have convinced me that nowhere is nature being destroyed so rapidly as in the
40 United States. Except within our conservation areas, an earthly paradise is being turned into an earthly hades; it is neither savages nor primitive men who are doing this but men and women who boast of their civilization. Air and water are polluted, rivers and streams serve as sewers
45 and dumping grounds, forests are swept away, and fish

are driven from the streams. Many birds are becoming extinct, and certain mammals are on the verge of extermination. Vulgar advertisements hide the landscape, and in all that disfigures the wonderful heritage of nature's beauty
50 today, we Americans are in the lead.

Fortunately the tide of destruction is ebbing, and the tide of conservation is coming in. Americans are practical. Like all other northern peoples, they love money and will sacrifice much for it, but they are also full of idealism and
55 moral and spiritual energy. The influence of the splendid body of Americans and Canadians, who have turned their best forces of mind and language into literature and into political power for the conservation movement, is becoming stronger every day. Yet we are far from the point where
60 the momentum of conservation is strong enough to arrest and roll back the tide of destruction, and this is especially true with regard to our quickly vanishing animal life.

11. What does the writer intend to accomplish with this passage?

   A. He wants to shock the reader with gruesome facts about the destruction of wildlife.

   B. He wants to introduce the reader to the concept of conserving wildlife.

   C. He wants to incite fear in the reader.

   D. He wants to provoke activism in the reader to conserve nature.

12. Who does the author blame most for the destruction of wildlife?

   F. People around the world

   G. Americans

   H. Southerners

   J. The reader

13. The author specifically mentions all of the following means of preservation EXCEPT:

    A. sentimental.
    B. legislative.
    C. economical.
    D. educational.

14. The author compares nature to:

    F. fine jewelry.
    G. fine art.
    H. a feather for fashion wear.
    J. a great battle.

15. It is implied throughout the entire passage that the author believes:

    A. nature is not just a part of the world, but rather nature is the world.
    B. living in harmony with nature should be every living being's first priority.
    C. the main job of human beings should be to protect the world in which they live.
    D. human beings have no capacity for compassion when it comes to nature.

16. The author urges the reader to evoke action by:

    F. appealing directly to the opposition.
    G. traveling to conservation areas to see nature's beauty.
    H. enforcing legislation about conservation and by raising awareness.
    J. starting violent protests against people who destroy nature.

17. The author uses lines 37–40 to:

    A. develop context for the rest of the paragraph.
    B. establish credibility and reliability in his passage.
    C. boast about all the places he has traveled to.
    D. encourage the reader to see places all over the world.

18. The overall tone of the passage can best be described as:

    F. angry and anxious.
    G. defensive and disdainful.
    H. honest and educational.
    J. determined and direct.

19. The final paragraph is vital to the passage because:

    A. it describes how conservationism is on the rise but emphasizes there is much work left to be done.
    B. it explains that humans are smart and innovative.
    C. it details how far humans still have to go in conservation efforts.
    D. it shows what efforts have already been made toward conserving nature.

20. The author compares his call for action to:

    F. an alarm clock.
    G. the sounding of a medieval bell tower.
    H. a battle.
    J. an imperative duty.

END OF MINI-TEST TWO
STOP! DO NOT GO ON TO THE NEXT PAGE
UNTIL TOLD TO DO SO.

Attempts: _____   Correct: _____

Passage III

HUMANITIES: This passage is adapted from *Architecture and Democracy* by Claude Bragdon (©1918 by A.A. Knopf).

Broadly speaking, there are not five orders of architecture—nor fifty—but only two: arranged and organic. These correspond to the two terms of that "inevitable duality" which bisects life. Talent and genius, reason and
5 intuition, bromide and sulfite are some of the names we know them by.

Arranged architecture is reasoned and artificial produced by talent and governed by taste. Organic architecture, on the other hand, is the product of some obscure
10 inner necessity for self-expression, which is subconscious. It is as though nature herself, through some human organ of her activity, had addressed herself to the service of the sons and daughters of men.

Arranged architecture in its finest manifestations is
15 the product of a pride, a knowledge, a competence, a confidence staggering to behold. It seems to say of the works of nature, "I'll show you a trick worth two of that." For the subtlety of nature's geometry, and for her infinite variety and unexpectedness, arranged architecture substitutes a
20 Euclidian system of straight lines and (for the most part) circular curves, assembled and arranged according to a definite logic of its own. It is created but not creative; it is imagined but not imaginative. Organic architecture is both creative and imaginative. It is non-Euclidian in the
25 sense that it is higher-dimensional—that is, it suggests extension in directions and into regions where the spirit finds itself at home but of which the senses give no report to the brain.

To make the whole thing clearer, it may be said that
30 arranged and organic architecture bear much the same relation to one another that a piano bears to a violin. A piano is an instrument that does not give forth discords if one follows the rules. A violin requires absolutely an ear—an inner rectitude. It has a way of betraying the man of talent
35 and glorifying the genius, becoming one with his body and his soul.

Of course it stands to reason that there is not always a hard and fast differentiation between these two orders of architecture, but there is one sure way by which each may
40 be recognized and known. If the function appears to have created the form, and if everywhere the form follows the function, changing as that changes, the building is organic; if on the contrary "the house confines the spirit," if the building presents not a face but however beautiful a mask,
45 it is an example of arranged architecture.

But in so far as it is anything at all, aesthetically, our architecture is arranged, so if only by the operation of the law of opposites, or alternation, we might reasonably expect the next manifestation to be organic. There are
50 other and better reasons, however, for such expectancy.

Organic architecture is ever a flower of the religious spirit. When the soul draws near to the surface of life, as it did in the two mystic centuries of the Middle Ages, it organizes life; and architecture, along with the other arts,
55 becomes truly creative. The informing force comes not so much from man as through him. After the war that spirit of brotherhood, born in the camps and bred on the battlefields and in the trenches of Europe, is likely to take on all the attributes of a new religion of humanity, prompting
60 men to such heroisms and renunciations, exciting in them such psychic sublimations, as have characterized the great religious renewals of time past.

If this happens it is bound to write itself on space in an architecture beautiful and new; one which "takes
65 its shape and sun-color" from the opulent heart. This architecture will of necessity be organic, the product not of self-assertive personalities but the work of the "patient demon" organizing the nation into a spiritual democracy.

The author is aware that in this point of view there
70 is little of the "scientific spirit," but science fails to reckon with the soul. Science advances facing backward, so what prevision can it have of a miraculous and divinely inspired future—or for the matter of that, of any future at all? The old methods and categories will no longer answer; the or-
75 derly course of evolution has been violently interrupted by the earthquake of the war; igneous action has superseded aqueous action. The casements of the human mind look out no longer upon familiar hills and valleys, but on a stark, strange, devastated landscape, the ploughed land
80 of some future harvest of the years. It is the end of the age, the Kali Yuga—the completion of a major cycle—but all cycles follow the same sequence: after winter, spring; and after the Iron Age, the Golden.

The specific features of this organic, divinely in-
85 spired architecture of the Golden Age cannot of course be discerned by any one any more than the manner in which the Great Mystery will present itself anew to consciousness. The most imaginative artist can imagine only in terms of the already-existent; he can speak only the
90 language he has learned. And yet some germs of the future must be enfolded even in the present moment. The course of wisdom is to seek them neither in the old romance nor in the new rationalism but in the subtle and ever-changing spirit of the times.

21. Which of the following questions is NOT answered in the passage?

   A. What are the two main orders of architecture?
   B. What are the qualities of arranged architecture?
   C. What was the name of the period before the Middle Ages?
   D. What are the qualities of organic architecture?

22. All of the following descriptions are used in the passage to characterize arranged architecture EXCEPT that it is:

   F. based on a Euclidian system of straight lines and circular curves.
   G. creative and imaginative.
   H. assembled and arranged.
   J. reasoned and artificial.

23. Paragraphs 1 through 4 (lines 1–36) establish all of the following about organic architecture EXCEPT its:

   A. origins.
   B. differences from arranged architecture.
   C. association with religion and spirituality.
   D. inevitably dual nature.

24. According to the passage, which of the following best describes the author's predictions about the architecture of the new "Golden Age"?

   F. The architecture of the future will likely be organic.
   G. The architecture of the future will likely be arranged.
   H. The architecture of the future will be for religious buildings.
   J. The architecture of the future will be the product of self-assertive personalities.

25. The author mentions the idea of how "the house confines the spirit" as part of his argument that:

   A. one can find clear signs to tell the difference between the two orders of architecture.
   B. the arranged form of architecture follows the law of opposites.
   C. the arranged form of architecture feels too closed in and claustrophobic.
   D. the arranged form of architecture is based on an outgrowth of spirit.

26. In the context of the passage, paragraph 9 (lines 69–83) is best described as presenting images of all of the following EXCEPT:

   F. disaster.
   G. devastation.
   H. war.
   J. mystery.

27. The author indicates that one reason he believed that the organic order of architecture was on the rise was that:

   A. since the current trend was arranged, it would alternate to being organic because of the law of opposites.
   B. a spiritual democracy would have a law that all architecture must be organic.
   C. organic architecture is best, so it is the wave of the future.
   D. the Iron Age was populated mainly with organic architecture.

28. Information in the passage suggests that the author believes the exact features of the future architectural style cannot be described primarily because:

   F. he is not sufficiently romantic or rational.
   G. we can only know what will come once the war is over.
   H. one can only imagine based on what already exists.
   J. even though he knows what it will look like, he cannot express it in words.

GO ON TO THE NEXT PAGE.

29. Based on paragraphs 1 through 4 (lines 1–36), which of the following statements indicates the author's opinion of the relationship between organic and arranged architecture?

   A. Though they are both styles of architecture, the arranged style is more structured, while the organic style is more imaginative.
   B. Both the organic and the arranged styles of architecture will soon give way to a spiritual form of architecture.
   C. All architecture is both organic and arranged.
   D. For thousands of years, mankind has alternated between an arranged and an organic architectural style.

30. The passage indicates that the violin described in paragraph 4 (lines 29–36) represents:

   F. the human spirit.
   G. arranged architecture.
   H. organic architecture.
   J. a lack of discord.

END OF MINI-TEST THREE
STOP! DO NOT GO ON TO THE NEXT PAGE
UNTIL TOLD TO DO SO.

This page is intentionally left blank.

18.4.4 Mini-Test 4

Attempts: _____   Correct: _____

Passage IV

NATURAL SCIENCE: This passage is adapted from *The Life Story of Insects* by George H. Carpenter (©1913 by G.P. Putnam's Sons).

Insects as a whole are preeminently creatures of the land and the air. This is shown not only by the possession of wings by a vast majority of the class but also by the mode of breathing through a system of branching air
5 tubes carrying atmospheric air with its combustion-supporting oxygen to all the insect's tissues. The air gains access to these tubes through a number of paired air holes or *spiracles* arranged segmentally in series.

It is of great interest to find that, nevertheless, a
10 number of insects spend much of their time under water. This is true of not a few in the perfect winged state, as for example aquatic beetles and water bugs ("boatmen" and "scorpions"), which have some way of protecting their spiracles when submerged and, possessing usually
15 the power of flight, can pass on occasion from pond or stream to upper air. But it is advisable in connection with our present subject to dwell especially on some insects that remain continually under water until they are ready to undergo their final molt and attain the winged state,
20 which they pass entirely in the air. The preparatory instars of such insects are aquatic; the adult instar is aerial. All mayflies, dragonflies, caddisflies, many beetles and two-winged flies, and a few moths thus divide their life story between the water and the air. For the present we confine
25 attention to the stoneflies, the mayflies, and the dragonflies.

In the case of many insects that have aquatic larvae, the latter are provided with some arrangement for enabling them to reach atmospheric air through the surface
30 film of the water. But the larva of a stonefly, a dragonfly, or a mayfly is adapted more completely than these for aquatic life; it can, by means of gills of some kind, breathe the air dissolved in water.

The aquatic young of a stonefly does not differ suf-
35 ficiently in form from its parent to warrant us in calling it a larva; the life history is like that of a cockroach, all the instars, however, except the final one—the winged adult or *imago*—live in the water. The young of one of our large species, a perla for example, has well-chitinized
40 cuticle, broad head, powerful legs, long feelers, and cerci like those of the imago; its wings arise from external rudiments, which are conspicuous in the later aquatic stages. But it lives completely submerged, usually clinging or walking beneath the stones that lie in the bed of a clear
45 stream, and examination of the ventral aspect of the thorax reveals six pairs of tufted gills, by means of which it is

able to breathe the air dissolved in the water wherein it lives. At the base of the tail-feelers or cerci also, there are little tufts of thread-like gills. An insect that is continually
50 submerged and has no contact with the upper air cannot breathe through a series of paired spiracles, and during the aquatic life period of the stonefly, these remain closed. Nevertheless, breathing is carried on by means of the ordinary system of branching air-tubes, the trunks of which
55 are in connection with the tufted hollow gill-filaments, through whose delicate cuticle gaseous exchange can take place, though the method of this exchange is as yet very imperfectly understood. When the stonefly nymph is fully grown, it comes out of the water and climbs to some con-
60 venient eminence. The cuticle splits open along the back, and the imago, clothed in its new cuticle, as yet soft and flexible, creeps out. The spiracles are now open, and the stonefly breathes atmospheric air like other flying insects. But throughout its winged life, the stonefly bears memori-
65 als of its aquatic past in the little withered vestiges of gills that can still be distinguished beneath the thorax.

31. The author's purpose for writing this passage can best be explained as:

  A. to create a literary manifestation of his love for insects.
  B. to educate readers on the life cycle of insects.
  C. to compare and contrast the stonefly with the dragonfly.
  D. to convince the reader to conserve insect habitats.

32. From the passage, the reader can infer that spiracles are most similar to:

  F. fins.
  G. lungs.
  H. gills.
  J. snorkels.

3

3

33. The overall tone of the passage is:

A. informative and insipid.
B. fascinated and educational.
C. scholastic and indifferent.
D. objective and pensive.

34. Which of the following insects is NOT described in this passage as adapting physical features necessary for breathing underwater?

F. Dragonfly
G. Stonefly
H. Beetle
J. Mosquito

35. Given that *molt* is a verb meaning "to lose feathers, hair, or skin to make way for new growth," the reader can infer that *instar* (lines 20–21) means:

A. phase.
B. scales.
C. wings.
D. life.

36. Lines 34–42 indicate that stoneflies:

F. spend almost all of their instars underwater.
G. prefer to lay their eggs underwater to protect them from non-aqueous prey.
H. only spend the first half of their life phases underwater.
J. hunt in the air but nest underwater.

37. The transformation of a stonefly from water insect to air insect is most like the transformation of:

A. a human fetus to a grown adult.
B. a caterpillar to a butterfly.
C. a tadpole to a frog.
D. a fish egg to a fish.

38. It can be reasonably inferred that "we confine attention" (lines 24–25) to three species of flies in order to:

F. provide examples of how typical flies go through some phases of their lives underwater.
G. prove that some flies are named incorrectly.
H. teach students about the larvae of all insects.
J. show that all insects fall into these three categories.

39. Based on the passage as a whole, it is implied that the author believes:

A. insects that can live in both the air and the water have a better chance of survival.
B. insects that mature underwater are more likely to develop wings than insects born above water.
C. insects who have the ability to lay eggs under water have higher offspring success rates.
D. the dual environments of these insects give them a varied life cycle.

40. In the first line of the passage, it can be inferred that the term *preeminently* is similar to all of the following definitions EXCEPT:

F. mostly.
G. primarily.
H. greatly.
J. predominantly.

END OF MINI-TEST FOUR
STOP! DO NOT GO ON TO THE NEXT PAGE
UNTIL TOLD TO DO SO.

Sum It Up

Reading Pacing

Goal Score

Have your goal raw score in mind on test day. You should know exactly how many questions you need to answer correctly to reach your goal.

Pacing Plan

Have your plan in place before you take the ACT reading test. Know how many minutes you should spend on each section and how many questions you need to attempt to achieve your goal score.

<u>Notes</u>

Reading Glossary

Author

The writer of a piece of content, whether fiction, nonfiction, memoir, etc.

Comparative adjectives

Adjectives that compare two nouns by adding *-er*, *-ier*, *more*, or *less*

Compare

To explain how something is similar to something else

Context

Words that surround a certain word or phrase; clarifies the meaning

Figurative

Metaphorical; using words as symbols

Hyperbole

A description that is exaggerated for emphasis

Idiom

An expression that cannot be understood from the meanings of its individual words but has a figurative meaning when taken as a whole phrase

Inference

A conclusion drawn from reasoning and available evidence

Literal

Using a word based on its exact definition; without metaphor or exaggeration

Main idea

The central idea of a text around which all events and information are focused

Metaphor

A word or phrase used to compare two unlike objects, ideas, thoughts, or feelings

Narrator

The person who recounts the events in a story; either a fictional character or the author of the piece

Personification

The act of assigning the qualities of a person to something that is not human or, in some cases, not even alive

Purpose

The author's intention and reason for writing; what the author hopes the work will accomplish

Scanning

Looking over all the parts of something carefully to detect some feature; the process of looking back to the passage to find a specific fact or detail

Simile

A phrase that uses the words *like* or *as* to describe someone or something by comparing it with someone or something else

Skimming

The process of reading through a text quickly, only determining the most important details rather than reading for thorough understanding

Superlative adjectives

Adjectives that compare three or more nouns and take the comparison of nouns to the highest degree by adding *-est*, *-st*, *-iest*, *most*, or *least*

Symbolism

The practice of giving special, non-literal meaning to objects, things, relationships, or events

Contributors

Chief Academic Officer
Oliver Pope

Lead Content Editor
Lisa Primeaux-Redmond

Assistant Content Editor
Allison Eskind

Lesson Writers
Lisa Primeaux-Redmond, Allison Eskind, Stephanie Bucklin, Nick Sweeney, Lori Martin

Question Editors
Jillian Musso, Allison Eskind, Emily DeYoung, Thomas Whittington

Question Writers
Jillian Musso, Lisa Primeaux-Redmond, Thomas Whittington, Pam Braud, Emily DeYoung, Anthony Mabrey, Tyler Munson, Allison Eskind, Lauren Pope, Wade Heaton, David Harr, Alex Moffatt, Patrick Ross

Art
Nicole St. Pierre, Eliza Todorova, Roland Parker, Kayla Manuel, Anne Lipscomb

Layout
Jeff Garrett, Elaine Broussard, Jeffrey Cappell, Ryan Herringshaw, Shannon Rawson, Nicole St. Pierre, Eliza Todorova

Proofreaders
Kristen Cockrell, Elaine Broussard, Allison Eskind, Jillian Musso, Lisa Redmond, Oliver Pope, Chrissy Vincent, Dan Marchese, Rhett Manuel, Catherine Tall, Jerelyn Pearson, Liz Baron, Jordan Sermon, Megan Reitzell, Diana Pietrogallo, Marcia Willis, Michael Laird

Interns
Kaitlyn Mattox, Rashaud Red, Jamaica Rhoden, Chelsey Smith

ACT® Mastery created by Craig Gehring

Made in the USA
Middletown, DE
08 January 2022

58191118R00186